First World War

and Army of Occupation

War Diary

France, Belgium and Germany

6 DIVISION
71 Infantry Brigade
Suffolk Regiment 9th Battalion
and Brigade Machine Gun Company
22 August 1915 - 31 January 1918

WO95/1625

The Naval & Military Press Ltd
www.nmarchive.com
Published in association with The National Archives

Published by

The Naval & Military Press Ltd

Unit 10 Ridgewood Industrial Park,

Uckfield, East Sussex,

TN22 5QE England

Tel: +44 (0) 1825 749494

www.naval-military-press.com

www.nmarchive.com

This diary has been reprinted in facsimile from the original. Any imperfections are inevitably reproduced and the quality may fall short of modern type and cartographic standards.

Contents

Document type	Place/Title	Date From	Date To
Heading	6 Div, 71 Inf Brigade. 9 Bn Suffolk Regiment. 1915 Aug To 1918 Feb. 71 Machine Gun Company 1916 Aug To 1918 Jan.		
Heading	WO95/1625/1 6th Div 9 Bn Suffolk Regt Aug 1915-Feb 1918		
Heading	6 Division 71 Bde 9 Bn Suffolk Regt 1915 Aug-1916 Dec		
Heading	71st Inf. Bde. 24th Div. Battn. Disembarked Boulogne From England 31.8.15 War Diary 9th Battn. The Suffolk Regiment. August And September (22.8.15 To 30.9.15) 1915		
War Diary	Blackdown	22/08/1915	31/08/1915
War Diary	Alette	01/09/1915	20/09/1915
War Diary	Alette Matringhen	21/09/1915	21/09/1915
War Diary	Matringhem	22/09/1915	22/09/1915
War Diary	Ham-En-Artois	23/09/1915	23/09/1915
War Diary	Le Cornet Bourdois	24/09/1915	24/09/1915
War Diary	Bethune	25/09/1915	25/09/1915
War Diary	Fosse 9 (Map 36 A)	25/09/1915	28/09/1915
War Diary	Ham-En-Artois	29/09/1915	30/09/1915
Heading	71st Inf. Bde. 6th Div. Battn. Transferred With Bde. From 24th Div. 14.10.15. War Diary 9th Battn. The Suffolk Regiment. October 1915		
War Diary	Ham-En-Artois	01/10/1915	01/10/1915
War Diary	Ham-En-Artois Proven	02/10/1915	02/10/1915
War Diary	Proven	03/10/1915	05/10/1915
War Diary	Brandhoek	05/10/1915	08/10/1915
War Diary	Trenches Brandhoek	09/10/1915	09/10/1915
War Diary	Trenches Brandhoek Reninghelst	10/10/1915	10/10/1915
War Diary	Reninghelst	11/10/1915	11/10/1915
War Diary	Watou	12/10/1915	14/10/1915
War Diary	Camp C (Sheet 28) A.30	15/10/1915	15/10/1915
War Diary	Camp C	16/10/1915	16/10/1915
War Diary	Trenches St Jean	17/10/1915	17/10/1915
War Diary	St Jean	18/10/1915	22/10/1915
War Diary	Camp A	23/10/1915	30/10/1915
War Diary	Trenches	31/10/1915	31/10/1915
Heading	71st Inf. Bde. 6th Div. War Diary 9th Battn-The Suffolk Regiment. November 1915		
War Diary	Trenches	31/10/1915	03/11/1915
War Diary	Camp A	04/11/1915	07/11/1915
War Diary	Trenches	08/11/1915	12/11/1915
War Diary	Rest Camps	13/11/1915	17/11/1915
War Diary	In Trenches	18/11/1915	19/11/1915
War Diary	Camp A	20/11/1915	26/11/1915
War Diary	Poperinghe	27/11/1915	30/11/1915
Heading	71st Inf. Bde. 6th Div. War Diary 9th Battn. The Suffolk Regiment. December 1915		
War Diary	Poperinghe	01/12/1915	02/12/1915
War Diary	Camp A	03/12/1915	18/12/1915

War Diary	In Trenches	19/12/1915	19/12/1915
War Diary	Trenches	21/12/1915	22/12/1915
War Diary	Poperinghe	23/12/1915	26/12/1915
War Diary	In Trenches St Jean	27/12/1915	27/12/1915
War Diary	In Trenches	28/12/1915	30/12/1915
War Diary	Camp A	31/12/1915	31/12/1915
Miscellaneous	9th Suffolk Vol 5		
War Diary	Camp A	01/01/1916	02/01/1916
War Diary	Camp A Trenches	03/01/1916	03/01/1916
War Diary	Trenches	04/01/1916	07/01/1916
War Diary	Poperinghe	08/01/1916	11/01/1916
War Diary	Trenches	12/01/1916	15/01/1916
War Diary	Camp A	16/01/1916	20/01/1916
War Diary	Trenches	21/01/1916	24/01/1916
War Diary	Poperinghe	25/01/1916	27/01/1916
War Diary	Trenches	28/01/1916	31/01/1916
War Diary	Camp A	01/02/1916	04/02/1916
War Diary	In Trenches	05/02/1916	08/02/1916
War Diary	Poperinghe	09/02/1916	12/02/1916
War Diary	In Trenches	13/02/1916	16/02/1916
War Diary	Camp A	17/02/1916	21/02/1916
War Diary	Trenches	22/02/1916	26/02/1916
War Diary	Poperinghe	27/02/1916	02/03/1916
War Diary	In Trenches	03/03/1916	07/03/1916
War Diary	Canal Bank.	08/03/1916	09/03/1916
War Diary	Poperinghe	10/03/1916	10/03/1916
War Diary	Canal Bank	10/03/1916	13/03/1916
War Diary	In Trenches	14/03/1916	18/03/1916
War Diary	Poperinghe	19/03/1916	19/03/1916
War Diary	Herzeele	20/03/1916	27/03/1916
War Diary	Camp M	28/03/1916	05/04/1916
War Diary	Calais	06/04/1916	15/04/1916
War Diary	Zutkerque	16/04/1916	16/04/1916
War Diary	Bollezeele	17/04/1916	17/04/1916
War Diary	Herzeele	18/04/1916	18/04/1916
War Diary	Camps	19/04/1916	26/04/1916
War Diary	Camp O	27/04/1916	02/05/1916
War Diary	In Support	03/05/1916	08/05/1916
War Diary	Camp O	09/05/1916	13/05/1916
War Diary	Trenches	14/05/1916	18/05/1916
War Diary	Camp O	19/05/1916	23/05/1916
War Diary	In Support	24/05/1916	28/05/1916
War Diary	Camp D	29/05/1916	31/05/1916
Miscellaneous	D.A.G. Base 9th Suffolk Vol 10	02/07/1916	02/07/1916
War Diary	Camp D	01/06/1916	02/06/1916
War Diary	Trenches	03/06/1916	07/06/1916
War Diary	Camp D	08/06/1916	13/06/1916
War Diary	Canal Bank	14/06/1916	17/06/1916
War Diary	Poperinghe	18/06/1916	19/06/1916
War Diary	Camp N	20/06/1916	30/06/1916
Diagram etc			
War Diary	Camp N	01/07/1916	02/07/1916
War Diary	Bollezeele	03/07/1916	14/07/1916
War Diary	Houtkerque	15/07/1916	15/07/1916
War Diary	Camp C	16/07/1916	23/07/1916
War Diary	Trenches	24/07/1916	27/07/1916

War Diary	Ypres	28/07/1916	31/07/1916
Heading	71st Brigade 6th Division 1/9 Battalion Suffolk Regiment August 1916		
War Diary	Camp M	01/08/1916	02/08/1916
War Diary	Beauval	03/08/1916	03/08/1916
War Diary	Arqueves	04/08/1916	04/08/1916
War Diary	Trenches	05/08/1916	11/08/1916
War Diary	Louvencourt	12/08/1916	12/08/1916
War Diary	Camp	13/08/1916	20/08/1916
War Diary	In Trenches	21/08/1916	27/08/1916
War Diary	In Camp	28/08/1916	28/08/1916
War Diary	Beauval	29/08/1916	29/08/1916
War Diary	Montonvillers	30/08/1916	31/08/1916
Heading	71st Brigade 6th Division. 9th Battalion The Suffolk Regiment September 1916.		
War Diary	Monton Villers	01/09/1916	06/09/1916
War Diary	Cardonnette	07/09/1916	07/09/1916
War Diary	Mericourt Lorre	08/09/1916	08/09/1916
War Diary	Sandpit Area	09/09/1916	11/09/1916
War Diary	Trenches	12/09/1916	19/09/1916
War Diary	Ville-Sur-Ancre	20/09/1916	22/09/1916
War Diary	Citadel	23/09/1916	23/09/1916
War Diary	Batt in Avelave	24/09/1916	26/09/1916
War Diary	Trenches	27/09/1916	30/09/1916
War Diary	Sandpits 7.18c Sheet Albert Combined	01/10/1916	08/10/1916
War Diary	Bivouacs in S29.c. Sheet 57 & SW	09/10/1916	09/10/1916
War Diary	Trenches	10/10/1916	13/10/1916
War Diary	Support Trenches	14/10/1916	17/10/1916
War Diary	Trenches	18/10/1916	19/10/1916
War Diary	Bwouace	20/10/1916	20/10/1916
War Diary	Camp F18c	21/10/1916	21/10/1916
War Diary	Corbie	22/10/1916	23/10/1916
War Diary	Merelessart	24/10/1916	28/10/1916
War Diary	Annezin	29/10/1916	31/10/1916
Map	Appendix (2)		
Map	Appendix 3 Shown		
War Diary	Annezin	01/11/1916	27/11/1916
War Diary	Levrreol	28/11/1916	30/11/1916
War Diary	Trenches	01/12/1916	07/12/1916
War Diary	Cuinchy	08/12/1916	11/12/1916
War Diary	Trenches	12/12/1916	15/12/1916
War Diary	Beuvry	16/12/1916	19/12/1916
War Diary	Noeux Les Mines	20/12/1916	25/12/1916
War Diary	Mazingarbe	26/12/1916	26/12/1916
War Diary	Trenches	27/12/1916	31/12/1916
Miscellaneous	10		
Heading	6th Division 9th Suffolk Reg 1917 Jan-1918 Feb Disbanded		
War Diary	Trenches	01/01/1917	08/01/1917
War Diary	Mazingarbe	09/01/1917	12/01/1917
War Diary	Trenches	13/01/1917	16/01/1917
War Diary	Support Trenches	17/01/1917	19/01/1917
War Diary	Front Line Trenches	20/01/1917	23/01/1917
War Diary	Mazingarbe	24/01/1917	27/01/1917
War Diary	Trenches	28/01/1917	31/01/1917
War Diary	Support Trenches	01/02/1917	04/02/1917

War Diary	Front Line Trenches	05/02/1917	08/02/1917
War Diary	Mazinegarbe	09/02/1917	12/02/1917
War Diary	Front Line Trenches	13/02/1917	17/02/1917
War Diary	La Bourse	18/02/1917	18/02/1917
War Diary	Bethune	19/02/1917	28/02/1917
War Diary	La Bourse	01/03/1917	01/03/1917
War Diary	Less.D. Coy	02/03/1917	03/03/1917
War Diary	Support Trenches	04/03/1917	05/03/1917
War Diary	Front Line Trenches	06/03/1917	09/03/1917
War Diary	Philosophe	10/03/1917	15/03/1917
War Diary	Front Line Trenches	16/03/1917	21/03/1917
War Diary	Support Trenches	22/03/1917	27/03/1917
War Diary	Front Line Trenches	28/03/1917	31/03/1917
Miscellaneous	Headquarters 71st Infantry Brigade	01/05/1917	01/05/1917
War Diary	Front Line Trenches	01/04/1917	02/04/1917
War Diary	Philosophe	03/04/1917	08/04/1917
War Diary	Front Line Trenches	09/04/1917	14/04/1917
War Diary	Reserve Trenches	15/04/1917	20/04/1917
War Diary	Front Line Trenches	21/04/1917	22/04/1917
War Diary	Support Trenches	23/04/1917	24/04/1917
War Diary	Front Line Trenches	25/04/1917	27/04/1917
War Diary	Support Trenches	28/04/1917	30/04/1917
Map	Taken from Lens Map 36 c S.W.I Scale 1-10.000		
War Diary	Support Trenches	01/05/1917	01/05/1917
War Diary	Mazingarbe	02/05/1917	02/05/1917
War Diary	Front Line Trenches	03/05/1917	10/05/1917
War Diary	Reserve Billet	11/05/1917	18/05/1917
War Diary	Front Line Trenches	19/05/1917	26/05/1917
War Diary	Support Trenches & Philosophe	27/05/1917	03/06/1917
War Diary	Front Line Trenches	04/06/1917	11/06/1917
War Diary	Verquin And Vaudricourt	12/06/1917	18/06/1917
War Diary	Maroc	19/06/1917	27/06/1917
War Diary	Aix Novlette	28/06/1917	30/06/1917
Miscellaneous	Appendix "A"		
Miscellaneous	Report On Raid By "B" Coy. Nigh Of 10/11th June 1917		
Miscellaneous	6th Divn G. O. 2/66. 71st I. B. No. 2384 71st Infantry Brigade.	12/06/1917	12/06/1917
Miscellaneous			
Miscellaneous	Headquarters, 71st Infantry Brigade.	01/08/1917	01/08/1917
War Diary	Sailly Labourse	01/07/1917	01/07/1917
War Diary	Front Line Trenches	02/07/1917	09/07/1917
War Diary	Philosophe	10/07/1917	19/07/1917
War Diary	Front Line Trenches	20/07/1917	24/07/1917
War Diary	Frevillers	25/07/1917	31/07/1917
Operation(al) Order(s)	Operation Order No. 50 by Major J. P. Wylie. D.S.O. Commanding 9th Battalion The Suffolk Regiment.	18/07/1917	18/07/1917
Operation(al) Order(s)	9th Battalion The Suffolk Regiment. Operation Order No. 52	22/07/1917	22/07/1917
War Diary	Frevillers	01/08/1917	25/08/1917
War Diary	Vaudricourt	26/08/1917	31/08/1917
Miscellaneous	Speech By The Corps Commander At The Presentation Of Model Riband Parade.	08/08/1917	08/08/1917
Miscellaneous			
Miscellaneous	Administrative Order-Issued With Operation order No.53.	24/08/1917	24/08/1917

Operation(al) Order(s)	Operation Order No. 53. Lieut-Co. F.Latham. D S.O. Commanding 9th Battalion The Suffolk Regt.	25/08/1917	25/08/1917
Miscellaneous	Headquarters, 71st Infantry Brigade.	01/10/1917	01/10/1917
War Diary	Vaudricourt	01/09/1917	03/09/1917
War Diary	Braquemont	04/09/1917	04/09/1917
War Diary	Trenches	05/09/1917	13/09/1917
War Diary	Mazingarbe	14/09/1917	14/09/1917
War Diary	Trenches	15/09/1917	22/09/1917
War Diary	Les Brebis	23/09/1917	23/09/1917
War Diary	S. Maroc	24/09/1917	30/09/1917
Operation(al) Order(s)	Operation Order No. 54. By Lieut Col. F. Latham. D.S.O. Commanding 9th Battalion The Suffolk Regt.	03/09/1917	03/09/1917
Operation(al) Order(s)	9th Battalion Suffolk Regiment. Operation Order No. 55	03/09/1917	03/09/1917
Operation(al) Order(s)	9th Bn. Suffolk Regiment Operation Order No. 56.	08/09/1917	08/09/1917
Operation(al) Order(s)	Operation Order No. 57 By Lieut Col. F. Latham D.S.O. Commanding 9th. Battalion The Suffolk Regiment.	13/09/1917	13/09/1917
Miscellaneous	Addendum To 9th Battalion Suffolk Regiment. Operation Order No. 57	14/09/1917	14/09/1917
Operation(al) Order(s)	Battalion Suffolk Regiment Operation Order No. 58	18/09/1917	18/09/1917
Operation(al) Order(s)	9th. Battalion The Suffolk Regiment. Operation Order No. 59	21/09/1917	21/09/1917
Miscellaneous	Reference O.O. No. 59 Para, 2. For 2/lieut. J. V. Tailby read 2/lieut. F. Bullen.	22/09/1917	22/09/1917
Operation(al) Order(s)	9th Battalion The Suffolk Regiment. Operation Order No. 60.	23/09/1917	23/09/1917
Miscellaneous	Headquarters, 71st Infantry Brigade.	01/11/1917	01/11/1917
War Diary	Maroc	01/10/1917	01/10/1917
War Diary	Vaudricourt	02/10/1917	08/10/1917
War Diary	Trenches	09/10/1917	21/10/1917
War Diary	Bully Grenay	22/10/1917	22/10/1917
War Diary	Auchy Au Bois	23/10/1917	31/10/1917
Operation(al) Order(s)	9th. Battalion The Suffolk Regiment. Operation Order No. 61	01/10/1917	01/10/1917
Operation(al) Order(s)	9th. Battalion The Suffolk Regiment. Operation Order No. 62.	08/10/1917	08/10/1917
Operation(al) Order(s)	9th Battalion The Suffolk Regiment. Operation Order No. 63.	18/10/1917	18/10/1917
Operation(al) Order(s)	9th Battalion The Suffolk Regiment. Operation Order No. 64	16/10/1917	16/10/1917
Operation(al) Order(s)	9th Battalion The Suffolk Regiment. Operation Order No. 65.	19/10/1917	19/10/1917
Operation(al) Order(s)	9th Battalion The Suffolk Regiment. Operation Order No. 66	20/10/1917	20/10/1917
Operation(al) Order(s)	9th Battalion The Suffolk Regiment. Operation Order No. 67	29/10/1917	29/10/1917
Operation(al) Order(s)	9th Battalion The Suffolk Regiment. Operation Order No. 68.	29/10/1917	29/10/1917
Miscellaneous	Drafts. Appendix I		
Miscellaneous			
Miscellaneous	Headquarters 71st Inf. Bde.	17/12/1917	17/12/1917
War Diary	Denier & Belrencourt	01/11/1917	15/11/1917
War Diary	Moisloins	16/11/1917	16/11/1917
War Diary	Bois Dessart	17/11/1917	19/11/1917
War Diary	Trenches	20/11/1917	30/11/1917

Operation(al) Order(s)	9th Battalion The Suffolk Regt. Operation Order No. 69.	13/11/1917	13/11/1917
Operation(al) Order(s)	9th Battalion The Suffolk Regt. Operation Order No. 70.	14/11/1917	14/11/1917
Operation(al) Order(s)	9th Battalion The Suffolk Regt. Operation Order No. 71.	19/11/1917	19/11/1917
Miscellaneous	Not To Be Taken Into Front Trenches.		
Miscellaneous	Infantry And Tank Operations. 1. General Principles.		
Miscellaneous	11. General Lines Of An Attack.		
Diagram etc	Diagram A. Normal Attack Formation.		
Diagram etc	Diagram B. Position When No. 1 N. B. Tank Is In The Wire.		
Miscellaneous	Training Note Tank And Infantry Operations Without Methodical Artillery Preparation		
Diagram etc	Diagram 1.		
Diagram etc	Diagram 2		
Diagram etc	Diagram 3		
Diagram etc	Diagram 4		
Diagram etc	Diagram 5		
Miscellaneous	O.C. Company.	18/11/1917	18/11/1917
Diagram etc	9th Suffolks		
Operation(al) Order(s)	9th Battalion The Suffolk Regiment. Operation Order No. 72.	22/11/1917	22/11/1917
Operation(al) Order(s)	9th Battalion The Suffolk Regiment. Operation Order No. 73.	26/11/1917	26/11/1917
Miscellaneous	A Form Messages And Signals.		
Miscellaneous	D.A.G. G.H.Q. 3rd Echelon.	16/12/1917	16/12/1917
Miscellaneous	9th Battalion The Suffolk Regiment. Nominal Roll Of Officers Of The Above Battalion December 1917.		
Miscellaneous	Headquarters, 71st Infantry Brigade.	11/12/1918	11/12/1918
War Diary	Trenches	01/12/1917	12/12/1917
War Diary	Etricourt	13/12/1917	14/12/1917
War Diary	Bailleulmont	15/12/1917	31/12/1917
Miscellaneous	Ref. Attached Operation Order No. 75. Cancel Para. 3 & Substitute. Appendix I	01/12/1917	01/12/1917
Operation(al) Order(s)	9th Battalion The Suffolk Regiment. Operation Order No. 75.	01/12/1917	01/12/1917
Operation(al) Order(s)	9th Battalion The Suffolk Regiment. Operation Order No. 76	04/12/1917	04/12/1917
Operation(al) Order(s)	9th Battalion The Suffolk Regiment. Operation Order No. 77.	12/12/1917	12/12/1917
Operation(al) Order(s)	9th Battalion The Suffolk Regiment. Addendum Operation Order No. 77.	12/12/1917	12/12/1917
Operation(al) Order(s)	9th Battalion The Suffolk Regiment. Operation Order No. 78	13/12/1917	13/12/1917
Miscellaneous	Nominal Roll Of Officers Who Were Actually With The Battalion On 31.12.1917.		
Miscellaneous	9th battalion the Suffolk Regiment. Nominal Roll Of Officers Who Were Actually brone on the strength of the above Battalion On 31.12.1917.		
Miscellaneous	Headquarters, 71st Infantry Brigade.	01/02/1918	01/02/1918
War Diary	Bailleulmont	01/01/1918	01/01/1918
War Diary	Camps Courcelles	02/01/1918	17/01/1918
War Diary	Fremicourt	18/01/1918	18/01/1918
War Diary	Trenches	19/01/1918	22/01/1918
War Diary	Lebucquiere	23/01/1918	31/01/1918

Map	Dis Position Map		
Operation(al) Order(s)	9th Battalion The Suffolk Regiment. Operation Order No. 80.	16/01/1918	16/01/1918
Operation(al) Order(s)	9th Battalion The Suffolk Regiment. Operation No. 70.	31/12/1917	31/12/1917
Operation(al) Order(s)	9th Battalion The Suffolk Regiment. Operation Order No. 81.	17/01/1918	17/01/1918
Operation(al) Order(s)	9th Battalion The Suffolk Regiment. Operation Order No. 82.	21/01/1918	21/01/1918
Miscellaneous	Table "A" to Accompany O.O. 82. Battn. H.Q.		
Operation(al) Order(s)	9th Battalion The Suffolk Regiment. Operation Order No. 83.	25/01/1918	25/01/1918
Miscellaneous	Nominal Roll Of Officers Of The 9th Battalion The Suffolk Regiment Who Were Present At The Officers Farewell Inner On 29/1/1918	01/02/1918	01/02/1918
Miscellaneous	Headquarters, "A" 6th Division.	18/02/1918	18/02/1918
War Diary	Lebucquiere	01/02/1918	05/02/1918
Miscellaneous		05/02/1918	05/02/1918
Miscellaneous	Ph Division	05/02/1918	05/02/1918
Miscellaneous	Dear Colonel Latham.	05/02/1918	05/02/1918
War Diary	Lebucquiere	06/02/1918	09/02/1918
War Diary	Courcelles	10/02/1918	16/02/1918
Miscellaneous	9th Battalion The Suffolk Regiment.	16/02/1918	16/02/1918
Operation(al) Order(s)	9th Battalion The Suffolk Regiment Operation Order No. 85	08/02/1918	08/02/1918
Heading	WO95/1625/2 6th Division List Machine Gun Coy.		
Heading	6th Division 11st M.G. Coy. January To December 1917 Aug 1916-Jan 1918		
Heading	71st Brigade. 6th Division. 71st Brigade Machine Gun Company August 1916		
War Diary	Euglebelmer	06/08/1916	06/08/1916
War Diary	In The Trenches	08/08/1916	11/08/1916
War Diary	Louvencourt	12/08/1916	12/08/1916
War Diary	In The Trenches	14/08/1916	27/08/1916
War Diary	Louvencourt	28/08/1916	28/08/1916
War Diary	Beauval	29/08/1916	29/08/1916
War Diary	Flesselles	30/08/1916	31/08/1916
Heading	71st Brigade 6th Division 71st Brigade Machine Gun Company September 1916.		
War Diary	Flesselles	01/09/1916	05/09/1916
War Diary	Allonville	07/09/1916	07/09/1916
War Diary	Mericourt L'Abbe	08/09/1916	08/09/1916
War Diary	Sandpit Area	09/09/1916	11/09/1916
War Diary	Briqueterie	12/09/1916	12/09/1916
War Diary	Guillemont	13/09/1916	15/09/1916
War Diary	Guinchy	16/09/1916	16/09/1916
War Diary	Chimpanzee Trench	16/09/1916	16/09/1916
War Diary	Treux	18/09/1916	18/09/1916
War Diary	Citadel Area	22/09/1916	22/09/1916
War Diary	Carnoy	24/09/1916	24/09/1916
War Diary	Arrow Head Copse	25/09/1916	25/09/1916
War Diary	Trenches	26/09/1916	29/09/1916
War Diary	Craters	30/09/1916	30/09/1916
War Diary	Sandpit Area	31/09/1916	31/10/1916
War Diary	Fouquereuil	01/11/1916	23/11/1916
War Diary	Le Preol	25/11/1916	20/12/1916
War Diary	Noeux Les Mines	21/12/1916	26/12/1916

War Diary	Vermelles	26/12/1916	14/04/1917
War Diary	Tharoc	01/05/1917	02/05/1917
War Diary	Vermelles	04/05/1917	18/05/1917
War Diary	Fouquereuil	19/05/1917	19/05/1917
War Diary	Vermelles	29/05/1917	19/06/1917
War Diary	Drouvin	20/06/1917	26/06/1917
War Diary	Bully Grenay	27/06/1917	29/06/1917
War Diary	Vermelles	30/06/1917	26/07/1917
War Diary	Villers Brulin	27/07/1917	26/08/1917
War Diary	Neoux Les Mines	27/08/1917	04/09/1917
War Diary	Les Brebis	05/09/1917	13/09/1917
War Diary	Loos	14/09/1917	23/09/1917
War Diary	Cite St. Pierre	24/09/1917	29/09/1917
Miscellaneous	Les Brebis	30/09/1917	30/09/1917
War Diary	Drouvin	01/10/1917	09/10/1917
War Diary	Thazengaile	16/10/1917	16/10/1917
War Diary	Loos	11/10/1917	18/10/1917
War Diary	Emile	18/10/1917	23/10/1917
War Diary	Noeux Les Mines	23/10/1917	23/10/1917
War Diary	La Timande	24/10/1917	28/10/1917
War Diary	Orlencourt	29/10/1917	29/10/1917
War Diary	Leincourt	30/10/1917	15/11/1917
War Diary	Dessert Wood	16/11/1917	16/11/1917
War Diary	Trenches	19/11/1917	30/11/1917
War Diary	Premy Chapel	01/12/1917	04/12/1917
War Diary	Ribecourt	05/12/1917	07/12/1917
War Diary	Valley Trench	08/12/1917	10/12/1917
War Diary	Etricourt	14/12/1917	14/12/1917
War Diary	Bellacourt	16/12/1917	31/12/1917
Heading	6th Division 71st M.G. Coy January Only 1918		
War Diary	Bellacourt	01/01/1918	01/01/1918
War Diary	Courcelles	02/01/1918	15/01/1918
War Diary	Fremicourt	16/01/1918	16/01/1918
War Diary	Doignies	17/01/1918	25/01/1918
War Diary	Lebucquiere	26/01/1918	31/01/1918

6 DIV, 71 INF BRIGADE.

9
~~6~~ BN SUFFOLK REGIMENT.

1915 AUG TO 1918 FEB.

71 MACHINE GUN COMPANY

1916 AUG TO 1918 JAN.

1625

6 DIV, 71 INF BRIGADE.

~~6~~ 9 BN SUFFOLK REGIMENT.
1915 AUG TO 1918 FEB.

71 MACHINE GUN COMPANY.
1916 AUG TO 1918 JAN.

1625

WO 95/1625/1

6TH DIV

9 BN SUFFOLK REGT

AUG 1915 - FEB 1918

6 DIVISION

71 BDE

9 BN SUFFOLK REGT

1915 AUG – 1916 DEC

71st Inf.Bde.
24th Div.

Battn. disembarked
Boulogne from
England 31.8.15.

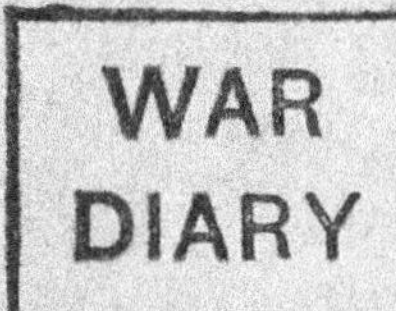

9th BATTN. THE SUFFOLK REGIMENT.

AUGUST AND SEPTEMBER

(22.8.15 to 30.9.15)

1 9 1 5

Instructions regarding War Diaries and Intelligence Summaries are contained in F. S. Regs., Part II. and the Staff Manual respectively. Title pages will be prepared in manuscript.

9th Battn. Suffolk Regt.

WAR DIARY
or
~~INTELLIGENCE SUMMARY.~~

(*Erase heading not required.*)

Army Form C. 2118.

Place	Date	Hour	Summary of Events and Information	Remarks and references to Appendices
Blackdown	22/8/15.	--	Battalion in Barracks.	
			15% of N C Os and men and 7 Officers away on final leave	
Blackdown	23/8/15	--	As above	
Blackdown	24/8/15	8.30 a.m.	Battalion proceeded to Chobham Common for exercise in Trench Warfare.	
			Troops Bivouacked on the Common	
			A further 15% of N C O's and men were recalled to Barracks and sent on 48 hours leave at 8 p m	
Blackdown	25/8/16		Battalion at Chobham Common.	
			A further 15% N. C O's and men sent on 48 hours leave at midday	
			Battalion returned to Barracks at 7.45 P.M.	
			12 NCOs to 12 Batt Suffolk Regt.	
			1 man to 10 "	
			15 men to 11 Essex	
			19 men to 8 Bedfordshire	
Blackdown	26/8/16		Battalion in Barracks.	
			remaining Officers and men who had not had leave, proceeded on 48 hours final leave.	
Blackdown	27/8/15		Battalion in Barracks.	
			50 men sent to fill in trenches at Chobham Common	
Blackdown	28/8/15		Battalion in Barracks. 200 men sent to fill in trenches at Chobham Common	

2353 Wt. W2544/1454 700,000 5/15 D. D. & L. A.D.S.S./Forms/C. 2118.

4

Instructions regarding War Diaries and Intelligence Summaries are contained in F. S. Regs., Part II. and the Staff Manual respectively. Title pages will be prepared in manuscript.

9th Batn Suffolk Regt.

WAR DIARY
~~or~~
~~INTELLIGENCE SUMMARY.~~
(Erase heading not required.)

Army Form C. 2118.

Place	Date	Hour	Summary of Events and Information	Remarks and references to Appendices
Blackdown.	28/8/15.		First draft of Battalion proceeded to Southampton. at night. consisting of:— Field Officer. Machine Gun Officer. Transport Officer. R.Q.M.Sgt. Transport Sgt. Sgt Shoemaker Drivers 37. Pioneers 2. Grooms 10. Machine Gun Section 34. Cooks 5. Signallers with cycles 9. Company Storeman 4.	
Blackdown.	29/8/15		Battalion in Barracks.	
Blackdown	30/8/15.		Battalion proceeded overseas. via. Folkestone A.T.B. Companies left Blackdown at to entrain 5.50 PM C.T.D " " " " to entrain 6.17 PM The Batn had an uneventfull crossing and landed at Boulogne about midnight, both embarkation and disembarkation was carried out very satisfactorily The C. O. was congratulated by G. O. C Division on having no absentees. Brig Gen Bartier having remained in England the Brigade was commanded by Col Mummsell Sherwin.	

2353 Wt. W2534/1454 700,000 5/15 D. D. & L. A.D.S.S./Forms/C. 2118.

3.

Army Form C. 2118.

WAR DIARY

or

~~INTELLIGENCE SUMMARY.~~

(Erase heading not required.)

Instructions regarding War Diaries and Intelligence Summaries are contained in F. S. Regs., Part II. and the Staff Manual respectively. Title pages will be prepared in manuscript.

Place	Date	Hour	Summary of Events and Information	Remarks and references to Appendices
Boulogne	31/8/15	–	On arrival at Boulogne the Batn was formed up on the quay and marched to "Ostrohove Large Rest Camp" where T. Camp was handed over to us. Blankets etc were issued and by 2 am the men had settled down. The morning was spent resting the men in camp. At 12.15. marched to Gare Central and entrained for MONTREUIL arriving at 5.57 P.M. after detraining orders were received to proceed to ~~[illegible]~~ ALETTE about 8 Kil N.E. MONTREUIL. After a rather trying march owing to large amount of dust from passing motors etc arrived ALETTE at 6.20 P.M. and found no arrangements had been made for billets. The Mayor was found, who requisitioned barn, outbuildings straw etc and the Batn was billeted by 7.40 P.M. D. Coy had to proceed on to ~~[illegible]~~ CLONLEU where they obtained ~~[illegible]~~ quarters. The Transport had not yet arrived but subsequently turned up at 9.35 P.M. They had detrained at MARESQUEL but	

2353 Wt. W2544/1454 700,000 5/15 D. D. & L. A.D.S.S./Forms/C. 2118.

4

Instructions regarding War Diaries and Intelligence Summaries are contained in F. S. Regs., Part II. and the Staff Manual respectively. Title pages will be prepared in manuscript.

WAR DIARY

or

~~INTELLIGENCE~~ ~~SUMMARY~~.

(*Erase heading not required.*)

Army Form C. 2118.

Place	Date	Hour	Summary of Events and Information	Remarks and references to Appendices
			owing to very hilly nature of the road on the points which had been given them they had great difficulty in proceeding. Horses and mules arrived very tired.	
			Capt. AP Mack left in Hosp Hospital Boulogne with a small bone broken in his left foot.	
Alette.	1/9/15.		The Batn in Billets in ALETTE. The day was spent in completing billeting arrangements and in perfecting commissariat arrangements and in attending to the comforts of the men.	
ALETTE	2/9/15.		Batn in billets in ALETTE. Assemblies were practiced at Company Alarm posts and times taken for collective assembly at Batn Alarm post. The Batn was afterwards route marched in full marching order, Transport Etc exercised also.	
ALETTE	3/9/15.		Batn in billets in ALETTE very wet day no out-door work was possible	
"	4/9/15.		do do do Coy Commanders held Kit inspections in morning to find out deficiencies in mens Kits	

2353 Wt. W2544/1454 700,000 5/15 D. D. & L. A.D.S.S./Forms/C. 2118.

5.

Instructions regarding War Diaries and Intelligence Summaries are contained in F. S. Regs., Part II. and the Staff Manual respectively. Title pages will be prepared in manuscript.

WAR DIARY
or
~~INTELLIGENCE SUMMARY.~~
(Erase heading not required.)

Army Form C. 2118.

Place	Date	Hour	Summary of Events and Information	Remarks and references to Appendices
Alette	5/9/15.		Sunday Batn attended church parade in open, at 11 A.M. At 3 P.M Brigadier Gen. Shewen had a Brigade assembly on St Omer Rd and inspected Batns in column of route.	
Alette	6/9/15.		Batn exercised under Company arrangements. At 11 A.M. Lt Gen R.C.B Haking K.C.B. saw Commanding Officer, 2nd in Command, Company Commanders Etc and welcomed ~~#~~ the Brigade to the 11th Army Corps and roughly explained ideas of future tactics of the Allies	
Alette	7/9/15		9 AM Brigade 'rendezvous' on St Omer Rd for a Divisional Scheme for attack watched by Lt Gen Haking. The attack was successfully delivered and Gen Haking expressed himself as being pleased with the manner it was carried out.	

6

Army Form C. 2118.

WAR DIARY
or
~~INTELLIGENCE SUMMARY.~~
(Erase heading not required.)

Instructions regarding War Diaries and Intelligence Summaries are contained in F. S. Regs., Part II. and the Staff Manual respectively. Title pages will be prepared in manuscript.

Place	Date	Hour	Summary of Events and Information	Remarks and references to Appendices
Alette	8/9/15.		Two Companies employed in digging instructional trenches, and two Companies firing at temporary range which has been arranged for the use of Batn whilst in ALETTE.	
ALETTE	9/9/15.		Exercises in entrenching, range firing etc under Company Commanders.	
ALETTE	10/9/15		Exercises in entrenching, etc under Coy Commanders	
		9 PM	At 9 P.M. a surprise alarm was given and the Batn assembled in column of route at Batn Headquarters, the assembly was carried out expeditiously and Batn moved off complete in 1 hour 40 mins.	
ALETTE	11/9/15.		An Instructional attack was carried out by the Brigade. This Batn was however in reserve and saw little of the proceedings.	
ALETTE	12/9/15		SUNDAY	
		9.30 AM	Church Parade.	
ALETTE	13/9/15.		Exercises in entrenching and range work under Coy Arrangements.	
			Corpl from Guards Division attached to Batn for three days for instruction in Bombing.	

2353 Wt. W2544/1454 700,000 5/15 D. D. & L. A.D.S.S./Forms/C. 2118.

1.

Instructions regarding War Diaries and Intelligence Summaries are contained in F. S. Regs., Part II. and the Staff Manual respectively. Title pages will be prepared in manuscript.

WAR DIARY
or
~~INTELLIGENCE~~ SUMMARY.
(Erase heading not required.)

Army Form C. 2118.

Place	Date	Hour	Summary of Events and Information	Remarks and references to Appendices
ALETTE	14/9/15.		A Divisional Field day had been arranged, and the Batn marched out to assist them but the scheme was abandoned on account of wet weather.	
ALETTE	15/9/15		Training under Company Arrangements. Men were paid in Afternoon.	
ALETTE	16/9/15.		Training under Company Arrangements.	
ALETTE	17/9/15.		Training under Company Arrangements. Batn Night march and practise of Attack Formation.	
ALETTE	18/9/15.		Batn practised in constructing Bivouac Shelters.	
ALETTE	19/9/15		Church Parade.	
ALETTE	20/9/15		Training under Company Arrangements.	
ALETTE } MATRINGHEN }	21/9/15		Colonel Ernest Stracey proceeded to Norfolk Regt and Command taken by Major Brettell of East Surrey Regt. Battn received orders to leave ALETTE. Paraded at 3.30 and marched during the night to MATRINGHEM a distance of 21 miles. The march was well carried out there being few stragglers.	

2353 Wt. W2544/1454 700,000 5/15 D. D. & L. A.D.S.S./Forms/C. 2118.

Instructions regarding War Diaries and Intelligence Summaries are contained in F. S. Regs., Part II. and the Staff Manual respectively. Title pages will be prepared in manuscript.

WAR DIARY
or
~~INTELLIGENCE~~ ~~SUMMARY~~.
(Erase heading not required.)

Army Form C. 2118.

Place	Date	Hour	Summary of Events and Information	Remarks and references to Appendices
MATRINGHEM	22/9/15	A.M. 2.30	Battn arrived at MATRINGHAM and was billeted in farm buildings etc. During day men were rested.	
		P.M. 1.30	Billeting party left at 1.30 for new area (1 officer 1 N.C.O).	
		5.0	Battn left MATRINGHAM and marched about 15 miles to HAM-EN-ARTOIS with Brigade. Men very tired owing to long march of previous night.	AW.
HAM-EN-ARTOIS	23/9/15		Battn arrived about 3.A.M. and went into billets. At 5.0 P.M. billeting party left for bivouac area at LE GORNET BOURDOIS.	
		7.P.M.	Battn left HAM-EN-ARTOIS for Brigade concentration bivouac area. Being fortunate in the allotment of areas all men were able to sleep in farm buildings. Storm during greater part of night.	AW.
LE GORNET BOURDOIS	24/9/15		Men rested during morning and afternoon. Billeting party left at 2 P.M for BETHUNE	
		4.0 P.M.	Battn marched off with Brigade to BETHUNE a distance of twelve miles arriving following morning.	AW.

2353 Wt. W2544/1454 700,000 5/15 D. D. & L. A.D.S.S./Forms/C. 2118.

Army Form C. 2118.

WAR DIARY
or
~~INTELLIGENCE~~ SUMMARY.

(*Erase heading not required.*)

Instructions regarding War Diaries and Intelligence Summaries are contained in F. S. Regs., Part II. and the Staff Manual respectively. Title pages will be prepared in manuscript.

Place	Date	Hour	Summary of Events and Information	Remarks and references to Appendices
BETHUNE	25/9/15	A.M. 1.0	Battn arrived at BETHUNE and proceeded to MONTMORENCY and FEUILLARDE BARRACKS. Men had very good quarters	
		11.0	An order was received for Battn move. Men were assembled and Battn ready to leave within half an hour. Battn proceeded in direction of front along the RUE D'AIRE. News had been received previously that after the heavy bombardment we had heard all night the German line had been pierced and trenches captured. Men in excellent spirits and all eager for the coming conflict. On the way up hundreds of German prisoners were met and also hundreds of wounded British Soldiers wounded in legs and arms showing that fighting had been in the open. Brigade formed up close to FOSSE No 9 on "QUALITY ST" and orders given for the attack.	REF 36B L 6.
			Extract from Corps Order.	
			"The twenty-fourth Division less seventy third Brigade will act as support to the 9th Division together with	

2353 Wt. W2544/1454 700,000 5/15 D. D. & L. A.D.S.S./Forms/C. 2118.

Instructions regarding War Diaries and Intelligence Summaries are contained in F. S. Regs., Part II. and the Staff Manual respectively. Title pages will be prepared in manuscript.

Army Form C. 2118.

WAR DIARY
or
~~INTELLIGENCE SUMMARY.~~
(Erase heading not required.)

Place	Date	Hour	Summary of Events and Information	Remarks and references to Appendices
BETHUNE FOSSE 9 (MAP 36 A)	25/9/15	P.M. 4.0	The 21st DIVISION on the right, advancing between LOOS & HULLUCH with objective ALLAY. Objective of 24 Div. VENDEN LE VEIL. The 24th Div. will keep touch on their right with the 21st DIVN. Advance will be made on line roughly:- Cross roads square G20 A 69 G23 D and S limit in VENDEN LE VEIL. General compass bearing 98° TRUE. 72 BDE will advance to crossroads in G15B and advance on VENDEN-LE-VEIL. HULLUCH is reported held by the bridges but this is not verified. 72 BDE will verify this. 71 BDE will follow 72 BDE in support. Particular attention will be paid to keeping touch with the 21st DIV. Essex & Suffolks will form first line with front of 1000 yds the Norfolks and Bedfords in second line. Casualties and walking cases to VERMELLES."	
		P.M. 8.0	The Battalion was moved up in double line of platoons A & B Coys in front C & D in rear. A steady advance was made in this formation until the third and second lines of English trenches. On reaching the first line English and first line German trenches the Battn was halted owing to an order coming from in front to retire.	

Army Form C. 2118.

WAR DIARY
or
~~INTELLIGENCE SUMMARY.~~
(Erase heading not required.)

Instructions regarding War Diaries and Intelligence Summaries are contained in F. S. Regs., Part II. and the Staff Manual respectively. Title pages will be prepared in manuscript.

Place	Date	Hour	Summary of Events and Information	Remarks and references to Appendices
	25/9/15	12.0 M'NT.	About midnight the advance was held up for reasons then unknown and between that hour and dawn the Battalion dug trenches in advance of German rear trench.	AW.
	26/9/15	A.M 5.0	At dawn the Battalion was ordered back to the German support trench and occupied this. During the early hours of the day these trenches were occupied also the communication trenches.	
		11.25	At 11.25 an order was received that 21st + 24th Division should attack at 11 A.M., 21st on right 24th on left. The 72nd Bde was detailed to attack the front allotted to 24th Div, with 11th Essex and 9th Suffolks in support, Suffolks on right, Essex on left, 600 yds in rear of 72nd Bde. The original of this order was subsequently lost. As the message was so late Lt Col Brettell at once sent down verbal messages for immediate advance and each section mounted the parapet and advanced under a heavy ~~shrapnel fire~~	

2353 Wt. W2544/1454 700,000 5/15 D. D. & L. A.D.S.S./Forms/C. 2118.

Army Form C. 2118.

Instructions regarding War Diaries and Intelligence Summaries are contained in F. S. Regs., Part II. and the Staff Manual respectively. Title pages will be prepared in manuscript.

WAR DIARY
or
~~INTELLIGENCE SUMMARY.~~

(Erase heading not required.)

Place	Date	Hour	Summary of Events and Information	Remarks and references to Appendices
	26/9/15		shrapnel fire towards the objective named in the order of the previous evening. Owing to the lack of time it was impossible to rally companies and organise the line but the various commanders did all they could during the advance to consolidate their units. A & C Coys were on the left B & D on the right some of each company being in each line. Owing to parts of the line being very far behind owing to late warning a very rapid advance had to be made on the left and it was found to be impossible to continue wearing packs and these were taken off. The advance continued × until the HULLUCH ~~LOOS~~-LENS Road was reached. Here the	

×The leading line advanced about 150 to 200 yards beyond this road

2353 Wt. W2514/1454 700,000 5/15 D. D. & L. A.D.S.S./Forms/C. 2118.

Instructions regarding War Diaries and Intelligence Summaries are contained in F. S. Regs., Part II. and the Staff Manual respectively. Title pages will be prepared in manuscript.

WAR DIARY
or
~~INTELLIGENCE SUMMARY.~~
(*Erase heading not required.*)

Army Form C. 2118.

Place	Date	Hour	Summary of Events and Information	Remarks and references to Appendices
26/9/15		P.M. 5.0	advance was held up for reasons then unknown and shortly afterwards the right flank began to retire. The centre held on to the road for about three hours and the flanks advanced and retired twice finally retiring about 5 P.M. the centre following and returning to the German support trench which was held during the night. The left flank reported that they had come under enfilade machine gun fire from HULLUCH and were forced to retire and here most of the casualties occurred. Both the C.O. and Adjutant were wounded and the orders were not recovered up to date of writing. An act of gallantry by Capt ~~[illegible]~~ Packard was reported to the Brigadier the following day.	

2353 Wt. W2514/1454 700,000 5/15 D. D. & L. A.D.S.S./Forms/C. 2118.

Instructions regarding War Diaries and Intelligence Summaries are contained in F. S. Regs., Part II. and the Staff Manual respectively. Title pages will be prepared in manuscript.

WAR DIARY
or
~~INTELLIGENCE SUMMARY.~~
(Erase heading not required.)

Army Form C. 2118.

Place	Date	Hour	Summary of Events and Information	Remarks and references to Appendices
26/9/15		7.0 P.M.	At 7.0 P.M. remaining portion of Battn under Capt Packard (3 officers and 100 men) was ordered to hold the enemy's second line against counter-attack and hold on until relieved. At about 8.30 the trench was occupied and the usual measures of conversion and defence were carried out with all dispatch. No attack was carried out during the night. Just before being relieved Capt Packard got into touch with another party of the Battn under Lieut Ellwood.	[illegible]
	27/9/15	A.M. 2.0	The party under Capt Packard was relieved by a Company of Coldstream Guards and returned towards Vermelles. Owing to the late hour the men were bivouacked for the rest of the night joining the remainder of the Battn at the Brigade encampment at SAILLY LABOURSE	
		A.M. 9.30	The roll of the Battn was called and the absentees duly recorded.	

2353 Wt. W2544/1454 700,000 5/15 D. D. & L. A.D.S.S./Forms/C. 2118.

Army Form C. 2118.

WAR DIARY
or
~~INTELLIGENCE SUMMARY.~~
(*Erase heading not required.*)

Instructions regarding War Diaries and Intelligence Summaries are contained in F. S. Regs., Part II. and the Staff Manual respectively. Title pages will be prepared in manuscript.

Place	Date	Hour	Summary of Events and Information	Remarks and references to Appendices
	27/9/15		As far as can be ascertained the following were casualties among officers: Killed: Lieut T. T. Stevens. Wounded: Lt Col R. V. Brettell, Maj L. C. Arbuthnot, Capt & Adjt F. Hedges, Capt H. F. Law, Lt R. England, Lt F. R. Cobbold Casualties – Men 9 Killed. Died of wounds 2. Wounded 81. Missing 45. The remainder of the day spent in rest and selection of bivouacs etc ~~at~~ near NOYELLES LES VERMELLES (SHEET 36B F11).	AW.
	28/9/15		During the day the bivouac area was changed twice and finally the battalion was ordered to entrain at once at NOEUX-LES-MINES and moved to BERGUETTE. Detraining at BERGUETTE the Battalion marched to HAM-EN-ARTOIS arriving about midnight. The following appointments were made by Maj. F. G. Davies 2/Lt C. Allerton to acting Adjt. 2/Lt A. Williamson to Acting Asst Adjt. Officer i/c M.G. Section Lt G. F. Beyts. To be Second in Command of Battn Capt Chas Packard.	

2353 Wt. W2544/1454 700,000 5/15 D. D. & L. A.D.S.S./Forms/C. 2118.

Instructions regarding War Diaries and Intelligence Summaries are contained in F. S. Regs., Part II. and the Staff Manual respectively. Title pages will be prepared in manuscript.

WAR DIARY
or
INTELLIGENCE SUMMARY.
(Erase heading not required.)

Army Form C. 2118.

Place	Date	Hour	Summary of Events and Information	Remarks and references to Appendices
HAM-EN-ARTOIS	29/9/15		Battn resting at HAM-EN-ARTOIS. aw.	
HAM-EN-ARTOIS	30/9/15		Battn resting at HAM-EN-ARTOIS. aw.	

2353 Wt. W2544/1454 700,000 5/15 D. D. & L. A.D.S.S./Forms/C. 2118.

71st Inf.Bde.
6th Div.

Battn. transferred
with Bde. from
24th Div. 14.10.15.

WAR DIARY

9th BATTN. THE SUFFOLK REGIMENT.

O C T O B E R

1 9 1 5

Instructions regarding War Diaries and Intelligence Summaries are contained in F. S. Regs., Part II. and the Staff Manual respectively. Title pages will be prepared in manuscript.

WAR DIARY
or
~~INTELLIGENCE SUMMARY~~.
(Erase heading not required.)

Army Form C. 2118.

Place	Date	Hour	Summary of Events and Information	Remarks and references to Appendices
HAM-EN-ARTOIS.	1/10/15		Battalion resting in billets Ham-en-Artois. Order received	
		A.M.	to prepare for move.	AW
		11.0	Transport ordered to prepare to leave	
		P.M. 12.40	Transport with cookers left HAM-EN-ARTOIS for CASSEL. Orders received for move on Oct 2nd.	
			Rest of Battn remained at HAM-EN-ARTOIS.	AW.
HAM-EN-ARTOIS } PROVEN	2/10/15	8 A.M.	Battalion moved from HAM-EN-ARTOIS at this hour and marched to BERGUET and entrained. Journey by rail to GODVAERSVELDE and marched thence to WATOU and PROVEN arriving in the evening. Billets and bivouacs arranged just outside PROVEN. The change from FRANCE to BELGIUM was made just before reaching WATOU.	AW
PROVEN	3/10/15		Battalion resting at PROVEN.	AW
PROVEN	4/10/15		Battalion resting at PROVEN. Inspection by Maj Gen Capper who announced his taking Command of 24th DIVISION. In an address to the men he asked for their co-operation with him and their	

2353 Wt. W2544/1454 700,000 5/15 D. D. & L. A.D.S.S./Forms/C. 2118.

Instructions regarding War Diaries and Intelligence Summaries are contained in F. S. Regs., Part II. and the Staff Manual respectively. Title pages will be prepared in manuscript.

WAR DIARY
or
INTELLIGENCE SUMMARY.
(Erase heading not required.)

Army Form C. 2118.

Place	Date	Hour	Summary of Events and Information	Remarks and references to Appendices
			officers and congratulated them on what they had done on Sept 25/26.	
PROVEN – BRANDHOEK	5/10/15	12.30	2/LTS COLLIS, HARDY & THEOBALD reported their arrival. Capt Sammons and Lt Byrne with party of 24 N.C.Os and men left to go in next to trenches for instruction. AW	
			Battalion left PROVEN with 71ST INF. BDE and marched to BRANDHOEK Huts provided by 7th INF. BDE. AW	Map 28 G18a 5.9.
BRANDHOEK	6/10/15		Battalion resting in billets. In afternoon A & B. Coys left to go into trenches for instruction with 7TH INF. BDE. C & D. Coys remaining in billets. AW	
BRANDHOEK	7/10/15		A & B. Coys in trenches in HOOGE salient with Wiltshire Regt and S Lancs. Working party of 100 men and 1 officer sent to H.Q. 7 INF BDE. Improving of trenches near same. AW.	

2353 Wt. W2544/1454 700,000 5/15 D. D. & L. A.D.S.S./Forms/C. 2118.

Instructions regarding War Diaries and Intelligence Summaries are contained in F. S. Regs., Part II. and the Staff Manual respectively. Title pages will be prepared in manuscript.

WAR DIARY
or
~~INTELLIGENCE SUMMARY.~~
(Erase heading not required.)

Army Form C. 2118.

Place	Date	Hour	Summary of Events and Information	Remarks and references to Appendices
BRANDHOEK	8/10/15	9.30 P.M	C & D. Coys received new greatcoats and other equipment for going to trenches and marched off to H.Q. 7 INF. BDE. ~~Halt made~~ for tea at H.Q. 7. INF BDE and in darkness the companies went into trenches. Guides were met and Companies conducted to their various trenches and dug-outs. C. Coy was with WILTS RGT. D. COY the [illegible] [illegible] DOWN. BELL. GARDNER & MACDONALD reported. ~~[illegible]~~ HARDY & THEOBALD ~~reported~~ arrived.	AW
TRENCHES BRANDHOEK	9/10/15		A. & B. Coys resting in billets at BRANDHOEK. C & D. COYS in trenches. Companies in trenches were given opportunity of seeing all the various activities in trench warfare and took part in work and support etc. During the night 9/10 Pte Bareham of C. Coy was killed whilst at work above a support trench.	AW
TRENCHES BRANDHOEK RENINGHELST	10/10/15	NOON 12.0	C & D. Coys in trenches. A & B resting in hutments at BRANDHOEK. A & B. Coys left BRANDHOEK at noon and marched to RENINGHELST. PTE BAREHAM C. COY buried near TRANSPORT FARM. D & C. Coys left trenches during the evening and returned to H.Q 7. INF. BDE.	AW

2353 Wt. W2544/1454 700,000 5/15 D. D. & L. A.D.S.S./Forms/C. 2118.

WAR DIARY
or
INTELLIGENCE SUMMARY.
(Erase heading not required.)

Army Form C. 2118.

Instructions regarding War Diaries and Intelligence Summaries are contained in F. S. Regs., Part II. and the Staff Manual respectively. Title pages will be prepared in manuscript.

Place	Date	Hour	Summary of Events and Information	Remarks and references to Appendices
			As the Battn had moved to RENINGHELST arrangements made for A C & D Coys to bivouac in transport field of S. LANCS, the companies arriving there after midnight.	
RENINGHELST. ~~PROVEN.~~ WATOU	11/10/15	P.M. 4.0	A & B. Coys left RENINGHELST at NOON for PROVEN leaving rations for C & D. Coys. A & B Coys arrived at billeting area at 4.0	
		P.M. 8.0	and C & D Coys at 8 P.M.	
			aw	
~~PROVEN~~ WATOU.	12/10/15		Battn resting in billets near PROVEN	
		P.M. 11.30	Inspection of drafts by Brigadier General Shewan. aw	
WATOU.	13/10/15	12.30	Inspection of Battalion by Maj. Gen. Congreve V.C. who expressed his satisfaction with the appearance of the Battn and emphasised the importance of work in the trenches to ensure comfort during winter.	
			aw	

2353 Wt. W2514/1454 700,000 5/15 D. D. & L. A.D.S.S./Forms/C. 2118.

Army Form C. 2118.

Instructions regarding War Diaries and Intelligence Summaries are contained in F. S. Regs., Part II. and the Staff Manual respectively. Title pages will be prepared in manuscript.

WAR DIARY
or
INTELLIGENCE SUMMARY.
(Erase heading not required.)

Place	Date	Hour	Summary of Events and Information	Remarks and references to Appendices
WATOU	14/10/15	3.30	Battalion left WATOU and marched via POPERINGHE to Divisional camp C where huts were provided. Arrived at 6.15 P.M. AW	
CAMP C (Sheet 28 A.30)	15/10/15		Battalion bathed at Divisional Baths POPERINGHE. Path improvement work carried out under Coy. arrangements. AW	
			Inspection of Unit by Commander ~~at noon~~ 6th Corps (Gen J.L. KEIR) AW	
CAMP C.	16/10/15	3.0	Battalion left Camp C for trenches at ST. JEAN. Companies took over at about 8.30 p.m. Allotment of trenches	SHEET 28 C 27 d
			A Coy. ST JEAN. X8. 12A.	
			B Coy. B 12.	
			C Coy X 8 X 9	
			D Coy B 11 S 12.	

Instructions regarding War Diaries and Intelligence Summaries are contained in F. S. Regs., Part II. and the Staff Manual respectively. Title pages will be prepared in manuscript.

Army Form C. 2118.

WAR DIARY
or
~~INTELLIGENCE SUMMARY.~~

(Erase heading not required.)

Place	Date	Hour	Summary of Events and Information	Remarks and references to Appendices
TRENCHES ST JEAN.	17/10/15		Battn in trenches. Day and night working parties improved drainage of trenches. No casualties	AW
ST JEAN	18/10/15		Battn in trenches. Enemy shrapnel prevented day working parties doing such work. In evening at 9.15 p.m enemy entered listening post of B Coy and opened fire, was repulsed by rapid fire of B. Coy. C.S.M. Thompson wounded. Casualties 2 wounded.	AW
ST JEAN	19/10/15		Battn in trenches. Nothing unusual to report. Some shell fire during day. Casualties 1 killed 3 wounded.	AW
ST JEAN	20/10/15		Battn in trenches. Artillery of both sides very active. Casualties 1 Died of wounds, 1 wounded.	AW

2353 Wt. W2544/1454 700,000 5/15 D. D. & L. A.D.S.S./Forms/C. 2118.

Instructions regarding War Diaries and Intelligence Summaries are contained in F. S. Regs., Part II. and the Staff Manual respectively. Title pages will be prepared in manuscript.

WAR DIARY
or
INTELLIGENCE SUMMARY.
(Erase heading not required.)

Army Form C. 2118.

Place	Date	Hour	Summary of Events and Information	Remarks and references to Appendices
St JEAN.	21/10/15		Battn in trenches. Constant shelling during the day but no casualties. AW	
St JEAN	22/10/15		Battn in trenches. Enemy aeroplane overhead most of day during bombardment of trenches. Bombardment increased during afternoon and a few men were struck by shrapnel Casualties 2 Killed 5 wounded. Battn relieved between 7 and 9 p.m by 9 NORFOLK R. Relief carried out during shrapnel bombardment without casualties. Companies returned to Camp A, C Coy remaining at Canal bank. AW	

2353 Wt. W2544/1454 700,000 5/15 D. D. & L. A.D.S.S./Forms/C. 2118.

Instructions regarding War Diaries and Intelligence Summaries are contained in F. S. Regs., Part II. and the Staff Manual respectively. Title pages will be prepared in manuscript.

WAR DIARY
or
INTELLIGENCE SUMMARY.
(Erase heading not required.)

Army Form C. 2118.

Place	Date	Hour	Summary of Events and Information	Remarks and references to Appendices
CAMP A	23/10/15		Battn less C. Coy resting in CAMP A. AW	
CAMP A	24/10/15		Battn less C. Coy resting in CAMP A. Church parade in morning at 11.0. Capt A. P. MACK reported arrival, rejoined fit for duty. AW	
CAMP A	24/10/15		Battn less C. Coy resting in CAMP A. Casualties 2 wounded. AW	
CAMP A	25/10/15		Battn less C. Coy resting in CAMP A. Battn went to POPERINGHE for baths AW	
CAMP A	26/10/15		A. B. & D. Coys resting in CAMP A. Adjt and Coy Commanders went up to trenches preparatory to taking over. Party under Capt Packard and 2/Lt Wilmot Johnson went to POPERINGHE for inspection by Army Commander. AW	

2353 Wt. W2544/1454 700,000 5/15 D. D. & L. A.D.S.S./Forms/C. 2118.

Instructions regarding War Diaries and Intelligence Summaries are contained in F. S. Regs., Part II. and the Staff Manual respectively. Title pages will be prepared in manuscript.

WAR DIARY
or
INTELLIGENCE SUMMARY.
(Erase heading not required.)

Army Form C. 2118.

Place	Date	Hour	Summary of Events and Information	Remarks and references to Appendices
29	27/10/15		Battn went up to trenches at Forward Cottage district A. Coy B14 & S14 B. Coy S13B S15A & B16 C. Coy Forward Cottage + B15. S14. D. Coy. B14 & S13B.	AW
	28/10/15		Battn in Trenches Casualties ~~nil~~ 2 wounded.	AW
	29/10/15		Battn in Trenches at Forward Cottage Casualties - Died of wounds 1.	AW
	30/10/15		Battn in Trenches - Very bad weather, trenches began to fall in. Casualties 8 wounded	AW

2353 Wt. W2544/1454 700,000 5/15 D. D. & L. A.D.S.S./Forms/C. 2118.

Army Form C. 2118.

Instructions regarding War Diaries and Intelligence Summaries are contained in F. S. Regs., Part II. and the Staff Manual respectively. Title pages will be prepared in manuscript.

WAR DIARY
or
INTELLIGENCE SUMMARY.

(Erase heading not required.)

Place	Date	Hour	Summary of Events and Information	Remarks and references to Appendices
TRENCHES.	31/10/15		Batt. in Trenches C.O ordered relief of C Coy fire trenches owing to bad condition relief in evening Major F. G. Davies having reported sick was sent to England Casualties Wounded 2	

W. H. [illegible] Major
Cmdg
9th ~~[illegible]~~ Suffolk Regt.

9.11.15.

2353 Wt. W2544/1454 700,000 5/15 D. D. & L. A.D.S.S./Forms/C. 2118.

71st Inf.Bde.
6th Div.

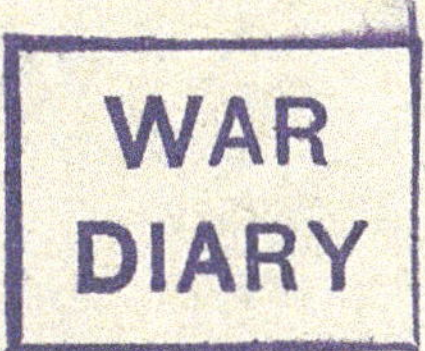

9th BATTN. THE SUFFOLK REGIMENT.

N O V E M B E R

1 9 1 5

Instructions regarding War Diaries and Intelligence Summaries are contained in F. S. Regs., Part II. and the Staff Manual respectively. Title pages will be prepared in manuscript.

WAR DIARY

or

INTELLIGENCE SUMMARY.

(Erase heading not required.)

Army Form C. 2118.

Place	Date	Hour	Summary of Events and Information	Remarks and references to Appendices
TRENCHES	31/10/15		Battn in Trenches. C.O. arranged relief of C. Coy's fire trenches owing to bad conditions. Relief in evening. Major F. G. Davies having reported sick was sent to England. Cas. Wounded 2. [illegible]	
TRENCHES	1/11/15		Battn in Trenches. Weather still very bad - much rain and damage to trenches. Much trouble with "Trench feet". Cas. Wounded 3. [illegible]	
	2/11/15		Battn relieved on night of 2nd by 9 Nor: R. Casualties Wounded 2. [illegible]	
	3/11/15		Battn resting in CAMP A. Major W. A. H. de la Pryme D.S.O. took over Command of Battn. [illegible]	

2353 Wt. W2514/1454 700,000 5/15 D. D. & L. A.D.S.S./Forms/C. 2118.

Instructions regarding War Diaries and Intelligence Summaries are contained in F. S. Regs., Part II. and the Staff Manual respectively. Title pages will be prepared in manuscript.

WAR DIARY
or
INTELLIGENCE SUMMARY.

(Erase heading not required.)

Army Form C. 2118.

Place	Date	Hour	Summary of Events and Information	Remarks and references to Appendices
CAMP A	4/11/15		Battn resting in CAMP A. AW	
CAMP A	5/11/15		Battn resting in CAMP. A. AW	
CAMP A	6/11/15		Battn resting in CAMP. A. Battn concert in evening. AW	
CAMP A	7/11/15		Battn at CAMP A. Church parade at 11.0 A.M. Battn went up to ST JEAN trenches at 5.0 P.M. AW.	

2353 Wt. W2544/1454 700,000 5/15 D. D. & L. A.D.S.S./Forms/C. 2118.

Instructions regarding War Diaries and Intelligence Summaries are contained in F. S. Regs., Part II. and the Staff Manual respectively. Title pages will be prepared in manuscript.

WAR DIARY
or
INTELLIGENCE SUMMARY.
(Erase heading not required.)

Army Form C. 2118.

Place	Date	Hour	Summary of Events and Information	Remarks and references to Appendices
Trenches	8/11/15		in Trenches taken over from 2nd SHERWOOD FORESTERS. Distribution of Batt. A. Coy 2 Platoons ST JEAN. 2 " B 11 & 12. B. Coy 2 " B12 2 " S13a & S13b. C. Coy in Canal Bank D Coy X 8 & X 9. No Casualties. B.A.	
Trenches	9/11/15		In trenches. enemy heavily bombarded LA BRIQUE & along road to ST JEAN. No Casualties. B.A.	
Trenches	10/11/15		In Trenches enemy quiet slight artillery action. No Casualties B.A.	
Trenches	11/11/15		In Trenches heavy artillery engagement enemy heavily shelled YPRES causing damage to the Tower. B.A.	

2353 Wt. W2514/1454 700,000 5/15 D. D. & L. A.D.S.S./Forms/C. 2118.

WAR DIARY
or
INTELLIGENCE SUMMARY.
(Erase heading not required.)

Army Form C. 2118.

Instructions regarding War Diaries and Intelligence Summaries are contained in F. S. Regs., Part II. and the Staff Manual respectively. Title pages will be prepared in manuscript.

Place	Date	Hour	Summary of Events and Information	Remarks and references to Appendices
Trenches	12/11/15.		In Trenches enemy quiet were relieved by 9th Norfolks at 9.20PM Batt moved to rest Camps. Headquarters & A Coy in H11. B Coy. Machine Gun Farm. C. Coy stopped on Canal Bank D Coy to POPERINGHE. ELA	
Rest Camps	13/11/15.		Batt Resting. D. Coy moved from POPERINGHE to Camp A in wood. 2 Platoon of C. Coy moved from Canal Bank to H11. our guns very busy weather very unsettled Batt supplying working parties for the trenches ELA	
Rest Camp	14/11/15.		Batt Resting. weather improving working parties supplied for trenches ELA	
Rest Camp	15/11/15.		Batt Resting working parties supplied for trenches artillery on both sides very active Casualties. 5. men. ELA	
Rest Camp	16/11/15.		Batt Resting. working parties supplied for trenches D Coy moved from Camp A to BRIELEN Casualties. 6. men Enemy Artillery very active. ELA	
Rest Camp	17/11/15.		Batt Resting. Batt proceeded to trenches at 6PM taken over from 2nd Sherwoods Foresters Distribution of Coys D. Coy FORWARD COTTAGE A Coy B14 & S14. B Coy B14. S14 & S13 C Coy S13 & S13 & LA BRIQUE. Relief finished at 9.10PM No Casualties ELA	

Army Form C. 2118.

Instructions regarding War Diaries and Intelligence Summaries are contained in F. S. Regs., Part II. and the Staff Manual respectively. Title pages will be prepared in manuscript.

WAR DIARY
or
INTELLIGENCE SUMMARY.
(Erase heading not required.)

Place	Date	Hour	Summary of Events and Information	Remarks and references to Appendices
In Trenches	18/11/15.		In Trenches enemy very quiet. Officers Commd 7th KRR. & Coy Commrs looking over trenches preparatory to taking over. 3 Casualties. CA CA.	
In Trenches	19/11/15		In Trenches. enemy quiet artillery active on occasion. Batt relieved by 7th KRR. relief finished by PM. Batt proceeded by train from YPRES. to Camp A in wood 4 Casualties. CA	
CAMP A.	20/11/15		Batt resting. Camp in bad state owing to the mud. CA	
CAMP. A.	21/11/15		Batt resting. CA	
CAMP A	22/11/15.		Batt resting. 8. Officers sent to LONDON. RE. Yard for instruction in revetments etc. CA	
CAMP A.	23/11/15.		Batt resting. 4. Other Officers sent for instruction to LONDON. R.E. weather cold but dry. CA	
CAMP A	24/11/15.		Batt resting. CA.	

2353 Wt. W2514/1454 700,000 5/15 D. D. & L. A.D.S.S./Forms/C. 2118.

Instructions regarding War Diaries and Intelligence Summaries are contained in F. S. Regs., Part II. and the Staff Manual respectively. Title pages will be prepared in manuscript.

WAR DIARY
or
INTELLIGENCE SUMMARY.
(Erase heading not required.)

Army Form C. 2118.

Place	Date	Hour	Summary of Events and Information	Remarks and references to Appendices
CAMP A.	25/11/15.		Batt. resting. Batt had short route march & were inspected by General Sir Herbert C.C. Plumer K.C.B. during the march. Band were with Batt for first time since LOOS.	[illegible]
CAMP A	26/11/15.		Batt resting. Batt proceeded to POPERINGHE to fresh billets.	[illegible]
POPERINGHE	27/11/15.		Batt resting.	[illegible]
POPERINGHE	28/11/15		Batt resting. Working Party of ~~145~~ men were sent to trenches to work with R.E of 14th Division. Casualties. 2. wounded. Batt went to Church at Cinema Poperinghe.	[illegible]
POPERINGHE	29/11/15.		Batt resting. Working Party of 145 & 350 men were sent to trenches to work with R.E of 14th Divis	[illegible]
POPERINGHE	30/11/15		Batt Resting. Working Parties suffered 3. Casualties.	

W.H.G. De la Rue Major
Commdg 9th Batt Suffolk Regt

2353 Wt. W2544/1454 700,000 5/15 D. D. & L. A.D.S.S./Forms/C. 2118.

71st Inf.Bde.
6th Div.

WAR DIARY

9th BATTN. THE SUFFOLK REGIMENT.

D E C E M B E R

1 9 1 5

Instructions regarding War Diaries and Intelligence Summaries are contained in F. S. Regs., Part II. and the Staff Manual respectively. Title pages will be prepared in manuscript.

WAR DIARY
or
INTELLIGENCE SUMMARY.

(Erase heading not required.)

Army Form C. 2118.

Place	Date	Hour	Summary of Events and Information	Remarks and references to Appendices
POPERINGHE	1/12/15.		Batt Resting. b.a.	
POPERINGHE	2/12/15.		Batt moved to Camp A. & relieved Norfolks D Coy going to Canal Bank. b.a.	
CAMP. A.	3/12/15		Batt Resting b.a.	
CAMP. A.	4/12/15.		Batt Resting. Casualties. Wounded. 2/LT. R.H. GUINNESS. do O.R. two. b.a.	
CAMP. A	5/12/15.		Batt. Resting. D Coy from Canal Bank. joined Batt in Camp A. Casualties. two (wounded) LIEUT. R. ENGLAND. joined Batt from Base [illegible]. b.a.	
CAMP. A	6/12/15		Batt Resting Casualties. two, (wounded) b.a.	
CAMP. A.	7/12/15.		Batt. Resting b.a.	
CAMP. A.	8/12/15		Batt. Resting 2/LT. C. H. BOX & 2/LT. W.F. FITCH. reported themselves & taken on Strength of Batt. b.a.	

Army Form C. 2118.

Instructions regarding War Diaries and Intelligence Summaries are contained in F. S. Regs., Part II. and the Staff Manual respectively. Title pages will be prepared in manuscript.

WAR DIARY
or
INTELLIGENCE SUMMARY.
(Erase heading not required.)

Place	Date	Hour	Summary of Events and Information	Remarks and references to Appendices
CAMP. A.	9/12/15		Batt resting	
do	10/12/15		do	
do	11/12/15		do	
do	12/12/15		do	
do	13/12/15		do	
do	14/12/15		do	
do	15/12/15		do CO.	
do	16/12/15		do	
do	17/12/15		do. Wire received from Brigade that Capt C.T. Packard. Capt G.B. Steward. Lieut C.F. Bartz awarded Military [Cross] for Bravery at Loos. No 13256. Serg. R. Bolingbroke. Pte 13395 Pte J.W. Mann No 17626 Pte G. Hales, awarded D.C.M. for same.	C.A.
do	18/12/15		Batt relieved 9th Norfolks in Trenches at St JEAN defences relief finished at 9.15 PM. Casualties Nil. Distribution of Coys. A Coy B 11.12 & 13. B. Fire & S Line C. St JEAN & Canal Bank. D Canal Bank	C.A.
In Trenches	19/12/15		At 5.30 AM. a Gas attack was made by the enemy. Gas was sent over from 5.30 AM to 6. A.M. & was followed by an very heavy bombardment of our Trenches & St JEAN. It continued through the day & night following. Attack failed. {D Coy & C Coy ordered to reinforce at 5.30 AM & after at 7.45 AM. Casualties. 2/Lt. B.F. COLLIS. wounded. O.R. Killed 4. Died of wounds 1. Died Gas poisoning 1. Wounded 40 Suffering Gas Poisoning 18.	C.A.
Trenches	20/12/15		Batt in Trenches. Bombardment kept up till 8 AM remainder of day fairly quiet. D Coy returned to Canal Bank. Casualties. 2/Lt. B F COLLIS. reported died of wounds. Killed 3. Wounded 7. Suffering Gas Poisoning 10. Died Wounds (1.) do Gas Poisoning (1)	C.A.
Trenches	21/12/15		Batt in Trenches. Quiet day. Casualties O.R. Died of wounds received on 19/12/15. (2)	C.A.
Trenches	22/12/15		2nd Sherwood Foresters relieved Batt in Trenches relief finished at 8.50 PM. Batt moved to rest Billets in Poperinghe.	C.A.

2353 Wt. W2544/1454 700,000 5/15 D. D. & L. A.D.S.S./Forms/C. 2118.

Instructions regarding War Diaries and Intelligence Summaries are contained in F. S. Regs., Part II and the Staff Manual respectively. Title Pages will be prepared in manuscript.

WAR DIARY
or
INTELLIGENCE SUMMARY
(Erase heading not required.)

Army Form C. 2118

Place	Date	Hour	Summary of Events and Information	Remarks and references to Appendices
POPERINGHE	23/12/15		Batt resting.	C.A.
POPERINGHE	24/12/15		do	C.A.
POPERINGHE	25/12/15		do	C.A.
POPERINGHE	26/12/15		Batt relieved 9th Norfolk in Trenches relief carried out & reported correct 8.50 PM. Distribution. D. Coy B9. B Coy B10 2 Platoons C Coy. B10A & 2 Platoon ✗ line 2 do A Coy S9A. 2 do Canal Bank.	
			Draft of 110. O.R. arrived from Base.	C.A.
In Trenches St JEAN.	27/12/15		Batt In Trenches Casualties. Wounded 2. O.R.	C.A.
In Trenches	28/12/15		Batt In Trenches Casualties nil.	C.A
do	29/12/15		Batt In Trenches Casualties O.R. wounded 3	C.A
In Trenches	30/12/15		Battn relieved. Relief completed without casualties at 8.30 P.M. Casualties O.R. Killed 1, Wounded 2.	AW
CAMP A	31/12/15		Battn resting. Casualties O.R. Wounded 1.	AW.

1.1.16. W.H.A. De La Poer Byrne Lt Col
Cmdg 9th Suffolk Regt.

1875 Wt. W593/826 1,000,000 4/15 J.B.C. & A. A.D.S.S./Forms/C. 2118.

9th Suffolks
Vol: 5

6th Dn

71st Bde

Instructions regarding War Diaries and Intelligence Summaries are contained in F. S. Regs., Part II. and the Staff Manual respectively. Title Pages will be prepared in manuscript.

WAR DIARY
or
INTELLIGENCE SUMMARY
(Erase heading not required.)

Army Form C. 2118

Place	Date	Hour	Summary of Events and Information	Remarks and references to Appendices
1916				
CAMP A	1/1/16		Battn resting in Camp A. AW.	
CAMP A	2/1/16		Battn resting in Camp A. AW.	
CAMP A / TRENCHES	3/1/16		Battn in Camp A. Relieved Norfolks on night of 3rd without casualties. AW.	
TRENCHES	4/1/16		Battn in Trenches. Casualties nil. AW.	
TRENCHES	5/1/16		Battn in Trenches. C.S.M. Putley killed by shell. Casualties Killed 1. Wounded 2. AW.	
TRENCHES	6/1/16		Batt in Trenches. GA.	
TRENCHES	7/1/16		Batt in Trenches. relieved by 2nd Sherwood Foresters. relief completed 9.30 PM Casualties Nil. GA.	

1875 Wt. W593/826 1,000,000 4/15 J.B.C. & A. A.D.S.S./Forms/C. 2118.

Army Form C. 2118

Instructions regarding War Diaries and Intelligence Summaries are contained in F. S. Regs., Part II. and the Staff Manual respectively. Title Pages will be prepared in manuscript.

WAR DIARY
or
INTELLIGENCE SUMMARY
(Erase heading not required.)

Place	Date	Hour	Summary of Events and Information	Remarks and references to Appendices
POPERINGHE	8/1/16		Batt resting.	
POPERINGHE	9/1/16		Batt resting. Draft of 100 NCOs & men arrived & taken on strength.	
POPERINGHE	10/1/16		Batt resting	
POPERINGHE	11/1/16		Batt resting. Batt relieved 9th Norfolks in Trenches relief complete at 7.45 PM Distribution B9. 2 Platoon B Coy B10. A Coy S10 A 2 Platoon B Coy S9 A 1½ do C do X line 1½ do C do Canal Bank. D Coy & 1 Platoon C Coy. Casualties Nil.	
TRENCHES.	12/1/16.		Batt in Trenches Casualties one wounded R.E	
TRENCHES	13/1/16		Batt in Trenches Casualties one wounded	
TRENCHES	14/1/15		Batt in Trenches Artillery very active on both sides Casualties 4. wounded (Four)	
TRENCHES	15/1/15.		Batt in Trenches. Batt relieved by 2nd Sherwood Foresters relief completed by 7.45 PM Casualties (2 Killed OR) 8 wounded	
Camp A	16/1/15		Batt at Rest	
Camp A	17/1/15		Batt at Rest 2/Lt. V. W. ORY. & 2/Lt G. CORNWALL reported & taken on strength	

1875 Wt. W593/826 1,000,000 4/15 J.B.C. & A. A.D.S.S./Forms/C. 2118.

Instructions regarding War Diaries and Intelligence Summaries are contained in F. S. Regs., Part II. and the Staff Manual respectively. Title Pages will be prepared in manuscript.

WAR DIARY
or
INTELLIGENCE SUMMARY
(Erase heading not required.)

Army Form C. 2118

Place	Date	Hour	Summary of Events and Information	Remarks and references to Appendices
CAMP 18/1/16			Batn in camp A.	
CAMP A	19/1/16		Batn in Rest Camp.	
CAMP A	20/1/16		Batn went up to Trenches. Relief at 8.20 without casualties	
TRENCHES	21/1/16		In trenches. Casualties nil.	
TRENCHES	22/1/16		In trenches. Casualties ~~nil~~. Killed 1 R.S. Wounded 1 R.S.	
TRENCHES	23/1/16		In trenches. Draft of 1 officer O.R. 30. (LIEUT. L.A. WHILLIER. taken on strength of Batt.) Casualties 1 wounded. R.S.	
TRENCHES	24/1/16		In trenches. Casualties 1. R.S.W. Relief by Notts + Derby Rgt 8.20.	
POPERINGHE	25/1/16		Batt at Rest.	
POPERINGHE	26/1/16		Batt at Rest	
POPERINGHE	27/1/16		Batt at Rest. Batt took over trenches from 9th Norfolks. Distribution: A8 2 Platoon C Coy one Platoon D Coy; B9 2 do C Coy; B10 3 do D Coy; S10.A. 2 do B Coy; S9A 1 do A Coy; S8. 1 Platoon B Coy; X Line 1 do B Coy, 2 do A Coy; Canal Bank 1 do A Coy. Relief complete 11.15 PM. Casualties NIL.	

Army Form C. 2118

Instructions regarding War Diaries and Intelligence Summaries are contained in F. S. Regs., Part II. and the Staff Manual respectively. Title Pages will be prepared in manuscript.

WAR DIARY
or
INTELLIGENCE SUMMARY
(Erase heading not required.)

Place	Date	Hour	Summary of Events and Information	Remarks and references to Appendices
Trenches	28 1/16.		Batt in Trenches ba	
Trenches	29 1/16.		Batt in Trenches Casualties - Gas alert. ordered by Division ba one O R. Killed R.S.W.	
Trenches	30 1/16		Batt in Trenches Casualties 2/Lt. A.G. DOUGLAS. Reported 1. ba one. O.R. wounded. R.S.W. as attached to the Regiment	
Trenches	31 1/16.		Batt in Trenches Batt relieved by 2nd Sherwoods. ba Casualties 2/Lt A WILLIAMSON. Killed Shell 2/Lt. S. KELSEY Wounded do O.R. two wounded	
Camb A.	1/2/16		Batt at Rest	
Ean				

W. H. de la Pryme Lt Col.
Commd 9th Suffolks

1875 Wt. W593/826 1,000,000 4/15 J.B.C. & A. A.D.S.S./Forms/C. 2118.

Instructions regarding War Diaries and Intelligence Summaries are contained in F. S. Regs., Part II. and the Staff Manual respectively. Title pages will be prepared in manuscript.

WAR DIARY
or
INTELLIGENCE SUMMARY.
(Erase heading not required.)

Army Form C. 2118.

Place	Date	Hour	Summary of Events and Information	Remarks and references to Appendices
Camp A.	1/2/16		Batt at Rest. Casualties one O.R. Killed, one O.R. Wounded. Capt. A.P. MACK. promoted Major vice London Gazette Feb 2nd 1916. Lieut S.W. CHURCH. promoted Capt. vice London Gazette Feb. CA	
Camp A	2/2/16		Batt at Rest. CA	
Camp A	3/2/16		Batt at Rest. CA	
Camp A	4/2/16		Batt at Rest. Batt relieved 9th Norfolks in Trenches. Distribution B 11 & 12. three Platoon B Coy; S 12 A one Platoon B Coy; X 8. one Platoon D Coy. Casualties one. O.R. wounded. Congreave Road. Two Platoon A Coy. St JEAN Defences. Two Platoon A Coy. Canal Bank 4 Platoon C Coy and three Platoon D Coy. CA	
In Trenches	5/2/16		Batt in Trenches. Casualties one O.R. Wounded. CA	
In Trenches	6/2/16		Batt in Trenches. Officer one wounded Capt. N.R. RAWSON. (RAMC) Shrapnell. CA	
In Trenches	7/2/16		Batt in Trenches. Casualties one Wounded O.R. CA	
In Trenches	8/2/16		Batt in Trenches. Casualties one. O.R. Killed, Two O.R. Wounded. Batt Relieved by 2nd Sherwoods. CA	

2353 Wt. W2544/1454 700,000 5/15 D. D. & L. A.D.S.S./Forms/C. 2118.

Army Form C. 2118.

Instructions regarding War Diaries and Intelligence Summaries are contained in F. S. Regs., Part II. and the Staff Manual respectively. Title pages will be prepared in manuscript.

WAR DIARY
or
INTELLIGENCE SUMMARY.
(Erase heading not required.)

Place	Date	Hour	Summary of Events and Information	Remarks and references to Appendices
Poperinghe	9/2/16		Batt at Rest.	
POPERINGHE	10/2/16		Batt at Rest.	
POPERINGHE	11/2/16		Batt at Rest	
POPERINGHE	12/2/16		Batt at Rest. "Stand to ready to move" ordered by Division at 4.30 PM "Stand to cancelled at" 6.15 PM. Batt relieved Norfolks in Trenches. Distribution as follows. A8 Three Platoons A Coy B9 one Platoon A and one B Coy B10 Three Platoons B Coy S10.A Two Platoon C Coy S9A one Platoon C Coy S8A one Platoon C Coy S7A Three Platoon D Coy S8. one Platoon D Coy. Casualties NIL.	
In Trenches	13/2/16		Batt in Trenches. Casualties. one. O.R. Killed R.S.W.	
In Trenches	14/2/16		Batt in Trenches. Heavy Bombardment on our right. SOS being sent from Hooge. Alert ordered at 6 P.M. 2/Lt L.T. Bright arrived with Draft of 30. O.R. Casualties. Three O.R. wounded 2 R.S.W. 1 [illegible]	
In Trenches	15/2/16.		Batt in Trenches. Casualties NIL	
In Trenches	16/2/16		Batt in Trenches. Casualties. Three O.R. wounded. R.S.W. Batt relieved by 2nd Sherwood.	
CAMP A	17/2/16		Batt at Rest	

2353 Wt. W2544/1454 700,000 5/15 D. D. & L. A.D.S.S./Forms/C. 2118.

Instructions regarding War Diaries and Intelligence Summaries are contained in F. S. Regs., Part II. and the Staff Manual respectively. Title pages will be prepared in manuscript.

WAR DIARY
or
INTELLIGENCE SUMMARY.
(Erase heading not required.)

Army Form C. 2118.

Place	Date	Hour	Summary of Events and Information	Remarks and references to Appendices
CAMP A.	18/2/16		Batt at Rest	
Camp A	19/2/16		Batt at Rest	
Camp A	20/2/16		Batt at Rest Casualties one O R wounded. R.S.W.	
Camp A	21/2/16		Batt at Rest Batt relieved Norfolks in Trenches Casualties NIL.	
Trenches	22/2/16		Batt in Trenches Casualties one. O.R. Died of Wounds	
Trenches	23/2/16		Batt in Trenches Gas alert ordered Casualties. NIL	
Trenches	24/2/16		Batt in Trenches Casualties. one. O.R. wounded R.S.W.	
Trenches	25/2/16		Batt in Trenches Casualties one O R wounded Shrapnell	
Trenches	26/2/16		Batt in Trenches Casualties two O.R. wounded Shell Draft of 20. O.R. ~~received~~ arrived Relieved by 2nd Sherwoods.	
Poperinghe	27/2/16		Batt at Rest.	
Poperinghe	28/2/16		Batt at Rest.	
Poperinghe	29/2/16		Batt at Rest.	
~~Poperinghe~~	~~1/3/16~~		~~Batt at Rest~~.	

W H De La Poer Lt Col.
Commd 9 Suffolks

2353 Wt. W2544/1454 700,000 5/15 D. D. & L. A.D.S.S./Forms/C. 2118.

Instructions regarding War Diaries and Intelligence Summaries are contained in F. S. Regs., Part II. and the Staff Manual respectively. Title pages will be prepared in manuscript.

WAR DIARY
or
INTELLIGENCE SUMMARY.
(Erase heading not required.)

Army Form C. 2118.

Place	Date	Hour	Summary of Events and Information	Remarks and references to Appendices
Poperinghe	1/3/16.		Batt at rest.	
Poperinghe	2/3/16		Batt at rest Battalion took over trenches from 9th Norfolks Casualties NIL	f.a.
			distribution of Coys A8. D Coy B9 one Platoon B Coy and one C Coy B10 Three Platoons B Coy S10A Two Platoons B Coy S9A one Platoon B Coy S7A Three Platoons A Coy S8 one Platoon A Coy	f.a.
In Trenches	3/3/16		Batt in Trenches Casualties NIL	f.a.
In Trenches	4/3/16		Batt in Trenches. Casualties NIL	f.a.
In Trenches	5/3/16		Batt in Trenches. Casualties NIL. No. 4/Serg WHITE. awarded D.C.M.	
In Trenches	6/3/16.		Batt in Trenches Casualties. Killed one O.R Wounded eleven six H.E. Shrapnel five R.G.W.	f.a.
In Trenches	7/3/16		Batt in Trenches. Casualties. Wounded one. O.R. Batt relieved by 2nd Sherwoods	f.a.
Canal Bank	8/3/16		Batt at Rest. working Parties of 10 officers and 500 men required. Casualties one. O.R accidentally wounded	f.a.
Canal Bank	9/3/16		Batt at Rest working Parties required. Casualties one. O.R wounded H.E. Shrapnell	f.a.

Army Form C. 2118.

Instructions regarding War Diaries and Intelligence Summaries are contained in F. S. Regs., Part II. and the Staff Manual respectively. Title pages will be prepared in manuscript.

WAR DIARY
or
INTELLIGENCE SUMMARY.
(Erase heading not required.)

Place	Date	Hour	Summary of Events and Information	Remarks and references to Appendices
Poperinghe Canal Bank	10/3/16		Batt at rest. Casualties one O.R. Killed 11. Wounded	[illegible]
Canal Bank	11/3/16		Batt at rest. Casualties Nil	[illegible]
Canal Bank	12/3/16		Batt at rest. Casualties three O.R. Wounded. 2/Lt. A. H. [illegible] reported himself and taken on strength	
Canal Bank	13/3/16		Batt at rest. Relieved [illegible] in trenches. Casualties. one O.R. Killed [illegible] wounded. Distribution: B.11 and 12 three [illegible] B Coy; S12A one " B Coy; X Line three " D Coy; S9A one " D Coy; [illegible] defences two " D Coy; Congreve Walk two " D Coy; LA BRIQUE one " C Coy; Canal Bank three " C Coy	[illegible]
In Trenches	14/3/16		Batt in Trenches. Casualties Nil	
In Trenches	15/3/16		Batt in Trenches. Casualties. one O.R. wounded. 2/Lt. A. H. [illegible] and 2/Lt. [illegible] promoted Lieutenants. Gazette March 15th 1916.	[illegible]
In Trenches	16/3/16		Batt in Trenches. Casualties two O.R. wounded	[illegible]
In Trenches	17/3/16		Batt in Trenches. Casualties two. O.R. wounded	[illegible]
In Trenches	18/3/16		Batt in Trenches. Casualties one. O.R. wounded. Batt relieved by [illegible] and [illegible]	[illegible]
Poperinghe	19/3/16		Batt at rest. Batt Paraded [illegible] Square and marched off at 10 A.M. to HERZEELE [illegible]. Draft of 2/Lt [illegible] and 30. O.R. reported and taken on strength	[illegible]
HERZEELE	20/3/16		Batt at rest	[illegible]
HERZEELE	21/3/16		Batt at rest. Batt was inspected by Commander in Chief General Sir Douglas HAIG. G.C.B. K.C.I.E. [illegible]	[illegible]
HERZEELE	22/3/16		Batt at rest	[illegible]
HERZEELE	23/3/16		Batt at rest	[illegible]
HERZEELE	24/3/16		Batt at rest	[illegible]
HERZEELE	25/3/16		Batt at rest	[illegible]

Instructions regarding War Diaries and Intelligence Summaries are contained in F. S. Regs., Part II. and the Staff Manual respectively. Title pages will be prepared in manuscript.

WAR DIARY
or
INTELLIGENCE SUMMARY.
(*Erase heading not required.*)

Army Form C. 2118.

Place	Date	Hour	Summary of Events and Information	Remarks and references to Appendices
HERZEELE	26/3/16		Batt at rest. Captain Church reported himself and was taken on the strength. DKM.	
HERZEELE	27/3/16		Batt: at rest. Batt. paraded at Herzeele and marched off at 10 a.m. to Camp M. DKM.	
CAMP 'M'	28/3/16		Batt at rest. DKM.	
CAMP 'M'	29/3/16		Batt at rest. Draft of twenty other ranks joined the Batt. DKM.	
CAMP 'M'	30/3/16		Batt at rest. DKM.	
CAMP 'M'	31/3/16		Batt: at rest. DKM.	

[illegible] 9th Suffolk Regt.
1.4.16

2353 Wt. W2544/1454 700,000 5/15 D. D. & L. A.D.S.S./Forms/C. 2118.

9. Suffolks
Army Form C. 2118
Vol 8

XX VI

Instructions regarding War Diaries and Intelligence Summaries are contained in F. S. Regs., Part II. and the Staff Manual respectively. Title Pages will be prepared in manuscript.

WAR DIARY
or
INTELLIGENCE SUMMARY
(Erase heading not required.)

Place	Date	Hour	Summary of Events and Information	Remarks and references to Appendices
CAMP. M.	1/4/16		Batt at rest. No 3/10133. SERGEANT ARTHUR FREDERICK SAUNDERS awarded VICTORIA CROSS for Gallantry at LOOS 2/LT. H.G. FROST attached R.F.C. reported missing	ba
CAMP. M	2/4/16		Batt at rest	ba
CAMP. M	3/4/16		Batt at rest. Casualties one O.R. wounded. Shrapnel	ba
CAMP. M.	4/4/16		Batt at rest. Casualties 2/LT. V.I. HARDY wounded. Still on duty. one O.R. wounded	ba
CAMP. M.	5/4/16		Batt at rest. Batt paraded at 8.45 P.M. and marched to HOPOUTRE, entrained and proceeded to CALAIS. detrained and marched to CAMP.	ba
CALAIS	6/4/16		Batt at rest.	ba
CALAIS	7/4/16		Batt at rest. G.O.C Brigade presented cards of recommendation to N.C.O's and men who had been chosen as having done good work in the country, since Battalion had left England.	ba
CALAIS	8/4/16		Batt at rest. Casualties. one O.R. hurt by bomb (accidentally)	ba
CALAIS	9/4/16		Batt at rest	ba
CALAIS	10/4/16		Batt at rest	ba
CALAIS	11/4/16		Batt at rest	ba
CALAIS	12/4/16		Batt at rest	ba
CALAIS	13/4/16		Batt at rest	ba
CALAIS	14/4/16		Batt at rest	ba
CALAIS	15/4/16		Batt proceeded by route march from CALAIS to ZUTKERQUE and there had billets for the night. (arrived at 3 PM)	ba
ZUTKERQUE	16/4/16		Batt proceeded by route march from ZUTKERQUE to BOLLEZEELE. and there had billets for night. (arrived at 3.30 PM)	ba
BOLLEZEELE	17/4/16		Batt proceeded by route march from BOLLEZEELE to HERZEELE. General Sir HERBERT C.O. PLUMER. G.C.M.G. K.C.B. inspected Batt as they marched past him.	ba
HERZEELE	18/4/16		Batt proceeded by route march from HERZEELE to CAMPS. E. of POPERINGHE.	ba
CAMPS	19/4/16		Batt at rest.	ba
CAMPS	20/4/16		Batt at rest.	ba

1875 Wt. W593/826 1,000,000 4/15 J.B.C. & A. A.D.S.S./Forms/C. 2118.

58

Instructions regarding War Diaries and Intelligence Summaries are contained in F. S. Regs., Part II. and the Staff Manual respectively. Title Pages will be prepared in manuscript.

WAR DIARY
or
INTELLIGENCE SUMMARY
(Erase heading not required.)

Army Form C. 2118

Place	Date	Hour	Summary of Events and Information	Remarks and references to Appendices
CAMP S.	21/4/16		Batt at rest.	bh
CAMP S	22/4/16		Batt at rest.	bh
CAMP S.	23/4/16		Batt at rest. Major P.B. NORRIS. 2nd D.C.L.I. reported and was attached to Batt,	bh
CAMP S.	24/4/16		Batt at rest	bh
CAMP S.	25/4/16		Batt at rest. Major P.B. NORRIS. 2nd D.C.L.I. attached to Batt. left Battalion.	bh
CAMP S.	26/4/16		Batt at rest. C and D Company in CAMP. were shelled Company were put in CAMP. O with A and B. Coys. Casualties one O.R Killed one wounded	bh
CAMP O.	27/4/16		Batt at rest	bh
CAMP. O.	28/4/16		Batt at rest. General Sir DOUGLAS. HAIG. G.C.B. K.C.I.E. K.C.V.O. inspected A and D. Company. Draft of 18. O.R arrived	bh
CAMP. O	29/4/16		Batt at rest	bh
CAMP. O.	30/4/16		Batt at rest. No 3/10052. Regimental Sergeant Major C.H. HURRELL. appointed Temporary Quartermaster of 12th Battalion ~~and left Batt~~	bh

1/5/16.

W.H.A. De la Pryme Lt Col.
Comm'd 9th Batt Suffolk Regt.

1875 Wt. W593/826 1,000,000 4/15 J.B.C. & A. A.D.S.S./Forms/C. 2118.

9th Suffolks

Vol 9

99

Instructions regarding War Diaries and Intelligence Summaries are contained in F. S. Regs., Part II. and the Staff Manual respectively. Title pages will be prepared in manuscript.

WAR DIARY
or
INTELLIGENCE SUMMARY.
(Erase heading not required.)

Army Form C. 2118.

Place	Date	Hour	Summary of Events and Information	Remarks and references to Appendices
CAMP. O	1/5/16.		Batt at rest.	fa
CAMP. O.	2/5/16.		Batt at rest. Batt took over support lines held by Sherwood Foresters.	fa
			Distribution Canal Bank. A and B Coys & 2 Platoons C. Coy.	fa
			Wilson's Farm. 2 Platoons. C. Coy.	
			Brielen D. Coy.	fa
In Support	3/5/16.		Batt in support. working parties supplied. Casualties one O.R. wounded	fa
do.	4/5/16		do do Casualties. one. O.R. Killed 4. O.R. wounded.	fa
do	5/5/16		do do Casualties. NIL.	fa
do	6/5/16		do do Casualties two O.R wounded.	fa
do	7/5/16		do do Casualties two O.R. wounded.	fa
do	8/5/16		do do Batt were relieved by 9th Norfolks. Casualties two O.R. wounded.	fa
Camp O	9/5/16		Batt at rest	fa
Camp O	10/5/16		do. LIEUT. F.R.C. COBBOLD. arrived & reported	fa
do	11/5/16		do	fa
do	12/5/16		do. Casualties one. O.R. wounded. Draft of 20. O.R arrived	fa
do	13/5/16		do Batt took over trenches from 1st Leicesters. Casualties two. O.R. wounded	
			Distribution B. 15, B 16 } A Coy. B14, S14 } D Coy. Forward Cottage, Lower and Macgregor Posts x9. x10 } B. Coy. B13, S13 } C. Coy.	fa

2353 Wt. W2544/1454 700,000 5/15 D. D. & L. A.D.S.S./Forms/C. 2118.

Army Form C. 2118.

Instructions regarding War Diaries and Intelligence Summaries are contained in F. S. Regs., Part II. and the Staff Manual respectively. Title pages will be prepared in manuscript.

WAR DIARY
or
INTELLIGENCE SUMMARY.

(Erase heading not required.)

Place	Date	Hour	Summary of Events and Information	Remarks and references to Appendices
Trenches	14/5/16		Batt in Trenches. Casualties. Lt Col W.H.A. DE. LA PRYME. D.S.O wounded. LIEUT. L. WILMOT. JOHNSON wounded (Suffering from Shell shock) 2/LT. C.H. BOX. wounded. wounded Three O.R	bq
do	15/5/16		Batt in Trenches. Casualties. LIEUT. F.R.C. COBBOLD. wounded. (Suffering from Shell Shock) O.R Killed 4. O.R wounded. 18.	bq
do	16/5/16		Batt in Trenches Casualties O.R. Killed 3. O.R wounded. 6.	bq
do	17/5/16		Batt in Trenches Casualties NIL.	bq
do	18/5/16		Batt in Trenches. Batt relieved by 9th Norfolks Casualties. NIL	bq
Camp O	19/5/16		Batt at rest. . Casualties. Capt M.F HEIGHAM. wounded 2/Lt. F.H. BRIGHT. wounded. O.R wounded -9.	bq
do	20/5/16		do	bq
do	21/5/16		do	bq
do	22/5/16		do 5. Officers reported their arrival. LIEUT. J.N. HARMER 2/LT H.W. SOULBY. 2/LT. E COLLYER. 2/LT. ST. ASKHAM 2/LT. B.B. CHRISTOPHES.	bq
do	23/5/16		do. Batt took over support lines from 1st Leicesters. Casualties NIL. LIEUT. E HOWES. JOINED Batt	bq
In Support	24/5/16		Battn in Support. Casualties NIL	bq
do	25/5/16		do Casualties one O.R. Killed one O.R. wounded. No 17846 PTE A.J. KEMP. awarded Military Medal for Gallantry on May 15th 1916	
do	26/5/16		Batt in Support. Casualties Two O.R. wounded.	bq

2353 Wt. W2544/1454 700,000 5/15 D. D. & L. A.D.S.S./Forms/C. 2118.

Instructions regarding War Diaries and Intelligence Summaries are contained in F. S. Regs., Part II. and the Staff Manual respectively. Title Pages will be prepared in manuscript.

Army Form C. 2118

WAR DIARY
or
INTELLIGENCE SUMMARY
(Erase heading not required.)

Place	Date	Hour	Summary of Events and Information	Remarks and references to Appendices
In Support.	27/5/16		Batt in Support. Casualties NIL	[illegible]
do	28/5/16		do. Casualties Two O.R. wounded. Batt relieved by 9th Norfolks. Capt. H.F. LAW reported his arrival.	[illegible]
Camp D	29/5/16		Batt at rest	[illegible]
do	30/5/16		do	[illegible]
do	31/5/16		do.	[illegible]

In the Field 1/6/16

[illegible] Major
Commd 9th Batt Suffolk Regt

1875 Wt. W593/826 1,000,000 4/15 J.B.C. & A. A.D.S.S./Forms/C. 2118.

10

9th Suffolk Vol 10.

VI

D. A. G.

Base

Herewith War Diary of the 9th (Service) Battalion Suffolk Regiment for the month ending 30th June 1916 with a copy of sketch of the trenches the Battalion occupied attached.

O.E. Mack Lt Col

O.C. 9th Suffolk Regt.

In the Field

2. 7. 16

Instructions regarding War Diaries and Intelligence Summaries are contained in F. S. Regs., Part II. and the Staff Manual respectively. Title Pages will be prepared in manuscript.

WAR DIARY
or
INTELLIGENCE SUMMARY
(Erase heading not required.)

Army Form C. 2118

Place	Date	Hour	Summary of Events and Information	Remarks and references to Appendices
CAMP. D	1/6/16		Batt at rest	
CAMP. D	2/6/16		Batt relieved 1st Leicesters in Trenches. Distribution A Coy FORWARD COTTAGE TOWER and MACGREGORS POSTS X9. X10. B Coy B14 and S14. C Coy B15 and B16. D Coy B13 and S13	bq bq
Trenches	3/6/16		Batt in Trenches	bq
Trenches	4/6/16		Batt in Trenches Casualties two O.R. wounded.	bq
Trenches	5/6/16		Batt in Trenches Casualties two O.R. wounded. → { Lieut. R. ENGLAND awarded Military Cross. 17751 L/Serg. S.H. Norton, 8659 L/Cpl W Fuer 12611 Pte T. Gay were awarded Military Medal	bq
Trenches	6/6/16		Batt in Trenches Casualties One O.R. wounded	bq bq
Trenches	7/6/16		Batt in Trenches. Batt were relieved by 9th Norfolks.	bq
Camp D	8/6/16		Batt at rest	bq
Camp D	9/6/16		Batt at rest	bq
Camp D	10/6/16		Batt at rest	bq
Camp D	11/6/16		Batt at rest	bq
Camp D	12/6/16		Batt at rest	bq
Camp D	13/6/16		Batt at rest. Batt relieved 1st Leicesters on Canal Bank X9. and ~~Wilson Farm~~ Prescott Farm	bq
Canal Bank	14/6/16		Batt in support	bq
Canal Bank	15/6/16		Batt in support. one O.R. wounded on working party	bq
Canal Bank	16/6/16		Batt in support	bq
Canal Bank	17/6/16		Batt in support. Batt were relieved by 1st Grenadier Guards	bq
Poperinghe	18/6/16		Batt at rest	bq

1875 Wt. W593/826 1,000,000 4/15 J.B.C. & A. A.D.S.S./Forms/C. 2118.

Army Form C. 2118

Instructions regarding War Diaries and Intelligence Summaries are contained in F. S. Regs., Part II. and the Staff Manual respectively. Title Pages will be prepared in manuscript.

WAR DIARY
or
INTELLIGENCE SUMMARY
(Erase heading not required.)

Place	Date	Hour	Summary of Events and Information	Remarks and references to Appendices
Poperinghe	19/6/16		Batt at rest. Batt proceeded by route march to camp. N.	ba
Camp N	20/6/16		Batt at rest. Lieut. C.F. Beyts proceeded to England to be transferred to Machine Gun Corps.	ba
Camp N.	21/6/16.		Batt at rest. Draft of 25. O.R. arrived.	ba
Camp N.	22/6/16.		Batt at rest. 500 O.R. took over posts occupied by 9th Norfolks. Distribution L4 A Coy L8 B and C Coys L2 D Coy. Major General. Batt was inspected by Lieut. General. F.R. The Earl of CAVAN. K.P. C.B. M.V.O.	ba
Camp N	23/6/16		Batt at rest.	ba
Camp N.	24/6/16		Batt at rest.	ba
Camp N	25/6/16		Batt at rest. Casualties Three O.R. wounded	ba
Camp N.	26/6/16		Batt at rest. Casualties one. O.R. wounded.	ba
Camp N	27/6/16		Batt at rest	ba
Camp N	28/6/16		Batt at rest	ba
Camp N.	29/7/16.		Batt at rest.	ba
Camp N.	30/7/16		Batt at rest.	

A. P. Mack Lt-Col
Commd 9th Suffolks

1. 7. 16

1875 Wt. W593/826 1,000,000 4/15 J.B.C. & A. A.D.S.S./Forms/C. 2118.

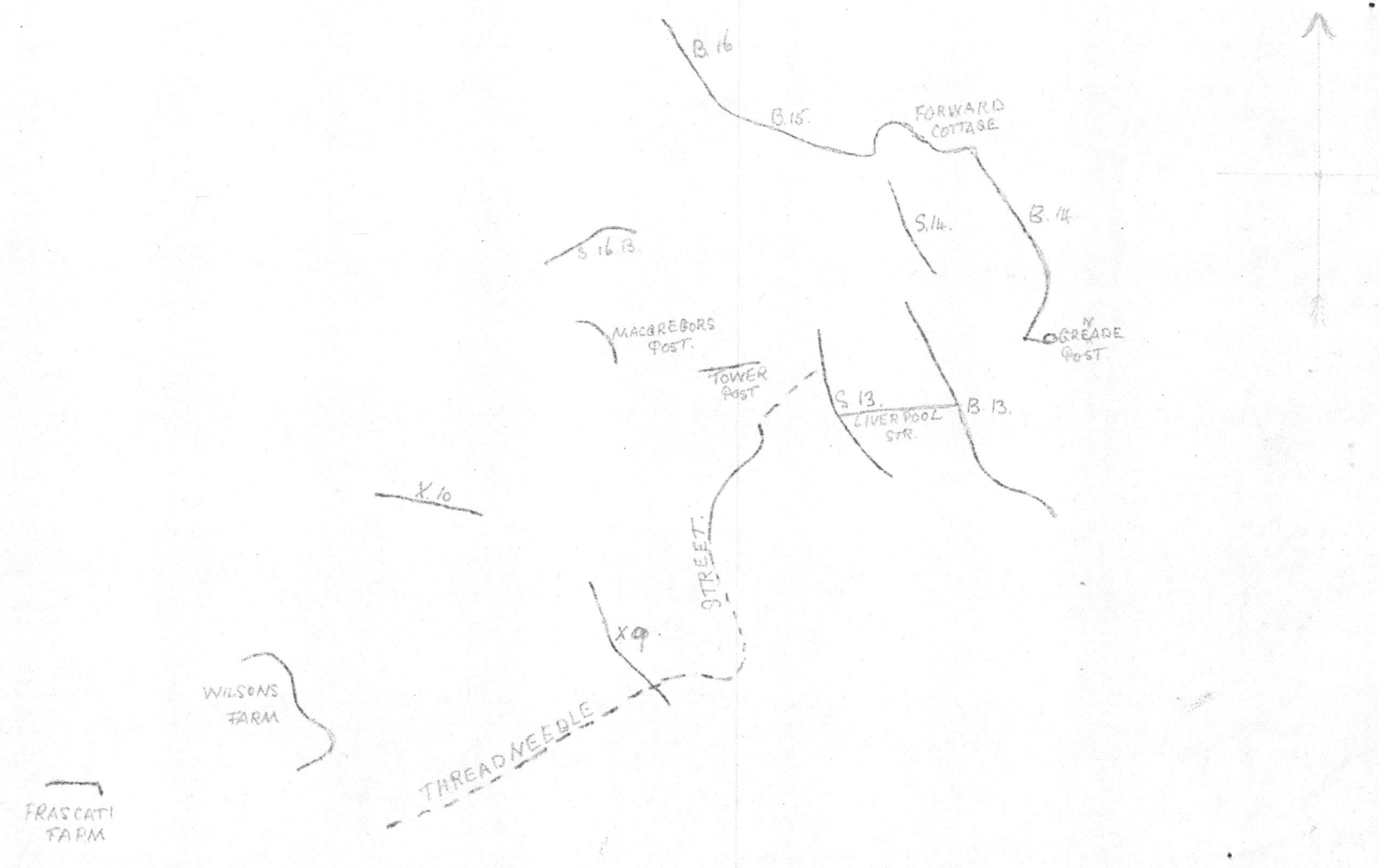

B.16
B.15.
FORWARD COTTAGE
B.14.
S.14.
S.16.B.
MACGREGORS POST.
McGREADE POST
TOWER POST
S.13.
LIVERPOOL STR.
B.13.
X.10
STREET.
X9.
WILSONS FARM
THREADNEEDLE
FRASCATI FARM

Army Form C. 2118.

Instructions regarding War Diaries and Intelligence Summaries are contained in F. S. Regs., Part II. and the Staff Manual respectively. Title Pages will be prepared in manuscript.

WAR DIARY
or
INTELLIGENCE SUMMARY

(Erase heading not required.)

Vol XI

119

Place	Date	Hour	Summary of Events and Information	Remarks and references to Appendices
CAMP. N.	1/7/16.		Batt. at rest. fa	
" N.	2/7/16.		" " " fa	
Bollezeele.	3/7/16.		" " " Batt moved by route march, to Bollezeele. fa	
"	4/7/16		Batt at rest. fa	
"	5/7/16		" " " fa	
"	6/7/16		" " " fa	
"	7/7/16		" " " fa	
"	8/7/16		" " " fa	
"	9/7/16		" " " fa	
"	10/7/16		" " " fa	
"	11/7/16		" " " fa	
"	12/7/16		" " " fa	
"	13/7/16		" " " fa	
"	14/7/16		" " " Batt moved by route march to Houtkerque fa	
Houtkerque	15/7/16		Batt at rest. Batt moved by route march to Camp C. fa	
Camp. C.	16/7/16.		Batt at rest fa	
" "	17/7/16		" " " fa	
" "	18/7/16		" " " fa	
" "	19/7/16		" " " fa	
" "	20/7/16		" " " fa	
" "	21/7/16		" " " fa	
" "	22/7/16		" " " Batt took over billets at YPRES from 11th Essex.	
	23/7/16		Batt in support. Batt took over trenches from 9th WEST YORKS. distribution A. Coy. A5a A6 and part of A7 B " remainder of A7 to A8 C " S8. X4 and X5 D " Congreve Walk fa.	

2449 Wt. W14957/M90 750,000 1/16 J.B.C. & A. Forms/C.2118/12.

Army Form C. 2118.

Instructions regarding War Diaries and Intelligence Summaries are contained in F. S. Regs., Part II. and the Staff Manual respectively. Title Pages will be prepared in manuscript.

WAR DIARY
or
INTELLIGENCE SUMMARY
(Erase heading not required.)

Place	Date	Hour	Summary of Events and Information	Remarks and references to Appendices
Trenches	24/7/16		Batt in trenches Casualties one O.R. wounded	
"	25/7/16		Batt in trenches	
"	26/7/16		Batt in trenches Casualties one O.R. Killed	
"	27/7/16		Batt in trenches Batt were relieved in trenches by 1st Leicesters and took over Billets in YPRES	
YPRES	28/7/16		Batt in support	
"	29/7/16		Batt in support. Casualties one O.R. wounded	
"	30/7/16		Batt in support	
"	31/7/16		Batt in support.	

31/7/16

A. P. Mack Lt-Col
Commd 9th Batt Suffolk Regt

2449 Wt. W14957/M90 750,000 1/16 J.B.C. & A. Forms/C.2118/12.

71st Brigade

6th Division $\frac{1}{2}$

1/9th BATTALION

SUFFOLK REGIMENT

AUGUST 1916

Army Form C. 2118.

9 Suffolk Regt

Vol 12

129

Instructions regarding War Diaries and Intelligence Summaries are contained in F. S. Regs., Part II. and the Staff Manual respectively. Title pages will be prepared in manuscript.

WAR DIARY
or
INTELLIGENCE SUMMARY.

(Erase heading not required.)

Place	Date	Hour	Summary of Events and Information	Remarks and references to Appendices
Camp M.	1/8/16		Batt at rest.	
Camp M.	2/8/16		Batt moved by Train to FIENVILLIERS - Candas and detrained and moved by route march to BEAUVAL	
BEAUVAL	3/8/16		Batt moved by route march to ARQUEVES	
ARQUEVES	4/8/16		Batt moved by route march to Camp in MAILLY-MAILLET Wood had dinner and then took over Trenches from 9th Batt. Loyal North Lancs distribution — "A" Coy 4 Platoons Essex Street "B" Coy 4 Platoons Pompadour St and St. Johns Road "C" Coy Wellington Trench and Fethard St. "D" Coy Marlborough and 5 line	
Trenches	5/8/16		Batt in Trenches	
Trenches	6/8/16		Batt in Trenches.	
Trenches	7/8/16		Batt in Trenches.	
Trenches.	8/8/16		Batt in Trenches. Casualties Two O.R. Killed 9 Wounded	
Trenches	9/8/16		Batt in Trenches. Casualties 2/Lieut A.H. Stole Suffering from Shell Shock one O.R. Wounded	
Trenches	10/8/16		Batt in Trenches.	
Trenches	11/8/16		Batt were relieved by 3rd Coldstream Guards and proceeded to LOUVENCOURT	
LOUVENCOURT	12/8/16		Batt at rest. Batt took over Camp in P.2.A	
Camp.	13/8/16		Batt at rest.	
Camp.	14/8/16		Batt at rest.	
Camp.	15/8/16		Batt at rest.	
Camp	16/8/16		Batt at rest.	
Camp	17/8/16		Batt at rest.	

2353 Wt. W2514/1454 700,000 5/15 D. D. & L. A.D.S.S./Forms/C. 2118.

Army Form C. 2118.

Instructions regarding War Diaries and Intelligence Summaries are contained in F. S. Regs., Part II. and the Staff Manual respectively. Title pages will be prepared in manuscript.

WAR DIARY
or
INTELLIGENCE SUMMARY.
(Erase heading not required.)

Place	Date	Hour	Summary of Events and Information	Remarks and references to Appendices
Camp.	18/8/16.		Batt at rest Casualties Three O.R. wounded.	
Camp.	19/8/16		Batt at rest	
Camp.	20/8/16		Batt at rest. Batt took over Trenches from 9th Norfolks distribution "A" Coy Wellington Trench and Fethard St. "B" Coy Marlborough St. and Fethard St. "C" Coy Pompadour. "D" Coy Essex Street	
In Trenches.	21/8/16.		Batt in Trenches Casualties one Officer missing believed killed 2/Lieut. S.T. Astham, one O.R. killed one Officer wounded LIEUT. A.H GUINNESS 5. O.R. wounded.	
In Trenches.	22/8/16.		Batt in Trenches.	
In Trenches.	23/8/16		Batt in Trenches. Casualties Three O.R. killed 7 wounded.	
In Trenches.	24/8/16.		Batt in Trenches. Casualties Two O.R. wounded.	
In Trenches.	25/8/16		Batt in Trenches. Casualties One. O.R. wounded.	
In Trenches.	26/8/16		Batt in Trenches. Casualties one O.R. killed one O.R. wounded.	
In Trenches.	27/8/16		Batt in Trenches. Batt were relieved by 6th GLOUCESTERS and proceeded to camp	
In Camp.	28/8/16		Batt. at rest. Batt proceeded by Route march to BEAUVAL	
BEAUVAL.	29/8/16		Batt at rest Batt proceeded by Route march to MONTONVILLERS	
MONTONVILLERS	30/8/16.		Batt at rest.	
MONTONVILLERS	31/8/16.		Batt at rest.	

Sept 1st 1916

A.H. Mack Lt Col
Commd 9th Suffolks

2353 Wt. W2544/1454 700,000 5/15 D. D. & L. A.D.S.S./Forms/C. 2118.

71st Brigade
6th Division.

9th BATTALION

THE SUFFOLK REGIMENT

SEPTEMBER 1916.

Instructions regarding War Diaries and Intelligence Summaries are contained in F. S. Regs., Part II. and the Staff Manual respectively. Title Pages will be prepared in manuscript.

WAR DIARY
or
INTELLIGENCE SUMMARY
(Erase heading not required.)

Army Form C. 2118.

9th Suffolks

Vol 13

Place	Date	Hour	Summary of Events and Information	Remarks and references to Appendices
MONTON-VILLERS.	1/9/16.		Batt at rest.	BA
do.	2/9/16.		Batt at rest. 2/Lt C. G. Gardner reported his arrival and taken on strength of Battn	BA
do.	3/9/16		Batt at rest. Draft of 41 O.R. arrived and taken on Strength of Battn.	BA
do.	4/9/16		Batt at rest. 2/Lt H. Almack, 2 Lt G. Hopkins, 2/Lt F. Buller, having reported were taken on Strength of Battn.	BA
do.	5/9/16		Batt at rest.	BA
do.	6/9/16.		Batt at rest. Batt moved by route march to CARDONNETTE.	BA
CARDONNETTE	7/9/16.		Batt at rest. Batt moved by route march to MERICOURT-L'ABBE	BA
MERICOURT-L'ABBE	8/9/16.		Batt at rest. Batt moved by route march to SANDPIT. AREA	BA
SANDPIT. AREA	9/9/16.		Batt at rest. Capt. V. W. Barrett joined Battn.	BA
SANDPIT AREA	10/9/16.		Batt at rest. 2/Lt R. T. Scott reported his arrival and taken on Strength of Battn.	BA
do.	11/9/16.		Batt at rest. Batt moved into Trenches and took over from 4th GRENADIER GUARDS Distribution — Front Line "C" & "D" Coys, Support Line "A" & "B" Coys	BA
TRENCHES.	12/9/16.		Batt in Trenches.	BA
TRENCHES	13/9/16.		Batt in Trenches. Batt. were ordered to attack enemy's Trenches. "B" "C" & "D" Coys attacked at 6.20 am. 1st. Two lines of enemy's trenches were captured, but owing to heavy Casualties from Artillery and M.G. Fire the situation could not be cleared up. At 7.30 pm. "A" Coy were ordered to attack the QUADRILATERAL but failed to reach their objective owing to very heavy M.G. fire. A new Trench was dug by the Battn which enabled them to get in touch with the 2nd. Sherwoods on the left and 8 Bedfords on the right. it also cleared up the situation, during these attacks the Battn behaved splendidly and it is regretted the casualties were heavy. Killed Capt. S. H. BYRNE 2/Lieut. G. D. GARDNER Wounded 2/Lieut C. WAYMAN 2/Lieut. A. G. DOUGLAS Capt. V. W. BARRETT 2/Lieut. G. COLLYER. 2/Lieut. D. K. MACDONALD 2/Lieut. H. E. FALKNER. 2/Lieut. A. FUDGE 2/Lieut. F. GOATCHER Killed O.R. 15. Wounded 185 2/Lieut. H. ALMACK Captain N. R. RAWSON. RAMC. attached 9th Suffolks	BA
TRENCHES	14/9/16		Batt in Trenches.	BA

2449 Wt. W14957/M90 750,000 1/16 J.B.C. & A. Forms/C.2118/12.

Army Form C. 2118.

Instructions regarding War Diaries and Intelligence Summaries are contained in F. S. Regs., Part II. and the Staff Manual respectively. Title Pages will be prepared in manuscript.

WAR DIARY
or
INTELLIGENCE SUMMARY

(Erase heading not required.)

Place	Date	Hour	Summary of Events and Information	Remarks and references to Appendices
Trenches.	15/9/16		Batt in Trenches. The Brigade were ordered to attack the enemy's Trenches, and to push on to their final objective which was between LESBOUCHS and MORVAL. and to establish a line on the ridge. The Brigade Ordered the 1st Leicesters and 9th Norfolk's to attack at 6·20am. The 2nd Sherwoods and 9th Suffolk's were in support. the 9th Suffolk's supporting 9th Norfolk's. The Battn lined up to move forward at 7·50 am. but owing to very heavy artillery and Machine Gun Fire half of "C" Coy could not leave their trench. The remainder of the Battn moved forward but were held up from heavy M.G. Fire which came from the enemy's strong position called the QUADRILATERAL. It was from the M. Guns that the Battn lost very heavily. Lieut. Col. A.P. MACK. was Killed at 8·30am. The remainder of Battn dug themselves in and got into touch with both Flanks. The enemy's barrage was extremely heavy and caused many more casualties. The Battn held the line they established till relieved by the 14th Durham Light Infantry at 11pm. and moved back to support trenches where they re-organized. Casualties were Killed Lieut. Col A.P. MACK LIEUT. J.T.C. FALLOWES LIEUT. L.A. WHILLIER 2/LIEUT. F. WILSON and 35 O.R. Wounded. Capt. L.E. ENSOR Capt. S.W. CHURCH LIEUT. J.N. HARMER 2/Lieut. W.H. HOILE 2/Lieut C.G. GARDNER 2/Lieut A. HOPKINS. 2/Lieut. R.T. SCOTT. and 99 O.R. Missing 2/Lieut. S.J. PRICE 2/Lieut. R.G. SMITH. and 93 O.R.	35 / 99 / 93 / 227
Trenches.	16/9/16		Batt in Trenches.	[initials]
Trenches.	17/9/16		Batt in Trenches. Batt were relieved by 11th Essex and moved to Trenches in support	[initials]
Trenches.	18/9/16		Batt in Trenches.	[initials]
Trenches.	19/9/16		Batt were relieved and moved by route march to VILLE-SUR-ANCRE	[initials]

2449 Wt. W14957/M90 750,000 1/16 J.B.C. & A. Forms/C.2118/12.

Army Form C. 2118.

Instructions regarding War Diaries and Intelligence Summaries are contained in F. S. Regs., Part II. and the Staff Manual respectively. Title Pages will be prepared in manuscript.

WAR DIARY
or
INTELLIGENCE SUMMARY
(Erase heading not required.)

Place	Date	Hour	Summary of Events and Information	Remarks and references to Appendices
VILLE-SUR-ANCRE	20/9/16.		Batt at rest.	[illegible]
do	21/9/16.		Batt at rest 212. O.R. arrived and were taken on Strength	[illegible]
do	22/9/16		Batt moved by route march to the CITADEL.	[illegible]
CITADEL	23/9/16		Batt moved by route march to A.8.A Sheet ALBERT	[illegible]
Batt in reserve	24/9/16		Batt in reserve 6 Officers Reported 2/Lieut C. L. Lucas. 2/Lieut L. C. Rae 2/Lieut A. J. Hoare. 2/Lieut H. T. Roberts 2/Lieut H. A. Jones. 2/Lieut G. V. Bryant	[illegible]
Batt in reserve	25/9/16		Batt in reserve	[illegible]
Batt in reserve	26/9/16		Batt took over trenches from 2nd YORKS and LANCS Distribution "C" Coy advanced posts "A" "B" + "D" front line (Casualties 2. O.R. wounded)	[illegible]
Trenches	27/9/16		Batt in trenches Casualties wounded 2/Lieut H. A. Jones. 2/Lieut L. C. Rae. 4. O.R. Killed 18. O.R. wounded 2 Officers reported 2/Lieut G. L. Wilson 3rd Batt Norfolk Regt. and 2/Lieut C. V. Canning	[illegible]
Trenches.	28/9/16		Batt in trenches 8. O.R. wounded (Casualties). Major F. Latham D.S.O. arrived and took Command of Bn	[illegible]
Trenches	29/9/16		Batt in trenches Casualties 1. O.R. Killed 9. O.R. wounded 3 Officers reported Lieut L. G. Thomas. 2/Lieut L. Hayne. 2/Lieut J. B. Morton 13. O.R. arrived.	[illegible]
Trenches	30/9/16		Batt in trenches Casualties wounded 2/Lieut W. Wilson 4. O.R. Killed 7. O.R. wounded. Battalion were relieved by Queens Westminsters	[illegible]

2/10/1916

F. Latham Major
Comdg 9th Bn Suffolk Regiment.

2449 Wt. W14957/M90 750,000 1/16 J.B.C. & A. Forms/C.2118/12.

Army Form C. 2118.

Instructions regarding War Diaries and Intelligence Summaries are contained in F. S. Regs., Part II. and the Staff Manual respectively. Title Pages will be prepared in manuscript.

WAR DIARY
or
INTELLIGENCE SUMMARY
(Erase heading not required.)

9th Suffolk Regt.

VOL 14

Place	Date	Hour	Summary of Events and Information	Remarks and references to Appendices
SANDPITS F.18.c. Sheet [illegible] ALBERT Combined	1/10/16		Batt at rest. draft of 14 O.R arrived and taken on strength. b.a.	
"	2/10/16		Batt at rest. 2/Lt. W.F. FITCH awarded Military cross for gallantry on Sept. 15 when he took command of the firing line and under very heavy Artillery and Machine gun fire consolidated the position. b.a.	
"	3/10/16		Batt at rest. draft of 24 O.R. arrived and taken on strength. b.a.	
"	4/10/16		Batt at rest. LIEUT and ADJUTANT C. ALLERTON awarded Distinguish service order for gallantry on Sept 15th when all the senior officers were either killed or wounded he took command of the Battalion until relieved by the 2nd in command. b.a.	
"	5/10/16		Batt at rest. draft of 75 O.R. arrived and taken on strength. b.a.	
"	6/10/16		Batt at rest. Batt moved to Camp at F.17.B. sheet ALBERT combined. b.a.	
	7/10/16		Batt at rest. b.a.	
	8/10/16		Batt at rest. Batt moved to bivouacs in BERNAFAY wood. S.29.c. Sheet 57.c. S.W. draft of 2 O.R. arrived. b.a.	
Bivouacs in S.29.c. Sheet 57.c.S.W.	9/10/16		Batt took over trenches from 2nd YORKS and LANCS. and 1st Kings SHROPSHIRE LIGHT INFANTRY. distribution as shown on attached map. Casualties. Two O.R. Killed. 7 wounded. b.a.	Appendix (1)
Trenches	10/10/16		Batt in trenches. draft of 10 O.R. arrived and taken on strength. Casualties. 7 O.R. Killed. 16 wounded. b.a.	
"	11/10/16		Batt in trenches. Casualties. 2 O.R. Killed. 14 wounded. b.a.	

2449 Wt. W14957/M90 750,000 1/16 J.B.C. & A. Forms/C.2118/12.

149

Army Form C. 2118.

Instructions regarding War Diaries and Intelligence Summaries are contained in F. S. Regs., Part II. and the Staff Manual respectively. Title Pages will be prepared in manuscript.

WAR DIARY
or
INTELLIGENCE SUMMARY
(Erase heading not required.)

9th Suffolk Regt.

Place	Date	Hour	Summary of Events and Information	Remarks and references to Appendices
Trenches	12/10/16		Batt in trenches. Draft of 5 O.R. arrived and taken on strength. Casualties. 13 O.R. Killed 34 wounded. G.A.	
"	13/10/16		Batt in trenches. Draft of 9 O.R. arrived and taken on strength. Batt was relieved by 2nd Sherwood Foresters and took over trenches in support as shown on attached map. Casualties. 2 O.R. Killed 8 wounded. G.A.	
Support Trenches	14/10/16		Batt in support. Casualties. One O.R. Killed. one missing. LIEUT. WILMOT. JOHNSON. and 10 O.R. reported arrival and taken on strength. G.A.	Appendix (2)
"	15/10/16		Batt moved to Camp at S.28.c. Sheet 57c S.W. after being relieved by 1st LEICESTERS. G.A.	
"	16/10/16		Batt took over support trenches from 1st Leicesters ~~[struck through]~~ G.A.	Appendix (2)
"	17/10/16		Batt took over trenches from 2nd Sherwood Foresters. distribution as shown in attached map. Casualties. 2 O.R. Killed 7 wounded. Major R.H. RADFORD. 3rd Bn Leicester Regt was attached for instruction to the Battalion. G.A.	Appendix (3)
Trenches	18/10/16		Batt in trenches. Casualties. 5 O.R. Killed 11 wounded. G.A.	
	19/10/16		Batt in trenches. Batt was relieved by 1st Sherwood Foresters and went into Bivouacs in B22.c. Sheet 57c S.W. Casualties one O.R. Killed 3 wounded. G.A.	
Bivouacs.	20/10/16		Batt moved to Camp at F.18.c. Sheet ALBERT. combined. G.A.	
Sandpits Camp. F.18.c	21/10/16		Batt moved by route march to CORBIE and went into billets. G.A.	
CORBIE	22/10/16		Batt at rest. G.A.	

2449 Wt. W14957/M90 750,000 1/16 J.B.C. & A. Forms/C.2118/12.

Army Form C. 2118.

Instructions regarding War Diaries and Intelligence Summaries are contained in F. S. Regs., Part II. and the Staff Manual respectively. Title Pages will be prepared in manuscript.

WAR DIARY
or
INTELLIGENCE SUMMARY
(Erase heading not required.)

9th Suffolk Regt.

Place	Date	Hour	Summary of Events and Information	Remarks and references to Appendices
CORBIE	23/10/16		Batt at rest. Batt proceeded by train to AIRAINES and from there marched to billets at MERELESSART.	
MERELESSART.	24/10/16		Batt at rest.	
"	25/10/16.		Batt at rest.	
"	26/10/16.		Batt at rest.	
"	27/10/16		Batt at rest. Draft of 4 O.R arrived and reported	
"	28/10/16		Batt at rest. Batt proceeded by train to FOUQUEREIL. and from there marched to billets at ANNEZIN.	
ANNEZIN.	29/10/16.		Batt at rest. Capt. C.T. Packard M.C. reported his arrival and taken on strength	
"	30/10/16		Batt at rest. Draft of 5 O.R arrived and taken on strength	
"	31/10/16.		Batt at rest.	

31. 10. 16.

[illegible] Major
Comm^d 9th Bn Suffolk Regt.

2449 Wt. W14957/M90 750,000 1/16 J.B.C. & A. Forms/C.2118/12.

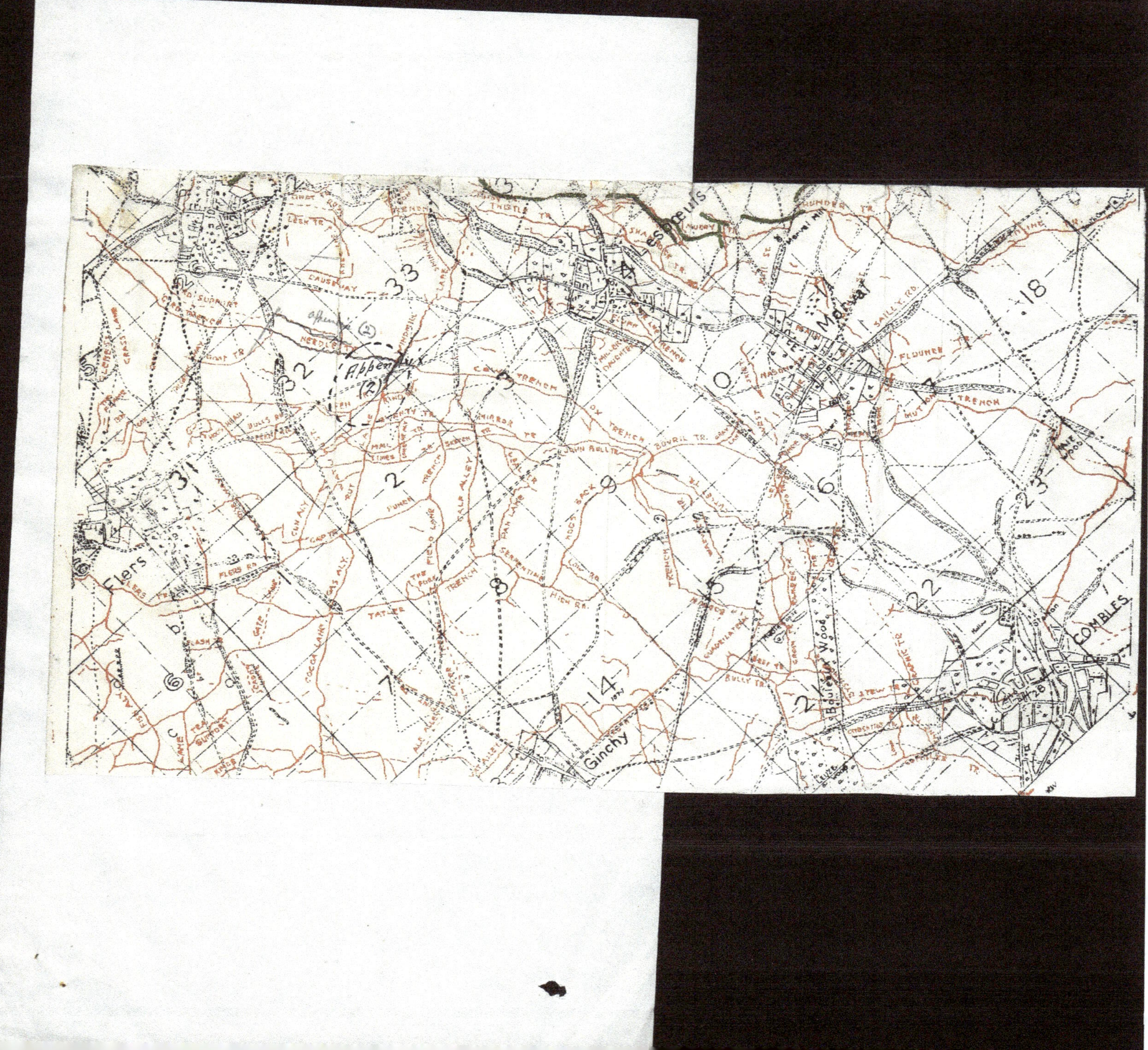
Les Boeufs
Morval
Flers
Ginchy
Bouleaux Wood
COMBLES

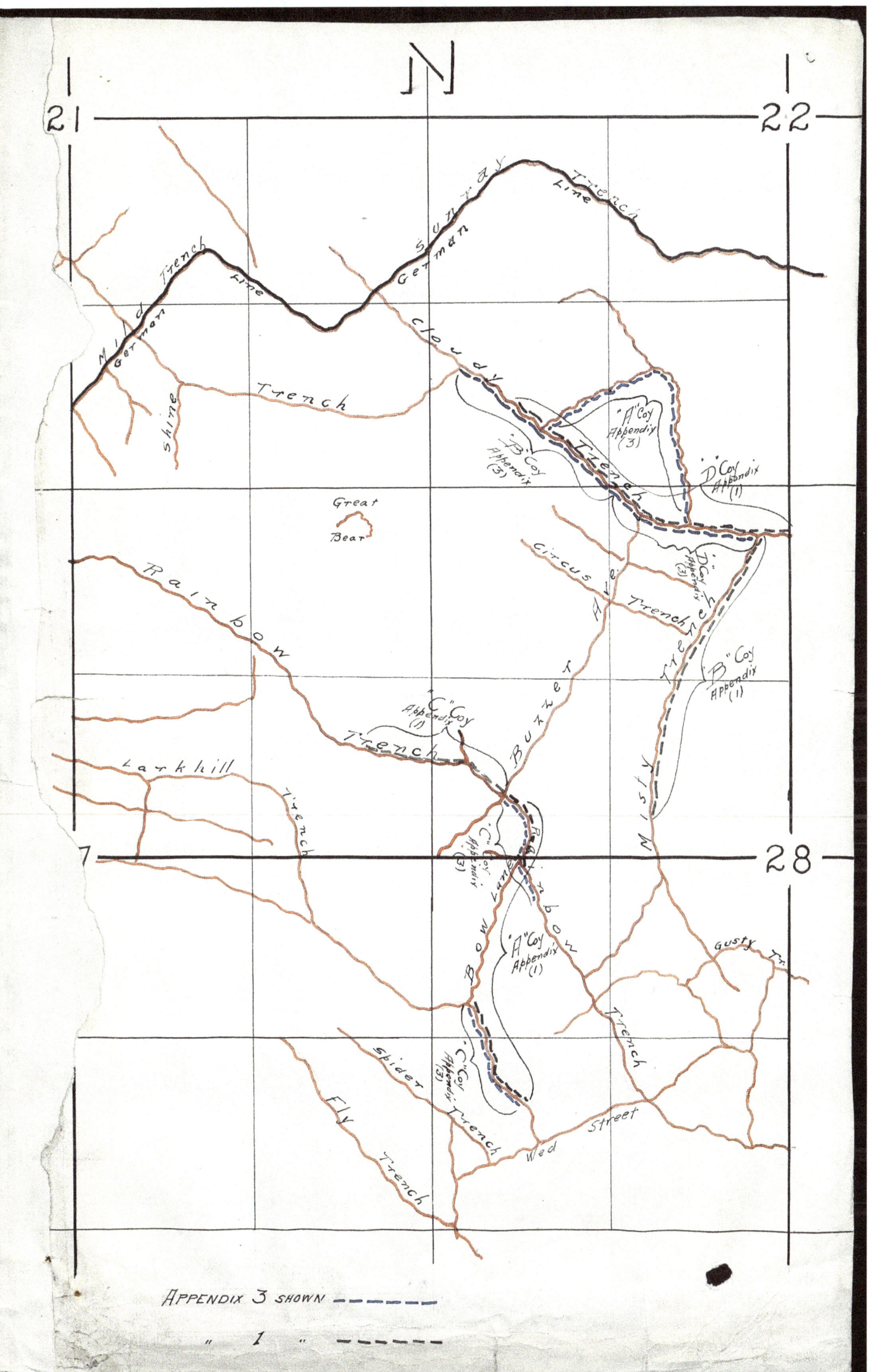
N
21
22
28
Mild German Trench Line
Sunray German Trench Line
Trench Line
Cloudy Trench
shine
Trench
"A" Coy Appendix (3)
"B" Coy Appendix (3)
"D" Coy Appendix (1)
"D" Coy Appendix (3)
Great Bear
Rainbow Trench
Circus Ave
Trench
Misty Trench
"B" Coy Appendix (1)
"C" Coy Appendix (1)
Butter
Larkhill Trench
"C" Coy Appendix (3)
Rainbow
Bow Lane
"A" Coy Appendix (1)
Rainbow Trench
Gusty Tr.
"C" Coy Appendix (3)
Spider Trench
Fly Trench
Wed Street
APPENDIX 3 SHOWN
" 1 "

Army Form C. 2118.

9 Suffolk Regt

Vol 13

159

Instructions regarding War Diaries and Intelligence Summaries are contained in F. S. Regs., Part II. and the Staff Manual respectively. Title pages will be prepared in manuscript.

WAR DIARY
or
INTELLIGENCE SUMMARY.
(*Erase heading not required.*)

Place	Date	Hour	Summary of Events and Information	Remarks and references to Appendices
ANNEZIN.	1/11/16.		Batt at rest.	ba
do	2/11/16.		Batt at rest.	ba
do	3/11/16.		Batt at rest. Capt C.T. PACKARD. M.C. attached to 18th Brigade HQ for instruction in duties of Staff Captain 2/Lts. J.V. TAILBY. H.C.S. THROSSELL. G.KING. J.A.BLANCH. J.R.COLTHORPE. having reported their arrival are taken on strength of Bn	ba
do.	4/11/16		Batt at rest.	ba
do	5/11/16.		Batt at rest. 2/Lt. C.H.MILLER having reported his arrival is taken on strength of Batt.	ba
do	6/11/16.		Batt at rest. working-parties of 5 officers and 412. O.R supplied. one officer and 103. O.R. to MOROC. remainder MAZINGARBE. Parties were under charge of Major R.H. RADFORD and were under orders of the 24th Division	ba
do.	7/11/16		working parties supplied in 24th Division area	ba
do	8/11/16		do do	ba
do	9/11/16		do do	ba
do	10/11/16		do do	ba
do	11/11/16		do do	ba
do	12/11/16.		do do	ba
do	13/11/16		do do	ba
do	14/11/16		Batt were relieved from working parties by 2nd DURHAM. LIGHT INFANTRY and returned to billets	ba
do	15/11/16		Batt at rest	ba
do	16/11/16		do [faint] 4 O.R. arrived and taken on strength	ba
do	17/11/16		do	ba
do	18/11/16		do . G.O.C. Brigade inspected the Battalion	ba
do	19/11/16		do	ba
do	20/11/16		do [faint] 3 O.R. arrived and taken on strength	ba
do	21/11/16		do 2/Lt. H.P. ROBERTS. sent to Field Ambulance sick.	ba

2353 Wt. W2544/1454 700,000 5/15 D. D. & L. A.D.S.S./Forms/C. 2118.

Army Form C. 2118.

Instructions regarding War Diaries and Intelligence Summaries are contained in F. S. Regs., Part II. and the Staff Manual respectively. Title Pages will be prepared in manuscript.

WAR DIARY
or
INTELLIGENCE SUMMARY
(Erase heading not required.)

Place	Date	Hour	Summary of Events and Information	Remarks and references to Appendices
ANNEZIN	22/11/16		Batt at rest. Draft of 3 O.R. arrived and taken on strength.	
do	23/11/16		do	
do	24/11/16		do	
do	25/11/16		do	
do	26/11/16		do	
do	27/11/16		do. Battalion moved by route march to billets in LE-PREOL. 3 Officers and 102 O.R. proceeded to ANNEQUIN to relieve 251 Tunnelling Coy. on working parties.	
LE-PREOL	28/11/16		Batt in reserve. B. Coy took over support trench (ESPERANTO-TERRACE) from 1st LEICESTER'S and was placed under orders of 1st LEICESTER'S. Draft of 3 O.R. arrived and taken on strength	
do	29/11/16		do. 2 Officers and 64 O.R. returned from working parties at ANNEQUIN and joined Battalion	
do	30/11/16		Batt in reserve. C and D Coy. and half Headquarters proceeded to trenches and took over from 1st LEICESTER'S (Two Platoons D Coy took over TOWER RESERVE Trench from 15th D.L.I.) D Coy in front line from BOYAU 30 to ROBERTSONS ALLEY – WILSONS WAY. C Coy Two Platoons TOWER RESERVE. Two Platoons VILLAGE LINE from junction with [illegible] LANE to junction with WILSONS WAY – VILLAGE LINE. B Coy was relieved in ESPERANTO TERRACE by 2nd Sherwood Foresters and proceeded to billets in LE-PREOL.	

1/12/16.

[signature] Lt Col
Comndg 9th (S) Bn Suffolk Regt

2449 Wt. W14957/M90 750,000 1/16 J.B.C. & A. Forms/C.2118/12.

Instructions regarding War Diaries and Intelligence Summaries are contained in F. S. Regs., Part II. and the Staff Manual respectively. Title Pages will be prepared in manuscript.

WAR DIARY
or
INTELLIGENCE SUMMARY
(Erase heading not required.)

9/Suffolks

Army Form C. 2118.

Vol 16

Place	Date	Hour	Summary of Events and Information	Remarks and references to Appendices
Trenches	1/12/16		Bn in trenches Casualties one OR wounded. Position A21B8.4 to A21d6.2½. Ref LA BASSEE 36c NW.1	[illegible]
	2/12/16		Bn in trenches do one OR do	[illegible]
	3/12/16		Bn in trenches do one OR killed & one OR wounded [illegible]	[illegible]
	4/12/16		Bn in trenches do one OR wounded Lt L. W Johnson sick to England	[illegible]
	5/12/16		Bn in trenches do 2/Lt Sedd[illegible] wounded	[illegible]
	6/12/16		Bn in trenches	[illegible]
	7/12/16		Bn in trenches Reinforcements 4 O.R	[illegible]
CUINCHY	8/12/16		Bn relieved by 9th Bn Norfolk Regt & moved to support in billets in HARLEY ST (CAMBRIN)	[illegible]
	9/12/16		Bn in support. Bn supplies working parties	[illegible]
	10/12/16		Bn in support Bn supplies working parties	[illegible]
	11/12/16		Bn in support Bn supplies working parties	[illegible]
Trenches	12/12/16		Bn relieved 9th Bn Norfolk Regt in the line from A21B8.4 to A21d6.2½ (LA BASSEE 36c NW) Reinforcements 2 OR	[illegible]
	13/12/16		Bn in trenches Casualties 1 OR (at duty)	[illegible]
	14/12/16		Bn in trenches Reinforcements 22 OR billeted at LE TREOL. LT COL J.T. COLLAS 2/1st London Regt attached to Bn for instruction 2Lt C MORBS rejoined Bn from FA	[illegible]
	15/12/16		Bn in trenches	[illegible]
BEUVRY	16/12/16		Bn relieved by 9th Bn Norfolk Regt & moves into billets in BEUVRY (Ref BETHUNE (comb. sheet 36A SE 36 SW 36B NE 36c NW) Reinforcements 35 O.R.	[illegible]
	17/12/16		Bn in Divisional reserve	[illegible]
	18/12/16		Bn in Divisional reserve	[illegible]
	19/12/16		Bn in Divisional reserve	[illegible]

Instructions regarding War Diaries and Intelligence Summaries are contained in F. S. Regs., Part II. and the Staff Manual respectively. Title Pages will be prepared in manuscript.

WAR DIARY or INTELLIGENCE SUMMARY

(Erase heading not required.)

Army Form C. 2118.

Place	Date	Hour	Summary of Events and Information	Remarks and references to Appendices
NOEUX LES MINES	20/12/16		Bn relieved by 1st Bn Norfolk Regt + moves into billets in NOEUX LES MINES + is in Army Reserve	1077
	21/12/16		Bn in Rest LT COL J J COLLAS returns to England	1077
	22/12/16		Bn in Rest - Training	1077
	23/12/16		Bn in Rest Training	1077
	24/12/16		Bn in Rest Training	1077
	25/12/16		Bn in Rest Training	1077
MAZINGARBE	26/12/16		Bn moves to MAZINGARBE + comes under orders of 62nd I.B.	1077
TRENCHES	27/12/16		Bn relieves 13th Bn NORTHUMBERLAND FUSILIERS in the line (QUARRIES RIGHT) Position G11 b 8.3 to G12 d 7.1 LOOS 36c NW 3	1077
	28/12/16		Bn in trenches	1077
	29/12/16		Bn in trenches casualties 2 O.R. killed	1077
	30/12/16		Bn in trenches casualty 1 O.R. wounded	1077
	31/12/16		Bn relieved by 9th Bn Norfolk Regt + moves into support trenches	1077

J Latham Lt. Col.
Comdg 9th Bn (S) The Suffolk Regt

2449 Wt. W14957/M90 750,000 1/16 J.B.C. & A. Forms/C.2118/12.

6th Division

9th Suffolk Reg.

~~January to December~~

~~1914~~

1917 JAN – 1918 FEB

DISBANDED

Instructions regarding War Diaries and Intelligence Summaries are contained in F. S. Regs., Part II. and the Staff Manual respectively. Title Pages will be prepared in manuscript.

WAR DIARY
or
INTELLIGENCE SUMMARY
(Erase heading not required.)

Army Form C. 2118.

9th Suffolks

Vol 17

179

Place	Date	Hour	Summary of Events and Information		Remarks and references to Appendices
Trenches	1/1/17.		Batt in support trenches. Casualties 2 O.R. wounded	ba	
"	2/1/17.		do do	ba	
"	3/1/17		Batt in do	ba	
"	4/1/17		Batt relieved 9th Norfolks in front line disposition D. Coy. 2 platoons front line E of BOYAU 78. one Platoon close support line S of HULLOCK ROAD one platoon by night in K. by day front line BOYAU 78. A Coy one Platoon NEWPORT CRATER one platoon LANCER. one platoon trench joining DEVON LANE and DUDLEY LANE one platoon Chapel Alley at Coy HQ B one platoon LOOKOUT Crater one platoon BRESLAU Crater. one platoon by BOYAU 92 and 93. one platoon GRINWOOD Trench at Coy HQ C. in support St GEORGES Trench.	ba	See attached map.
Trenches	5/1/17		Batt in front line trenches	ba	
"	6/1/17		do do Casualties one O.R. wounded	ba	
"	7/1/17		do do	ba	
"	8/1/17		do do Batt was relieved by 9th Norfolks and proceeded to billets in MAZINGARBE 2nd LIEUT R.H. STOCKMAN reports his arrival and taken on strength.	ba	
MAZINGARBE	9/1/17		Batt at rest billets. working parties found. 2/Lt E.L.G. ARKELL reports his arrival and taken on strength draft of 112 O.R. arrived and taken on strength.	ba	
do	10/1/17		Batt at rest billets working parties found	ba	
do	11/1/17		do do do	ba	
do	12/1/17		do. do Batt took over front line trenches from 9th Norfolks. disposition same as 4/1/17. with exception that C and D. change over	ba	
Trenches	13/1/17		Batt in front line trenches Lt Col F. LATHAM. took temporary command of 71 Brigade Major M.F. HEIGHAM took do do do Battalion	ba	

Army Form C. 2118.

Instructions regarding War Diaries and Intelligence Summaries are contained in F. S. Regs., Part II. and the Staff Manual respectively. Title Pages will be prepared in manuscript.

WAR DIARY
or
INTELLIGENCE SUMMARY

(Erase heading not required.)

Place	Date	Hour	Summary of Events and Information	Remarks and references to Appendices
Trenches	14/1/17		Batt in front line trenches	[illegible]
do	15/1/17		do do	[illegible]
do	16/1/17		do do Batt was relieved by 9th Norfolks and took over Support trenches. disposition:– A Coy 3 Platoons O.B4 one Platoon Chapel Alley B " 1 Platoon O.B.1. one Platoon O.B4 2 Platoon O.B5. C " 2 Platoon O.B.1. 2 Platoon DEVON LANE at junction of O.B1 D " 1 Platoon O.G.1 3 Platoons DEVON LANE	[illegible]
Support trenches	17/1/17		Batt in Support trenches	[illegible]
do	18/1/17		do Casualties one O.R. killed 4 O.R. wounded	[illegible]
do	19/1/17		do Batt took over front line trenches from 9th Norfolks disposition same as 12/1/17 with exception that B and D Coys changed	[illegible]
Front line trenches	20/1/17		Batt in front line trenches	[illegible]
do	21/1/17		do do Casualties two O.R. wounded	[illegible]
do	22/1/17		do	[illegible]
do	23/1/17		do Batt was relieved in trenches by 9th Norfolks and proceeded to billets in MAZINGARBE.	[illegible]
[illegible] (…ZINGARBE?)	24/1/17		Batt at rest	[illegible]
do	25/1/17		do LT.COL.F.LATHAM returned from Brigade and took command of Battalion	[illegible]

2449 Wt. W14957/M90 750,000 1/16 J.B.C. & A. Forms/C.2118/12.

Instructions regarding War Diaries and Intelligence Summaries are contained in F. S. Regs., Part II. and the Staff Manual respectively. Title Pages will be prepared in manuscript.

WAR DIARY
or
INTELLIGENCE SUMMARY

(Erase heading not required.)

Army Form C. 2118.

Place	Date	Hour	Summary of Events and Information	Remarks and references to Appendices
MAZINGARBE	26/1/17		Batt at rest. 2/LIEUT. G. HOPKINS arrived and taken on strength	ba
do	27/1/17		Batt at rest. Batt took over Front line trenches from 9th Norfolks disposition same as 19/1/17 with exception that A and B changed over	ba
Trenches	28/1/17		Batt in Front line trenches - Casualties one O.R. wounded.	ba
do	29/1/17		do do	ba
do	30/1/17		do do	ba
do	31/1/17		do do Batt was relieved by 9th Norfolks and proceeded to Support trenches.	ba

1/2/17.

[signature] Lt Col
Commd 9th (S) Bn Suffolk Regt

2449 Wt. W14957/M90 750,000 1/16 J.B.C. & A. Forms/C.2118/12.

189

Army Form C. 2118.

Instructions regarding War Diaries and Intelligence Summaries are contained in F. S. Regs., Part II. and the Staff Manual respectively. Title Pages will be prepared in manuscript.

WAR DIARY
or
INTELLIGENCE SUMMARY
(Erase heading not required.)

9th (S) Bn Suffolk Rgt.

Vol 18

Place	Date	Hour	Summary of Events and Information	Remarks and references to Appendices
SUPPORT. TRENCHES.	1/2/17.		Batt^n in support trenches	ba
do	2/2/17		do. do.	ba
do.	3/2/17.		do do	ba
do	4/2/17.		do do. Batt^n took over front line trenches from 9th Norfolks. disposition of Coys:- A Coy. 2 Platoons front line trench E of BOYAU.78. one platoon close support line S. of HULLOCK ROAD. one platoon by night in K. by day front line BOYAU.78. B.Coy. one platoon NEWPORT. one platoon LANCER. one platoon in trench joining DEVON.LANE. and DUDLEY.LANE one platoon CHAPEL.ALLEY. C.COY. 4 Platoons ST GEORGES.TRENCH. D.COY. one platoon LOOKOUT. one platoon BRESLAU. craters. one platoon 92 and 93. BOYAU. one platoon GRIMWOOD.TRENCH. Casualties. 2/LT. J.R.COLTHORPE. wounded.	ba ba
FRONT.LINE.TRENCHES.	5/2/17.		Batt in front line trenches	ba
do	6/2/17.		do do. Casualties 2.O.R. wounded. Lt Col. F. LATHAM. DSO. left Batt^n to take temporary command of 71st Brigade Major M.F. HEIGHAM. took over temporary command of Batt^n.	ba
do	7/2/17.		Batt in front line trenches. Casualties one. O.R. wounded.	ba
do	8/2/17.		do do. 9th Norfolks relieved Batt^n in trenches. Batt^n proceeded to billets in reserve at MAZINGARBE.	ba
MAZINGARBE.	9/2/17.		Batt^n in reserve	ba
do	10/2/17.		do	ba
do	11/2/17.		do	ba
do	12/2/17.		do. Batt^n took over front-line trenches from 9th Norfolks. disposition of Coys. same as on 4/2/17. with exception that C. and D Coys changed over. Casualties one O.R. killed 4. wounded.	ba
FRONT.LINE.TRENCHES.	13/2/17.		Batt in front line trenches. Batt. had following casualties from the 71st Brigade raiding party which raided enemy trenches night of 12/13. 2/LT. E.KINE. Killed. one O.R. Killed 2.O.R. wounded.	ba

2449 Wt. W14957/M90 750,000 1/16 J.B.C. & A. Forms/C.2118/12.

Army Form C. 2118.

Instructions regarding War Diaries and Intelligence Summaries are contained in F. S. Regs., Part II. and the Staff Manual respectively. Title Pages will be prepared in manuscript.

WAR DIARY
or
INTELLIGENCE SUMMARY
(Erase heading not required.)

Place	Date	Hour	Summary of Events and Information	Remarks and references to Appendices
Front line Trenches	14/2/17.		Batt in front line trenches. Casualties 2. O.R. wounded	fa
do	15/2/17.		do do	fa
do	16/2/17		do do Casualties 3. O. R. wounded.	fa
do	17/2/17.		do do. Batt was relieved in trenches by the 12th Northumberland Fusiliers and after relief went to rest billets at LA BOURSE.	fa
LA BOURSE.	18/2/17.		Batt at rest. Batt proceeded by route march to BETHUNE where they were billeted in the ORPHANAGE.	fa
BETHUNE.	19/2/17		Batt at rest 13 O. R. arrived and taken on strength	fa
do	20/2/17.		do	fa
do	21/2/17		do.	fa
do	22/2/17		do	fa
do	23/2/17		do	fa
do	24/2/17		do Major M F HEIGHAM. took up duties of Town Major. Major J. P. WYLIE took over command of Bn	fa
do	25/2/17		do one O.R. wounded (accidently) by Rifle Grenade.	fa
do	26/2/17		do	fa
do	27/2/17		do LT COL J P O TRIMBLE, M.C. took over command of Bn from Major J P WYLIE	fa
do	28/2/17		do. Bn proceeded by Route march to Billets at LA BOURSE	fa

1/3/17.

[signature] Lt Col
Commanding 9th (S) Bn The Suffolk Regt

2449 Wt. W14957/M90 750,000 1/16 J.B.C. & A. Forms/C.2118/12.

Instructions regarding War Diaries and Intelligence Summaries are contained in F. S. Regs., Part II. and the Staff Manual respectively. Title Pages will be prepared in manuscript.

WAR DIARY
or
INTELLIGENCE SUMMARY
(Erase heading not required.)

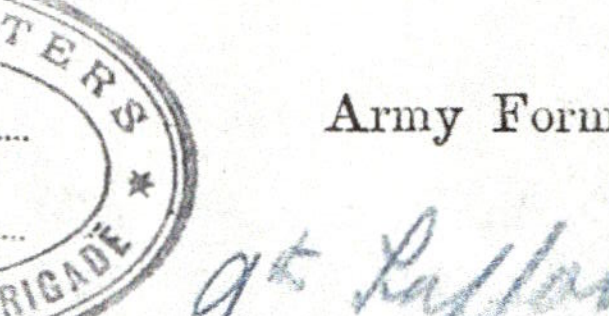

Army Form C. 2118.

9th Suffolks
Vol 19

Place	Date	Hour	Summary of Events and Information	Remarks and references to Appendices
LA.BOURSE.	1/3/17		Batt in reserve. D Coy took over support trenches from 12th and 13th NORTHUMBERLAND FUZILIERS. Disposition:- one platoon O.B1. between CHAPEL ALLEY and STAFFORD LANE. 2 Platoons CHAPEL ALLEY, one Platoon OB1 between CHAPEL ALLEY and DEVON LANE.	
do. LESS D Coy	2/3/17		Three Coys of Bn in reserve	
do	3/3/17		do Batt less D Coy, took over support trenches from 13th ROYAL FUZILIERS, disposition:- A Coy. 2 Platoons TENTH AVENUE, 1 Platoon VENDIN ALLEY, 1 Platoon DUFFERS DRIFT. B Coy. 2 do do between ESSEX LANE and HAY ALLEY, 2 Platoon TENTH AVENUE between HAY ALLEY and WINGS WAY C Coy 2 do do 2 Platoon LONE TREE, redoubt	
SUPPORT TRENCHES	4/3/17		Bn in Support trenches	
do	5/3/17		do Bn took over front line trenches from 9/Norfolks, disposition:- A Coy. 3 Platoons ST GEORGES TRENCH, one Platoon DEVON LANE. B Coy. 2 do NEWPORT CRATER by night one by day. one platoon unnamed trench one Platoon CHAPEL ALLEY. C Coy. one do between BOYAU 92 and LAMBIES LANE. one Platoon between LAMBIES LANE and BOYAU 87 one do do do 87 and 85. one Platoon GRIMWOOD Trench. D Coy. one do head of BOYAU 78 one Platoon K. dump one Platoon DUDLEY dump. one Platoon in Support trench.	
Front line trenches	6/3/17		Bn in Front line trenches. Casualties 2/CAPTAIN L.C. SCHOLFIELD wounded one O.R. wounded.	
do	7/3/17		do do one O.R. wounded	
do	8/3/17		do do one O.R. do. LIEUT A.A. GUINNESS. arrived and taken on strength.	
do	9/3/17		do Bn was relieved by 9/Norfolks and proceeded to billets in PHILOSOPHE. T/Col. LATHAM DSO assumed Command of the Battalion from Command the Brigade, Major J.B.S. TRIMBLE M.C. took up duties of 2nd in Command.	
PHILOSOPHE.	10/3/17.		Batt in reserve 2/Lt EWV TAYLOR reported and taken on strength	
do	11/3/17.		do.	
do	12/3/17		do Casualties one O.R. wounded	
do	13/3/17		do 2/Lt E.N.G. ARKELL reported and taken on strength.	
do	14/3/17		do Casualties one O.R. wounded	
do	15/3/17		do Bn took over front line trenches from 9/Norfolks disposition same as 5/3/17 with exception that A and B Coys changed over.	

2449 Wt. W14957/M90 750,000 1/16 J.B.C. & A. Forms/C.2118/12.

199

Instructions regarding War Diaries and Intelligence Summaries are contained in F. S. Regs., Part II. and the Staff Manual respectively. Title Pages will be prepared in manuscript.

WAR DIARY
or
INTELLIGENCE SUMMARY
(Erase heading not required.)

Army Form C. 2118.

Place	Date	Hour	Summary of Events and Information	Remarks and references to Appendices
Front line trenches	16/3/17		Bn in front line trenches. Casualties one O.R. Killed one wounded	[illegible]
do	17/3/17		do Casualties 2/Lt. H.C.S. THROSSELL Killed one O.R wounded	[illegible]
do	18/3/17		do Casualties 5 O.R. wounded	[illegible]
do	19/3/17		do	[illegible]
do	20/3/17		do Casualties 2 O.R. wounded	[illegible]
do	21/3/17		do Bn was relieved in front line trenches by 9/Norfolks and after relief took over support trenches	
			Disposition :- A Coy. 4 Platoons O.B.1.	
			B Coy 4 Platoon TENTH AVENUE between HAY ALLEY and WINGS WAY.	
			C. Coy. 4 Platoons do do VENDIN ALLEY and HAY ALLEY.	
			D Coy. 1 Platoon DEVON LANE one O.B.4 2. CHAPEL ALLEY.	[illegible]
			Casualties A/Capt L.G. THOMAS. wounded (GAS poisoning)	[illegible]
SUPPORT Trench	22/3/17		Bn in SUPPORT trench	[illegible]
do	23/3/17		do	[illegible]
do	24/3/17		do 2/LT. H.E. FALKNER reported his arrival and taken on strength	[illegible]
do	25/3/17		do	[illegible]
do	26/3/17		do	
do	27/3/17		do Bn took over front line trenches from 2nd SHERWOOD FORESTERS and 9th NORFOLKS, disposition :-	
			A.COY. one platoon head of BOYAU 78 one platoon K one platoon and 1 section NEWPORT ½ Platoon dugout between DUDLEY & K ½ Platoon DUDLEY	
			B.Coy one platoon NORTHERN TUNNEL exits and No 5 CRATER Post one platoon STRAW ALLEY DUGOUT and entrance to STRAW ALLEY. one platoon SOUTHERN TUNNEL exits and No 1 CRATER Post one platoon GREEN CURVE dugout and entrance to GREEN CURVE	
			C Coy one platoon St. GEORGES TRENCH WINGS WAY to HULLUCH ROAD one HULLUCH ROAD to DUDLEY LANE. one DUDLEY LANE to DEVON LANE one DEVON LANE to CHAPEL ALLEY	[illegible]

2449 Wt. W14957/M90 750,000 1/16 J.B.C. & A. Forms/C.2118/12.

Instructions regarding War Diaries and Intelligence Summaries are contained in F. S. Regs., Part II. and the Staff Manual respectively. Title Pages will be prepared in manuscript.

WAR DIARY
or
INTELLIGENCE SUMMARY

(Erase heading not required.)

Army Form C. 2118.

Place	Date	Hour	Summary of Events and Information	Remarks and references to Appendices
	27/3/17		D. COY. one Platoon head of CHAPEL ALLEY one platoon LANCER. one Platoon LOOKOUT. one platoon QUARRY BAY and GRIMWOOD TRENCH. Casualties one O.R. wounded	[illegible]
Front line trenches	28/3/17		Battn in front line trenches. Casualties one O R wounded	[illegible]
do	29/3/17		do	[illegible]
do	30/3/17		do Casualties one O.R. wounded	[illegible]
do	31/3/17		do Casualties 4 O.R. wounded	

1/4/17

Latham Lt Col
Commd 9th (S) Battn The Suffolk Regt

2449 Wt. W14957/M90 750,000 1/16 J.B.C. & A. Forms/C.2118/12.

CONFIDENTIAL.

Headquarters.
71st Infantry Brigade

Herewith War Diary of the Bn. under my Command for period 1st to 30th April 1917.

Latham Lt-Colonel,
Comd'g 9th Battalion Suffolk Regt.

1. 5. 17

Army Form C. 2118.

Instructions regarding War Diaries and Intelligence Summaries are contained in F. S. Regs., Part II. and the Staff Manual respectively. Title Pages will be prepared in manuscript.

WAR DIARY
or
INTELLIGENCE SUMMARY
(Erase heading not required.)

9 Suffolk Regt

Vol 20

Place	Date	Hour	Summary of Events and Information	Remarks and references to Appendices
Front line trenches	1/4/17		Battn in front line trenches Casualties one O.R wounded	
do	2/4/17		do Bn was relieved by 9th Norfolks and took over reserve billets in PHILOSOPHE	
PHILOSOPHE	3/4/17		Battn in reserve billets	
do	4/4/17		do Casualties 3 O.R. wounded (accidental)	
do	5/4/17		do	
do	6/4/17		do Casualties 1. O.R. wounded	
do	7/4/17		do Casualties 2. O. R. wounded	
do	8/4/17		do Battn took over front line trenches from 9th Norfolks. disposition as follows.	ref LOOS Map. 36c N.W 3. 1.10.000
			A COY one platoon head of BOYAU 78 one Platoon K. dump. one Platoon NEWPORT one Platoon close support line and BOYAU 78	
			B COY one platoon NORTHERN TUNNEL EXIT and No 5 Crater Post one Platoon STRAW ALLEY TUNNEL dugout and sap to STRAW ALLEY	
			~~B COY~~ one platoon SOUTHERN TUNNEL EXIT and No 1. Crater Post two Platoon GREEN CURVE TUNNEL dugout and sap to GREEN CURVE	
			one Platoon LOOKOUT one Platoon QUARRY BAY and GRIMWOOD	
			C COY one platoon head of CHAPEL ALLEY one Platoon LANDER	
			D COY 4 platoons ST GEORGES Trench.	
			Casualties 2/LT J.R. COLTHORPE wounded Killed 4 O.R wounded 6. O.R	
Front line trenches	9/4/17		Battn in Front line trenches Casualties one O. R. wounded	
do	10/4/17		do D Coy raided the enemys trenches behind LOOKOUT Crater in three parties. owing to heavy barrage only one of two parties who were to enter enemy trenches succeeded in doing so. one German was killed and 2 others believed wounded and one dugout was blown up. no identification was secured. our Casualties were slight. several of these being very slight wounds Casualties 2/LT C H MILLER wounded one O R killed 9 wounded (2 remaining at duty)	
			Casualties 2. O. R. wounded	
do	11/4/17		Battn in front line trenches Casualties one O.R killed 7 wounded Lieut. W F FITCH M.C. wounded (Remained at duty)	
do	12/4/17		do	
do	13/4/17		do Casualties one O. R. wounded	

209

Instructions regarding War Diaries and Intelligence Summaries are contained in F. S. Regs., Part II. and the Staff Manual respectively. Title Pages will be prepared in manuscript.

WAR DIARY
or
INTELLIGENCE SUMMARY
(Erase heading not required.)

Army Form C. 2118.

Place	Date	Hour	Summary of Events and Information	Remarks and references to Appendices
Front line trenches	14/4/17		Batt in front line trenches. Batt was relieved by 9th Bn NORFOLK Regt and took over reserve trenches from 2nd SHERWOODS. Disposition:- A COY 9th and 10th AVENUE. B COY RESERVE line from 7th AVENUE to DEVON LANE. C. COY. RESERVE line from EXETER CASTLE in O.B.1 to GORDON ALLEY. D. COY RESERVE line from DEVON LANE. to EXETER CASTLE	ba
RESERVE trenches	15/4/17		Batt in reserve. 2/Lt H. A. SHAW. reported and was taken on strength of Bn. Casualties. 2. O.R. wounded.	ba
do	16/4/17		Batt in reserve	ba ba
do	17/4/17		do do	ba
do	18/4/17		do do Casualties one. O.R. wounded	ba
do	19/4/17		do do	
do	20/4/17		do do Batt relieved 2nd SHERWOOD FORESTERS in front line trenches disposition:- A. COY. one platoon HULLUCH POST. one platoon GORDON Post by night STANSFIELD road by day one platoon DRUMMOND trench one platoon STANSFIELD Road B. COY one platoon BRESLAU. one platoon FOSSE TUNNEL and front line one platoon STANSFIELD TUNNEL and front line one platoon STANSFIELD TUNNEL C. COY one platoon RAT. CREEK. one platoon NORTHERN CRATER one platoon SOUTHERN CRATER one platoon Sentries in TUNNEL EXITS. D. COY 2. Platoon QUARRY. BAY. 2 Platoons O.G.1. entrance Casualties one. O.R. wounded	ba.

Army Form C. 2118.

Instructions regarding War Diaries and Intelligence Summaries are contained in F. S. Regs., Part II. and the Staff Manual respectively. Title pages will be prepared in manuscript.

WAR DIARY
or
INTELLIGENCE SUMMARY.
(Erase heading not required.)

Place	Date	Hour	Summary of Events and Information	Remarks and references to Appendices
Front line trenches	21/4/17		Battn in front line trenches Casualties 2 O.R. wounded.	
Front line trenches	22/4/17		Battn in front line trenches Battn was relieved by 2nd SHERWOOD FORESTERS and after relief took over support	[illegible]
			trenches disposition the same as 14/4/17. Casualties 3 O.R. Killed 2 O.R. wounded	[illegible]
Support trenches	23/4/17		Battn proceeded to MAROC and after a halt for a few hours in billets took over the Support trenches in LOOS	
			SUB-SECTION from 2nd YORKS and LANCS Regt. Disposition All 4 Coys in OG1. Battn came under the orders of	
			G.O.C. 16th Infantry Brigade. Casualties 7 O.R. wounded.	[illegible]
Support trenches	24/4/17		Battn in Support trenches. Battn relieved 1st BUFFS in front line trenches Disposition:-	
			A Coy. Three Platoons in SUNKEN ROAD Trench one platoon in support at BREWERY LOOS.	
			B Coy Four Platoons in NOVEL TRENCH. Capt R.H. GRIFFITHS 2nd Sherwood Foresters took up duties of 2nd in Command	
			C Coy Four Platoons between CAMERON TRENCH ALLEY and BLACKWATCH ALLEY	See attached map
			D Coy Four Platoons in OG1 and NATAL TRENCH and BOYAUS adjoining same	
			Casualties 2/Lt. A.H.L. HOWELL and 2/Lt F.N. PAINER wounded. 2 O.R. Killed 19 wounded.	[illegible]
Front line trenches	25/4/17		Battn in front line trenches Casualties 4 O.R. wounded	[illegible]
"	26/4/17		Battn in front line trenches. Casualties 3 O.R. Killed 3 wounded.	[illegible]
"	27/4/17		Battn in front line trenches. Battn was relieved by 2nd Sherwood Foresters and after relief took over Support trenches	
			Disposition:- A and B Coys in ENCLOSURE. G.5. 8. 100/80. C Coy. CELLARS Affaire [illegible] central D Coy. 2½ Platoons	See Map 36 C S.W. 1 Scale [illegible]
			SOLENT TUNNEL 1½ Cellars N.W. end of SLAG HEAP Casualties 1 O.R. Killed 8 wounded	[illegible]

A6945 Wt. W11422/M1160 350,000 12/16 D. D. & L. Forms/C./2118/14.

Instructions regarding War Diaries and Intelligence Summaries are contained in F. S. Regs., Part II. and the Staff Manual respectively. Title pages will be prepared in manuscript.

WAR DIARY
or
INTELLIGENCE SUMMARY.
(Erase heading not required.)

Army Form C. 2118.

Place	Date	Hour	Summary of Events and Information	Remarks and references to Appendices
Support trenches	28/4/17		Battn in Support trenches. Casualties NIL	
do	29/4/17		do Casualties 3 O.R. wounded	
do	30/4/17		do Two Companys A and B took over Support trenches from 1st Leicestershire Regt. Disposits. A Coy 4 Platoons MUSIC Trench. B Coy 4 Platoons KINGS ST. Batt HQ No 2 under 2nd in Command ~~~~ Harrison's TUNNEL	
			1/5/17. T Latham Lt-Col Commanding 9th Battalion Suffolk Regt	

A6945 Wt. W11422/M1160 350,000 12/16 D. D. & L. Forms/C./2118/14.

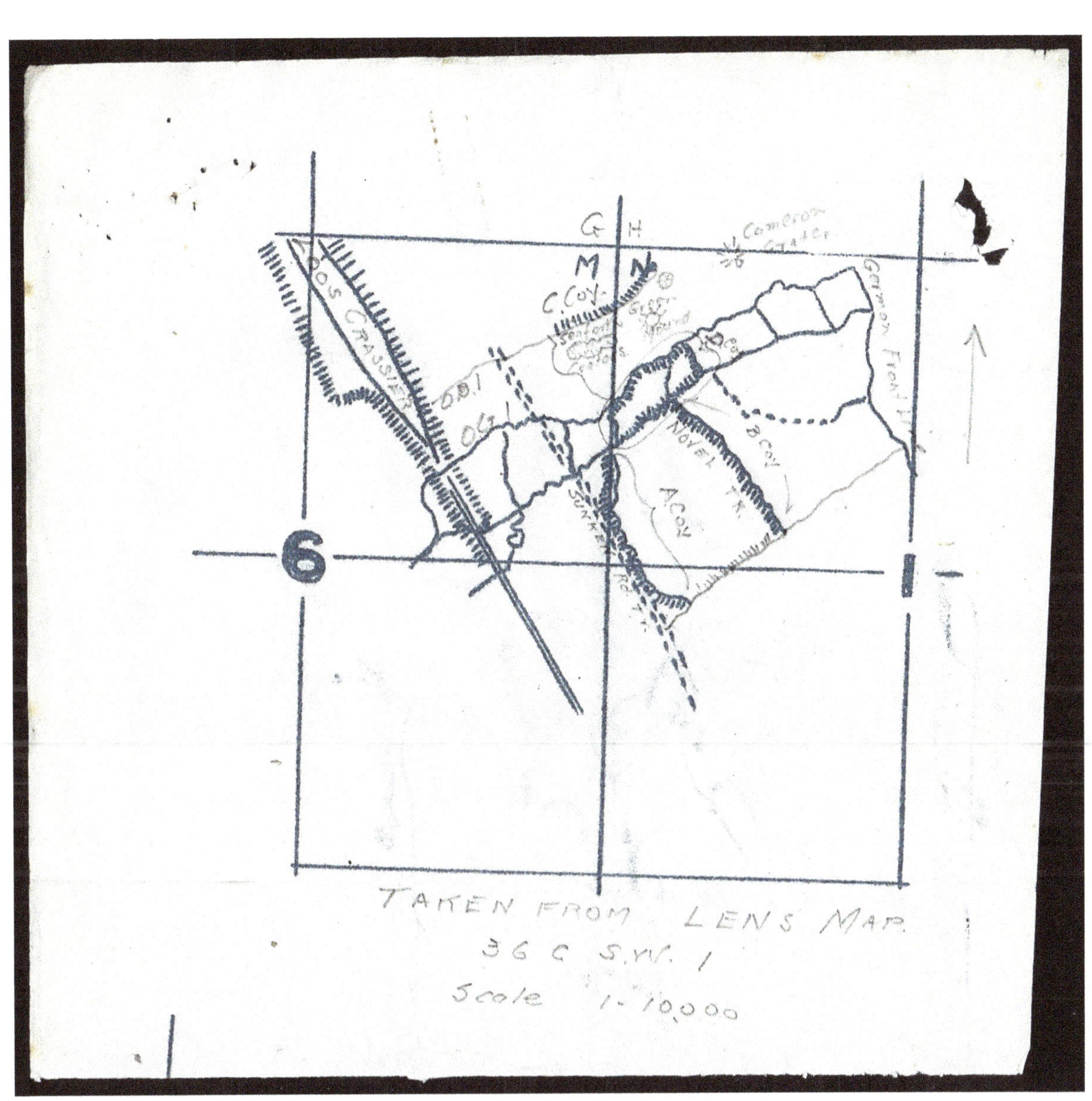
G
H
M
N
Cameron Crater
Loos Crassier
C. Coy.
OG.1
OG.1
D Coy
German Front Line
B Coy
Novel Tk.
A. Coy
Sunken Rd Tr.
6
1
TAKEN FROM LENS MAP
36 C S.W. 1
Scale 1-10,000

Instructions regarding War Diaries and Intelligence Summaries are contained in F. S. Regs., Part II. and the Staff Manual respectively. Title pages will be prepared in manuscript.

WAR DIARY
or
INTELLIGENCE SUMMARY.
(Erase heading not required.)

Army Form C. 2118.

9 Suffolk Rgt

Vol 21

Place	Date	Hour	Summary of Events and Information	Remarks and references to Appendices
Support Trenches	1/5/17		Battn in support trenches Battn was relieved as follows A and B Coy by 1/5th LINCOLNS C and D 2nd DURHAM LIGHT INFANTRY and after relief proceeded to billets in MAZINGARBE 2/Lt C. H. MILLER was awarded Military Cross for gallantry in raid made by D Coy on April 4th 1917 17720 Cpl. W GOSHAWK and 44031 Pte C ANDREWS awarded Military Medal for the same raid Reinforcements of 46 O.R joined divisional training Coy.	AA
MAZINGARBE	2/5/17		Battn in reserve Battn took over front line trenches from 8th BEDFORDS disposition: A Coy 2 platoon NEWPORT by night one platoon from there by day in CHAPEL ALLEY one platoon DEVON DUMP one platoon CHAPEL ALLEY	
			B. COY. 4 Platoons ST GEORGES Trench	
			C. COY one platoon LANCER one platoon LOOKOUT one platoon BRESLAU one platoon Tunnel exits	
			D Coy one platoon BOYAU 78 one platoon close support trench one platoon Dump one platoon DUDLEY dump.	
			Trench strength Officers 20 O.R. 473	AA
Front line trenches	3/5/17		Battn in front line trenches Casualties one O.R. wounded	AA
do	4/5/17		do do 2/Lt P. BRAIN wounded and 7 O.R	AA
do	5/5/17		do do Casualties 2 O.R killed 8 wounded (remaining at duty) 2/Lt A.G. DOUGLAS joined Battn from divisional training Coy	AA
do	6/5/17		Battn in front line trenches Casualties 3 O.R. wounded 58 O.R. arrived from divisional training Coy and taken on strength	AA

21

A6945 Wt. W11422/M1160 350,000 12/16 D. D. & L. Forms/C./2118/14.

Instructions regarding War Diaries and Intelligence Summaries are contained in F. S. Regs., Part II. and the Staff Manual respectively. Title pages will be prepared in manuscript.

WAR DIARY
or
INTELLIGENCE SUMMARY.
(Erase heading not required.)

Army Form C. 2118.

Place	Date	Hour	Summary of Events and Information	Remarks and references to Appendices
front line trenches	7/5/17		Batt in front line trenches. Casualties one O.R. killed 3 wounded. 51 O.R. joined Battalion from Divisional Training Coy.	[illegible]
do	8/5/17		do do do 2 O.R. wounded one remained at duty.	[illegible]
do	9/5/17		do do	[illegible]
do	10/5/17		do do Batt was relieved by 9th Norfolks and after relief proceeded to billets as follows	[illegible]
do			A. C and D Coys at VAUDRICOURT. B Coy DROUVIN. Bn HQ VERQUIN.	[illegible]
RESERVE billets	11/5/17		Batt in reserve. Major H.B. BROWN. DSO. 1st Leicestershire Regt. arrived to take T/command of Bn while Lt Col F. Latham DSO went on leave	[illegible]
do	12/5/17		do Draft of 12 O.R. arrived from base and reported taken on strength.	[illegible]
do	13/5/17		do	[illegible]
do	14/5/17		do	[illegible]
do	15/5/17		do	[illegible]
do	16/5/17		do	[illegible]
do	17/5/17		do	[illegible]
do	18/5/17		do Batt took over front line trenches from 9th Norfolks. disposition same as 4/5/17.	[illegible]
front line trenches	19/5/17		Batt in front line trenches. Casualties one O.R. killed one wounded	[illegible]
do	20/5/17		do do Casualties Three O.R. wounded	[illegible]
do	21/5/17		do do Casualties Nil	[illegible]

A6945 Wt. W11422/M1160 350,000 12/16 D. D. & L. Forms/C./2118/14.

Instructions regarding War Diaries and Intelligence Summaries are contained in F. S. Regs., Part II, and the Staff Manual respectively. Title pages will be prepared in manuscript.

WAR DIARY
or
INTELLIGENCE SUMMARY.
(Erase heading not required.)

Army Form C. 2118.

Place	Date	Hour	Summary of Events and Information	Remarks and references to Appendices
Front line Trenches	22/5/17		Battn in front line trenches Casualties one O.R. wounded	
do	23/5/17		do do Lt-Col. F. Latham DSO returned from leave and reassumed command of Battalion	
do	24/5/17		do do Extract from London Gazette 24.5.17 Temp Major (Acting Lt-Col) F. LATHAM D.S.O. (Capt LEICESTERSHIRE Regt) from LEICESTERSHIRE REGT. to command a Battalion and to be temporary Lt-Colonel 22/5/1917 seniority 19/11/16	
do	25/5/17		do do Casualties 2 O.R. Killed 2 wounded	
do	26/5/17		do do Battn was relieved by 9th Norfolks and after relief B Coy went in support trenches under tactical command of O/c 2nd Sherwood Foresters and D Coy went in support trenches under tactical command of O/c 9th Norfolks A. C. Coys and HQ went to reserve billet in PHILOSOPHE.	
			Casualties one Cadet Rifle (attached) Killed	
Support Trenches & PHILOSOPHE	27/5/17		Battn in brigade reserve	
do	28/5/17		do	
do	29/5/17		do	
do	30/5/17		do B and D Coys were relieved in support trenches by A and C Coys and after relief took over billets in PHILOSOPHE 12 O.R arrived from Divisional training Coy. Casualties 2 O.R wounded	
do	31/5/17		Battn in brigade reserve	

1/6/17.

F Latham Lt Col
Commanding 9th (S) Bn Suffolk Regt

A6945 Wt. W11422/M1160 350,000 12/16 D. D. & L. Forms/C./2118/14.

Instructions regarding War Diaries and Intelligence Summaries are contained in F. S. Regs., Part II. and the Staff Manual respectively. Title pages will be prepared in manuscript.

WAR DIARY
or
INTELLIGENCE SUMMARY.
(*Erase heading not required.*)

Army Form C. 2118.

9 Suffolk R

Vol 22

Place	Date	Hour	Summary of Events and Information	Remarks and references to Appendices
Support Trenches and PHILOSOPHE	1/6/17		Batt in Brigade reserve	fd.
do	2/6/17		do do	fd
do.	3/6/17		do do. Batt took over front-line trenches from 9th Norfolks. disposition:	
			A. Coy 2 Platoons NEWPORT by night one platoon from these to CHAPEL ALLEY by day one platoon DEVON DUMP. one platoon CHAPEL ALLEY	
			B Coy. 4 platoons ST GEORGES Trench. Coy finds garrisons at FREUND shaft and ST ELIE shaft.	
			C. Coy one platoon CANCER. one platoon LOOKOUT. one platoon BRESLAU one platoon QUARRY BAY and GRIMWOOD tunnel exit	
			D. Coy one platoon BOYAU 78 one platoon CLOSE support one platoon K. dump one platoon DUDLEY DUMP	
			Trench strength Officers 16. O.R. 512	fd
Front line trenches	4/6/17.		Batt in front line trenches Casualties 6 O.R. wounded	fd.
do	5/6/17.		do. do. Casualties one O.R. wounded.	fd
do	6/6/17		do do Casualties 3 O.R. wounded.	fd
do	7/6/17		do do. Casualties Nil.	fd
do	8/6/17		do do Casualties 1 O.R. Killed in Action 2. O.R. Wounded.	RHG
do	9/6/17		do do. A party of about 25 enemy attempted to raid	

229

A6945 Wt. W11422/M1160 350,000 12/16 D. D. & L. Forms/C./2118/14.

Instructions regarding War Diaries and Intelligence Summaries are contained in F. S. Regs., Part II, and the Staff Manual respectively. Title pages will be prepared in manuscript.

WAR DIARY
or
INTELLIGENCE SUMMARY.
(Erase heading not required.)

Army Form C. 2118.

Place	Date	Hour	Summary of Events and Information	Remarks and references to Appendices
Front Line Trenches	9/6/17		NEWPORT Sap at 1.30 a.m but were repulsed leaving 4 of their dead in front of our wire, taking their wounded back to their own lines. A smoke barrage and Bombardment was put up by our artillery and T.Ms and under cover of this a party went out and brought in the dead who were buried and identification obtained. Casualties 2 O.R. wounded.	RHG.
— do —	10/6/17		Battalion in Front Line Trenches. Casualties Nil	RHG.
— do —	11/6/17		— do — — do — 3 Officers and 94 O.R. made a raid on Enemy Front and Support Line, gained both objectives and did material damage to enemy's dugouts etc. Casualties 15 O.R. wounded 1 O.R. Missing; Total Casualties for the day 17 O.R. wounded 1 O.R. Missing	See Appendix "A" RHG.
VERQUIN and VAUDRICOURT	12/6/17		Battalion in Divisional Reserve. Bn HQrs "A" and "B" Companies at VERQUIN "C" and "D" Companies at VAUDRICOURT.	RHG.
— do —	13/6/17		Battalion in Divisional Reserve	RHG.
— do —	14/6/17		— do — — do —	RHG.
— do —	15/6/17		— do — — do —	

A6945 Wt. W11422/M1160 350,000 12/16 D. D. & L. Forms/C./2118/14.

Army Form C. 2118.

Instructions regarding War Diaries and Intelligence Summaries are contained in F. S. Regs., Part II. and the Staff Manual respectively. Title pages will be prepared in manuscript.

WAR DIARY
or
INTELLIGENCE SUMMARY.
(Erase heading not required.)

Place	Date	Hour	Summary of Events and Information	Remarks and references to Appendices
VERQUIN and VAUDRICOURT	16/6/17		Battalion in Divisional Reserve.	RHG
— do —	17/6/17		— do — — do —	RHG
— do —	18/6/17		At 6.30 pm the Battalion marched from VERQUIN and VAUDRICOURT to Billets at MAROC and the Battalion became temporarily attached to the 18th Inf. Bde for tactical digging purposes.	RHG
MAROC	19/6/17		Battalion employed in Tactical Digging Operations.	RHG
— do —	20/6/17		— do — — do —	RHG
— do —	21/6/17		— do — — do —	RHG
— do —	22/6/17		— do — — do —	RHG
— do —	23/6/17		— do — — do — Casualties 2 O.R. Killed 1 O.R. Wounded. Reinforcements of 1 Officer (LIEUT. G. F MOSELEY 6th Battalion) and 19 Other Ranks reported from No. 15. I.B.D.	RHG
— do —	24/6/17		Battalion employed in Tactical Digging Operations. Casualties 6. Other Ranks Killed 14 Other Ranks Wounded (1 at duty).	RHG RHG
do	25/6/17		Battalion employed in Tactical digging operations Casualties 2 O.R. Killed 11 wounded	[illegible]
do	26/6/17		do do Casualties one O.R. Killed 1 wounded. 2nd Lieut J.M. SOMERVILLE (3rd Battalion) joined Battalion	[illegible]

Instructions regarding War Diaries and Intelligence Summaries are contained in F. S. Regs., Part II. and the Staff Manual respectively. Title pages will be prepared in manuscript.

WAR DIARY
or
INTELLIGENCE SUMMARY.
(Erase heading not required.)

Army Form C. 2118.

Place	Date	Hour	Summary of Events and Information	Remarks and references to Appendices
MAROC	27/6/17		Batt employed in Lateral digging operations. Battn moved into Corps reserve to AIX NOULETTE	
			Following Officers reported their arrival 2/Lt A.H. STOTLE. 2/LT. R.B. COOK 2/LT. E.L TURNER	
			2/LT. W.J. FUTTER. 2/LT. H. SIMMONS.	Ed
AIX NOULETTE	28/6/17		Battn in Corps reserve	Ed
do	29/6/17		do do 2/Lt J.A SIMMONS joined Battalion also 8 O.R	Ed
do	30/6/17		do do Battalion moved to billets in SAILLY LABOURSE	Ed
	1/7/17		[signature] Lt Col Commanding 9th Bn Suffolk Regt	

A6945 Wt. W11422/M1160 350,000 12/16 D. D. & L. Forms/C./2118/14.

APPENDIX "A".

1. Casualties 1 O.R, Missing and 12 O.R. Wounded.
As regards the 1 Missing -
It is assumed that this Lance Corporal is a prisoner as he and another man when returning missed their direction and worked too far to the West and eventually found themselves half way through the German wire just North East of LANCER when an enemy appeared. The man who got away fired at the Boche and then ran off, but what happened to the Lance Corporal is unknown.

2. Stokes opened 45 seconds early, M.Gs. commenced shortly after, the Artillery correctly waited until Zero - 4 minutes before commencing.

3. With exception of one 77 mm battery which fired on raiders the enemy's barrage of 4.25, 77s T.Ms. and M.Gs. was scattered in neighbourhood of our reserve line. It is estimated that 2 H.T.Ms. were firing from the direction of HULLUCH Road and about 4 from the direction of the QUARRIES. M.Gs. and T.Ms. which might have thrown on raided area appeared to have been ~~satisfactory silenced~~ satisfactorily silenced.

4. A sketch Map is attached with notes thereon shewing all information obtained about enemy territory. It will be noticed that patrols were sent out as close to our box barrage as possible.

5. Our Artillery barrage was excellent, and the waves approached as close as possible before it lifted when they advanced straight forward. The smoke shell which it was suggested might be used at Zero 20 minutes as an additional recall signal could not be distinguished.

6. Torrents of rain commenced to decend at Zero and continued until Zero 30 minutes. If it had not been for the fact that the F.C.O. was in possession of a patrol lighter it would have been impossible to set off the rockets.

7. Great keenness was shewn by all ranks, and they were much disappointed at not encountering the enemy.

8. Although no enemy are known to havebeen killed much valuable information has been obtained concerning the enemy's lines and the feeling of security when covered by a good barrage has improved the morale of the men. The attack under fire is new to about 50 % of the men and the movement forward in waves has given them increased confidence.

9. (a) Enemy S.O.S. - Twin Green Lights.
(b) Enemy S.O.S. South of HULLUCH Road appears to be a single Red light.

10. 16th I.B. drew retaliation from same T.Ms. which otherwise would probably have been on this Sub-Section.

11. The O.C. Raid arranged and carried out the scheme excellently and showed sound initiative in sending a patrol back to raided area after our Artillery had ceased. It is regretted that the raid did not obtain any prisoners or identifications.

Report on Raid by "B" Coy. nigh of 10/11th June, 1917.

1. OBJECT -

Identification
To Kill enemy.
To destroy dug-outs etc.
To foster an offensive spirit.

2. OBJECTIVES.

Enemy Front Line from G.12.d.22.97 to G.12.a.87.08, and enemy close support line from G.12.b.22.14 to G.12.a.87.17.

3. STRENGTH.

3 Officers, 94.O.R. in two waves.

4. TIME.

12.30.a.m. 11th June.

5. ARTILLERY.

Field Artillery barraged enemy front line at point of assault and to the flanks from Zero - 4 to Zero at which time barrage lifted to enemy second line system forming box barrage around point of assault, and continued to Zero   35.

Howitzers bombarded trench junctions in enemy second line system, T.M. and M.G. emplacements for Zero - 4 to Zero   35.

6. STOKES GUNS.

Stokes Guns barraged flanks of assault, T.M. and M.G. emplacements from Zero - 4 to Zero   35.

7. MACHINE GUNS.

M.Gs barraged enemy communication trenches and parapets in rear and to right flank of assault from Zero - 4 to Zero   35.

8. NARRATIVE.

The raiders formed up in two waves in front of our own wire. At Zero - 4 they advanced under cover of our barrage, and at Zero advanced immediately on their objectives. First wave to second objective and second wave to first objective, establishing blocks to the West and East of the two objectives. Both objectives were reached without opposition and without difficulty. The wire had been effectively cut and broken up. No enemy were seen in either line, but about 5 were seen retiring to enemy second line system as the waves advanced. The bombing parties of each flank then worked along enemy line - about 50 Yds on the right and 70 Yds on the left but still no enemy were seen. Two patrols were sent forward from 1st wave to examine as far as possible enemy second line system. They approached as near as barrage would allow and found the ground open with few shell holes. Enemy wire reported low and thick and post located about G.12.b.50.18 in that line.

The enemy trenches attacked were much damaged by shell fire, being in places only waist or breast high. The close support line was practically a chain of shell holes only on right - on the left this line contained trip wire and did not show signs of recent occupation. One dug-out was destroyed by mobile charge in this line. Four dugouts were destroyed in enemy front line, one of these being entered before being destroyed. The dug-out was apparently in use but found unoccupied at time of assault. No prisoners were taken, and no identifications secured.

The Artillery barrage was excellent throughout.

The signal for withdrawal was given by sending up Mortar Rockets, bursting into thr e white lights on a string. This was plainly seen and proved satisfactory. The raiders returned in good order and all casualties were brought back.

Copy.

6th Divn G.O.2/66.
71st I.B. No.2384.

71st Infantry Brigade.

Your 2384 of 11/6/17 :-

The Divisional Commander directs me to say that he considers the reports rendered by the 9th Suffolk Regt. excellent.

The raid appears to have been well planned and well executed. It is unfortunate that the Battalion did not have the satisfaction of coming to blows with the enemy or of capturing some prisoners. At the same time the Divisional Commander agrees with the view of the Commanding Officer that the troops engaged cannot fail to have benefitted by the experience.

General Staff.
12.JUN.1917.
6th Division.

(Sgd.) T.T. ~~Wood.~~ Lieut-Colonel.,
General Staff.

(2)

9th Suffolks.

For information.

12/6/17.

(Sgd.) B.T. Burbury, Major,
Bde. Major, 71st. I. B.

Our casualties were 12 wounded, mostly slight, and one man missing.

Enemy retaliation was strong, but did not commence until ten minutes after our barrage opened. Enemy fired 77 mm. shells on his own front line.

A Patrol of 1 Officer and 5 O.R. went out half an hour after raiders returned to search ground, and to see if any enemy returned to raided portion, in which case to secure an identification.

The Patrol went over the whole front raided and waited on enemy parapet until 3.a.m. No movement of any kind observed.

CONFIDENTIAL.

Headquarters,

71st Infantry Brigade.

Herewith War Diary of the Battalion under my Command, for the month of July 1917.

Hatham Lieut-Colonel.,

1.8.17. Commanding 9th Battalion The Suffolk Regiment.

Instructions regarding War Diaries and Intelligence Summaries are contained in F. S. Regs., Part II. and the Staff Manual respectively. Title pages will be prepared in manuscript.

WAR DIARY
or
~~INTELLIGENCE SUMMARY.~~
(*Erase heading not required.*)

Army Form C. 2118.

9 Suffolk Rgt
Vol 23

Place	Date	Hour	Summary of Events and Information	Remarks and references to Appendices
SAILLY LABOURSE	1/7/17		Bn in reserve. Bn took over front line trenches from 1/5 Duke of Wellington (W Riding) Regt.	
			Disposition 'A' Coy 2 pltns by night NEWPORT by day one – 2 pltns DEVON by day –	
			one pltn CHAPEL ALLEY – 1 DEVON DUMP 'B' Coy 4 pltns ST GEORGES TR less 1 L G Sect	
			FREUND SHAFT 'C' Coy 1 pltn LANCER – 1 pltn LOOKOUT – 1 pltn BRESLAU – 1 pltn	
			QUARRY BAY + GRIMWOOD TRENCH 'D' Coy 1 pltn BOYAU 78 – 1 pltn CLOSE SUPPORT 78.	
			1 pltn 'K' DUMP 1 pltn DUDLEY DUMP	[initials]
Front line trenches	2/7/17		Bn in front line trenches. 2/Lt A.G. Douglas & 2/Lt J.A Bramley reported & taken on strength	
			Casualties 2 OR wounded. 2/Lt Stockman evacuated S. to Engl	[initials]
	3/7/17		" " " 3 OR killed 2 wounded	[initials]
	4/7/17		" " " 1 OR wounded (accidental)	[initials]
	5/7/17		" " " 2 ORs wounded Capt ^Dod^ Allerton D.S.O evacuated	
			to F.A. 2/Lt Bridewell reported to Div Training	
			Coy + is taken on strength	[initials]
	6/7/17		" " 2 OR wounded ~~Capt~~ A/Capt H.A Shaw evacuated ~~[illegible] wounded~~	
			~~on 1st Army course~~ S. to Eng [initials]	[initials]
	7/7/17		" " 1 OR killed	[initials]

A6945 Wt. W11422/M1160 350,000 12/16 D. D. & L. Forms/C./2118/14.

239

Instructions regarding War Diaries and Intelligence Summaries are contained in F. S. Regs., Part II. and the Staff Manual respectively. Title pages will be prepared in manuscript.

WAR DIARY
or
~~INTELLIGENCE SUMMARY~~.
(Erase heading not required.)

Army Form C. 2118.

Place	Date	Hour	Summary of Events and Information	Remarks and references to Appendices
Front line trenches	8/7/17		Bn in front line trenches Casualties 3 ORs wounded	[initials]
	9/7/17		" " " 2 ORs wounded	[initials]
PHILOSOPHE	10/7/17		Bn relieved by 9th Norfolks. HQs. 'B' & 'C' Coys withdraw to PHILOSOPHE in Bde reserve. 'A' in support to left sub section (ST ELIE) 'D' Coy in support to right sub section. Bn provides working parties. Lt Col J Latham DSO assumes temporary command of the 71st I.B during the absence of Brig Gen E Feetham CB CMG. Capt J.W.E. Mosse MC. 1st Leicestershires assumes temporary command of the Bn.	[initials]
	11/7/17		'B' Coy attached to 2nd Bn Sherwood Foresters in left sub-section as Bn reserve. 'C' Coy 1st Leicestershires attached to the Bn. Bn provides working parties. Major J.P. Wylie 2nd Sherwood Foresters relieves Capt J.W.E. Mosse MC in temporary command of Bn	[initials]
	12/7/17		'C' Coy relieves 'A' Coy in left sub section & 'A' Coy withdraws to PHILOSOPHE. Bn provides working parties. 2/Lt E.V. Harvey reports & is taken on strength	[initials]
	13/7/17		Bn in reserve	[initials]
	14/7/17		'A' Coy relieves 'D' Coy in right sub section. 'D' Coy withdraws to PHILOSOPHE. Bn provides working parties	[initials]
	15/7/17		Bn in reserve.	[initials]

A6945 Wt. W11422/M1160 350,000 12/16 D. D. & L. Forms/C./2118/14.

Army Form C. 2118.

Instructions regarding War Diaries and Intelligence Summaries are contained in F. S. Regs., Part II. and the Staff Manual respectively. Title pages will be prepared in manuscript.

WAR DIARY
or
~~INTELLIGENCE SUMMARY.~~
(Erase heading not required.)

Place	Date	Hour	Summary of Events and Information	Remarks and references to Appendices
PHILOSOPHE	16/7/17		'D' Coy relieves 'C' Coy in the left sub-section 'C' Coy withdraws to PHILOSOPHE Bn provides working parties Casualties 2 ORs killed 2 ORs wounded. 2/Lt R H Cock + 2/Lt F Goatcher reported + taken on strength.	WF
	17/7/17		Bn in reserve	WF
	18/7/17		" Capt Donaldson RAMC joins to 67th Heavy Group + Capt J.A. Sheary reports for duty as M.O. i/c Bn.	WF
	19/7/17		Bn in reserve, Bn takes over front line trenches from 9th Norfolks. O.O. No 50 attached	WF Appendix A.
Front line trenches	20/7/17		Bn in front line trenches	WF
	21/7/17		" " Casualties 2 ORs wounded	WF
	22/7/17		" " " 1. OR killed 8 ORs wounded (4 gassed by shells)	WF
	23/7/17		" " " 1 OR wounded (at duty)	WF
	24/7/17		" " " 1 OR killed 2 ORs wounded. Bn relieved by 6th Bn Sherwood Foresters + moves to training area at FREVILLERS. O.O. 52 attached.	WF Appendix B
FREVILLERS	25/7/17		Bn in rest. Lt Col F Latham D.S.O returns to the command of the Bn. Maj. J.T. Wylie rejoins his Bn.	WF
	26/7/17		Bn in training. 2/Lt G.G. Cooper, 2/Lt R.H. Phillips + 2/Lt C.C. Dew reported + taken on strength	WF

A6945 Wt. W11422/M1160 350,000 12/16 D. D. & L. Forms/C./2118/14.

Army Form C. 2118.

Instructions regarding War Diaries and Intelligence Summaries are contained in F. S. Regs., Part II, and the Staff Manual respectively. Title pages will be prepared in manuscript.

WAR DIARY
or
~~INTELLIGENCE SUMMARY~~.
(Erase heading not required.)

Place	Date	Hour	Summary of Events and Information	Remarks and references to Appendices
FREVILLERS	27/7/17		Bn in training. 2/Lt F. Goatcher admitted to F.A.	AFT
	28/7/17		" Capt G. M. Brown + 2/Lt. B. F. Packer reported + taken on strength. Capt	
			R England reports back to Bn from Div. Training Coys.	AFT
	29/7/17		" 2/Lt H. Alnack admitted to FA	AFT
	30/7/17		" 5 ORs reinforcements reported + taken on strength	AFT
	31/7/17		" Bn inspected by Brig. Gen E. Feetham CB. CMG. Commanding Brigade	AFT

31. 7. 17

F Latham Lt. Col.
Comdg 9th Bn Suffolk Regt

A6945 Wt. W11422/M1160 350,000 12/16 D. D. & L. Forms/C./2118/14.

SECRET. Copy No..........

OPERATION ORDER No.50.
by
M[illegible] J.P.WYLIE.D.S.O. Commanding 9th Battalion The Suffolk Regiment.

---

1. To-morrow, night of 19/20th inst. the Battalion will releive 9/Norfolks in the front line trenches - Right Sub-Section as under.

Right front Coy.	"A" Coy.	will relieve	"A" Coy.	Norfolks.
Centre Coy.	"C" Coy.	" "	"B" Coy.	"
Left front Coy.	"D" Coy.	" "	"D" Coy.	"
Support Coy.	"B" Coy.	" "	"C" Coy.	"

2. Battalion will move off as follows :-
   "A" & "D" Coys. from Support Trenches at 9.p.m.
   "C" Coy. from PHILOSOPHE at 9.p.m.
   "B" Coy. from Battalion Support of 2nd Sherwood Foresters, at 8.p.m.

3. Os. C. Coys. will arrange to send an advance party to take over all Trench Stores etc.

4. All Trench Stores, Aerpplane Photos, Maps, etc., will be taken over.

5. All Lewis Gun Boxes, Drums and ammunition will be taken into the front line trenches by Coys.

6. Officers' Trench Kit, Coy. and Hd. Qtrs. Stores for trenches must be ready to load by 8.30.p.m. outside Coy. Hd. Qtrs. and Hd. Qtr. Billets.

7. O.C. "C" Coy. and Hd. Qtrs. will each arrange for 4 men to help Drummers push up bogies.

8. Packs and Blankets of "C" Coy. and Hd. Qtrs. for Transport, will be ready to load outside Coy. and Hd. Qtr. Billets at 3.p.m.
   Officers' Valises to be ready at 5.30.p.m.
   Transport Officer will arrange accordingly.

9. Tunnel Warders will be attached to "B" Coy. during next tour of trenches for rations.

10. Relief Complete will be wired to Battalion Hd. Qtrs. by B.A.B. code.

11. ACKNOWLEDGE.

Lieut.,

18.7.17. A/Adjutant, 9th Battalion The Suffolk Regiment.

Copy.No.1..C.O.	Copy No.6..O.C.Hd.Qtrs.	Copy No.11..9/Norfolks.
" No.2.."A" Coy.	" " 7..Trans.Offr.	" " 12..2/Sherwood Forts.
" No.3.."B" Coy.	" " 8..Qr. Mr.	" " 13..Retained.
" No.4.."C" Coy.	" " 9..Med.Offr.	" " 14..Retained.
" No.5.."D" Coy.	" "10..A/R.S.M.	" " 15..War Diary
		" " 16..War Diary.

A

SECRET. 9th Battalion The Suffolk Regiment. Copy No.....

OPERATION ORDER. No. 52.

REF. SHEET. 36.B. 1/40.000.

1. 6th Div., less Artillery, will be relived in the line by 46th Div., less Artillery, Relief to be complete by 6.a.m. 25.7.17.
 On the night 24/25th inst., the Battalion will be relieved by 6th Battalion Sherwood Foresters, 139th Infantry Brigade.

2. On relief, the Battalion will move by busses from PHILOSOPHE CROSS ROADS to FREVILLERS, and will be in Corps Reserve.

3. The O.Rs. attached to 459th Field Coy. R.E. will re-join their Coys. at PHILOSOPHE CROSS ROADS on night of 24/25th inst. at midnight.
 N.C.Os. and men at present in charge of Keeps, will rejoin their Coys. on the 24th inst.

4. Os.C.Coys. will detail one guide per Platoon to report to Battalion Headquarters at 7.p.m. on 24th inst. They will meet platoons of 6th Sherwood Foresters, and guide them to their Coys. via CHAPEL ALLEY.

5. Battalion Commander, Coy. Commanders, and 1 N.C.O per Coy. of 6th Sherwood Foresters, will visit the Battalion on the morning of 23rd July. The Coy. Commanders and 1 N.C.O per Coy. will remain with Coys. until relief.

6. 2/Lieut. Bullen and 1 man per Headquarters and Coy. (to be detailed by O.C.Headquarters and Coys) and 2 Tunnel Warders will remain in the trenches till the 26th inst. They will parade at PHILOSOPHE CROSS ROADS at 9.a.m. 26th inst. to embus for the rest area.

7. A Billeting party, consisting of Quartermaster, 4 C.Q.M.Sgts. and Sgt. Dent, will report to the Secretary MAIRIE (V.1.b.3.1.) FREVILLERS by noon 24th inst., and will await the Battalion.

8. All trench stores, S.A.A., grenades, etc., in line; secret maps, photographs, defence schemes and documents dealing with the area will be handed over. Receipts will be forwarded to the Orderly Room by 10.a.m. 25th inst. 3 Trench Store Cards are attached, one to be forwarded to the Adjutant by 12 noon 24th inst., one handed over, and one as above. Great care must be taken in the checking and listing of all stores.

9. Surplus baggage is to be stored in Div. Stores, RUE DES ROSES, NOEUX LES MINES, and one caretaker to be detailed by the Quartermaster left in charge. He will be rationed by No.1.Coy. Div. Train.
 Only articles which are really worth keeping are to be stored. Spare clothing, ammunition, or rations are not to be left.

10. One lorry will be provided for transport of extra kit. Date and time of rendezvous will be wired to Quartermaster as soon as possible.

11. Transport will leave LABOURSE at 11.a.m. 24th inst., and proceed via NOEUX LES MINES - BARLIN - MAISNIL - RANCHICOURT to FREVILLERS.
 Transport will be parked at FREVILLERS.

P...T..P.

12. The strictest march discipline is to be observed by the Transport Officer during the move. The special points to be watched are :-
No overloading, no unauthorised personnel with the Transport. Any parties accompanying the Transport will be marched in formed bodies properly armed and equipped.

13. The Quartermaster will arrange for all rations for consumption on the 24th inst. to be cooked at Transport. Sergeant Master Cook will report to the Quartermaster on the morning of the 23rd inst.

14. All cooking utensils and Coy. stores now in trenches, will be sent down to Transport on night of 23/24th inst. The minimum of Officers' Kit and messing to be retained, the surplus being sent down on night of 23/24th inst. by empty ration bogies. Transport Officer will arrange for limbers to remain at MANSION HOUSE DUMP to convey same to Transport. Officers' Kit and messing urgently required will be carried out on relief and taken in the busses.

15. 2/Lieut. E.L. Lucas will be at the Cross Roads PHILOSOPHE from 11.p.m. on the night of 24th inst., and will superintend in embussing of Battalion.

16. Relief complete to be wired to Battalion Headquarters by B.A.B. code.

17. ACKNOWLEDGE.

Issued at...............

W Fitch Lieut.,

22/7/17. A/Adjutant, 9th Battalion The Suffolk Regiment.

Copies to :-

No. 1....Commanding Officer.
No. 2....O.C. "A" Company.
No. 3....O.C. "B" Company.
No. 4....O.C. "C" Company.
No. 5....O.C. "D" Company.
No. 6....O.C. Headquarters.
No. 7....Transport Officer.
No. 8....Quartermaster.
No. 9....Medical Officer.
No.10....R.S.M.
No.11....6th Battn. Sherwood Foresters.
No.12....Retained.
No.13....War Diary.
No.14....War Diary.

9th Suffolk Regt

Army Form C. 2118.

Instructions regarding War Diaries and Intelligence Summaries are contained in F. S. Regs., Part II, and the Staff Manual respectively. Title pages will be prepared in manuscript.

WAR DIARY
or
INTELLIGENCE SUMMARY.
(Erase heading not required.)

Vol 24

Place	Date	Hour	Summary of Events and Information	Remarks and references to Appendices
FREVILLERS	1/8/17		Bn in training. 2 Lieuts G.M.T. Head, & C. Sneesby reported & are taken on the strength of the Bn. Maj. W.R. Whitson reported & assumes the duties of 2nd in Com.	W.H.
	2/8/17		" " 2 Lieut C.C. Dew admitted to F.A. sick.	W.H.
	3/8/17		" " Capt. H Tylden-Wright 2nd/1st Derbyshire Yeo. reported & is attached to the Bn supernumerary. 2 Lieut H.P. Roberts left Bn to report to H.Qrs R.F.C. 2 Lieut H Almack rejoined Bn from F.A.	W.H.
	4/8/17		" "	W.H.
	5/8/17		" "	W.H.
	6/8/17		" "	W.H.
	7/8/17		" "	W.H.
	8/8/17		" " Capt. A H Guinness admitted to F.A. sick. Bde. inspected at presentation of medal ribbons by the Corps Commander. Bn Sports held.	W.H. Appendix A.
	9/8/17		" "	W.H.
	10/8/17		" "	W.H.
	11/8/17		" "	W.H.
	12/8/17		" " 2 Lieut. F. Gratcher rejoined Bn from F.A.	W.H.
	13/8/17		" "	W.H.

249

A6945 Wt. W11422/M1160 350,000 12/16 D. D. & L. Forms/C./2118/14.

Instructions regarding War Diaries and Intelligence Summaries are contained in F. S. Regs., Part II. and the Staff Manual respectively. Title pages will be prepared in manuscript.

WAR DIARY
or
INTELLIGENCE SUMMARY.
(Erase heading not required.)

Army Form C. 2118.

Place	Date	Hour	Summary of Events and Information	Remarks and references to Appendices
FREVILLERS	14/8/17		Bn in training. Capt V.E. Lloyd RAMC joins Bn as M.O. Div Sports held	AH
	15/8/17		" " Capt J.J.A. Sherry R.A.M.C. left Bn. Capt A.H. Guinness evacuated to Eng.	AH
	16/8/17		" " 2 Lieut C.C. Dew rejoined Bn from F.A. 2 Lieut A.G. Douglas admitted F.A. sick	AH
	17/8/17		" "	AH
	18/8/17		" " Lieut L. Wilmot-Johnson reported & is taken on strength of the Bn. Div Rifle meeting	AH
	19/8/17		" " Div Rifle meeting. Lewis Gun team of "A" Coy No 1 Ptn won the silver bugle (1st prize)	AH
	20/8/17		" "	AH
	21/8/17		" "	AH
	22/8/17		" "	AH
	23/8/17		" "	AH
	24/8/17		" "	AH
	25/8/17		" "	AH
VAUDRICOURT	26/8/17		Bn in Div. Reserve Bn moved to VAUDRICOURT. O.O. No 53. attached	AH Appendix B
	27/8/17		" " & training.	AH
	28/8/17		" " " 2 Lieut A.H. Stoyle & 26 O.Rs. attached to 459th Field Coy R.E.	AH
	29/8/17		" " " 2 Lieut H. Almack admitted F.A. sick	AH

A6945 Wt. W11422/M1160 350,000 12/16 D. D. & L. Forms/C./2118/14.

Instructions regarding War Diaries and Intelligence Summaries are contained in F. S. Regs., Part II, and the Staff Manual respectively. Title pages will be prepared in manuscript.

WAR DIARY
or
INTELLIGENCE SUMMARY.
(Erase heading not required.)

Army Form C. 2118.

Place	Date	Hour	Summary of Events and Information	Remarks and references to Appendices
VAUDRICOURT	30/8/17		Bn in Dw. Reserve & training	[illegible]
	31/8/17		6 ORs reported & are taken on strength of Bn	[illegible]
			1.9.17 [illegible signature] Lt Col Commanding 9th Bn Suffolk Regt	

A6945 Wt. W11422/M1160 350,000 12/16 D. D. & L. Forms/C./2118/14.

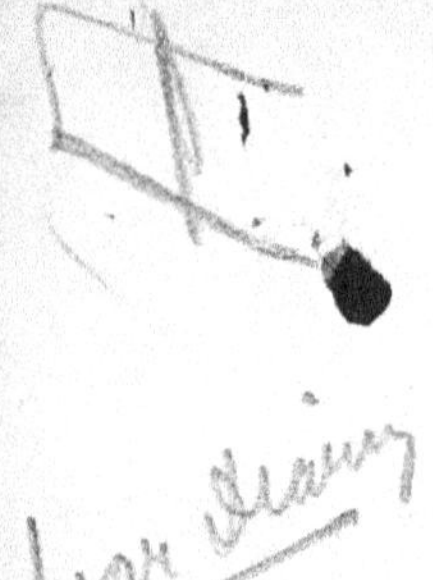

SPEECH BY THE CORPS COMMANDER

at the presentation of Medal Riband Parade.

War Diary

In the course of one's service one has to do many things, but nothing one has to do is a greater privilege than to come to a Brigade like this, and, in the name of His Majesty the King, to present the Medals and decorations which have been so well earned. You, to-day however, have added an additional pleasure to my visit, because I must heartily congratulate your Commander and yourselves upon a very excellent turnout, and upon the excellent physical appearance of the men whom I see before me to-day. I am not in the least surprised at seeing such a good turn-out - it is what I expected. I expected it because whenever you have had anything to do in this campaign you have done it. I expected it, because you belong to one of the celebrated old Divisions which made for themselves such a glorious reputation at the beginning of this War.

It is an enormous asset, and a tremendous privilege to belong to one of the old Divisions and consequently to be heir to all their old glories and traditions. There is no shadow of doubt that the example and discipline of the old six Divisions exercised a predominating influence on the new armies, and were the greatest factors in forming that fine spirit in those Armies which has enabled them during the last year to carry to success offensive operations on a grand scale. I do not think, therefore, that it is possible to place too high a value upon the traditions of the 6th Division. We look to it, although there are not many old soldiers left, to set an example of soldierly conduct, discipline and courage to the rest of the Corps.

I am now about to present inthe name of His Majesty the King decorations which have beenwon by some of your comrades. Before doing this, I want all here to understand that these decorations are not mere pieces of ribbon, but that those Ribbons are the Hall mark of the approval of your Sovereign and your Country for deeds of Courage, for deeds of Leadership, and for deeds of Initiative which have added to the traditions and to the glory of the 6th Division. There is no question whatever that it rests with the junior leaders, (junior officers and N.C.Os) whether there shall be success or failure in the operations which you are ordered to carry out. Our junior officers and N.C.Os are continually, during the course of battle, faced with the responsibility of solving important tactical problems and that responsibility can only be successfully undertaken when we have initiative and fearless leading in our junior ranks, and in the rank and file that determined disciplined courage which is only found in trained soldiers living up to the highest traditions. I want you to remember that we have now done with defensive warfare - practically everything that you will be asked to do in the future will be in the nature of an Offensive. Every leader must therefore so train himself that the will for victory, and forward movement under all conditions become in each individual a sub-concious habit of mind. It is a great thing to hold your trenches inviolate from any attempt of the enemy to get into them, but it is a far greater thing that when you are ordered to take a trench that that trench shall be taken, and even yet greater that the trench shall be held against all counter-attacks.

Now men, I will not keep you any longer, except to repeat how great an honour we all look upon it to come and see these decorations presented to men, who have, under the supreme test of battle, displayed all those qualities which I have been trying to put before you.

Those men who stand here to-day have proved their courage, their initiative and their right to be considered as leaders of men under the supreme test of war.

****

P.T.O.

The following ORs of the Bn received ribbons at the ~~demonstration~~ presentation

DCM

15083 C.S.M. Potter F.

MM

21270 Sgt Denton F. O

50298 Pte Baxter G. F

15436 Cpl Bunn C

12670 L/Cpl Bradley E M

16159 Cpl Miles L. J.

30746 Pte Annees. H.

[illegible]

ADMINISTRATIVE ORDER - ISSUED WITH OPERATION ORDER No.53.

---

1. The vehicles and Stores will be ready for loading at Places and times as follows :-

Maltese Cart, Aid Post.	7.a.m.
Officers Mess Cart, H.Qrs.Mess.	7.a.m.
Officers Spare Mess Cart Bath House.	7.a.m.
No.1.G.S.Wagon.Canteen (Officers Kit to be inside Canteen)	6.45.a.m.
No.2.G.S.Wagon. Orderly Room.	6.45.a.m.
Lorry. Q.M.Stores.	7.a.m.

2. Limbers (10) 1 Bombs,2 Tools, 3 S.A.A. - 4 Lewis Guns.
Water Carts (2) -Filled, with water Cans empty.
Trav: Kitchens (4)Fuel bunkers filled. Remainder of days rations, (Sgt.Clarke i/c.)
Headquarters Cooking utensils and remainder of day's rations will be carried on No.2.G.S.Wagon.
Transport Cooking Utensils and remainder of day's rations will be carried on limbers-Transport Officer to arrange distribution.
Maltese Cart - Medical Stores. (Sgt.Potter i/c.)
Officers Mess Cart - H.Q. Mess. (Sgt.Newson i/c.)
Officers Spare Cart-Coy Messes. (L/C.Stevenson "A" Coy.i/c.)
Kit not turning up to time will not be taken. On no condition will the cart wait.

3. G.S.Wagons. (2)
No.1. Officers Kits and Canteen Stores. (Cpl.Gallant i/c.)
No.2. Orderly Room - Band Packs and Rifles - Headquarters Cooking utensils, remainder of day's rations and Stores not carried on Hand Cart. (Sgt.Dent i/c.)
Handcarts (7) 1 per Coy -Hqtrs - Pioneers - Sanitary Squad.
Lorry.(1) Quartermasters Stores.
Shoemakers and Tailor's Stores.
Pioneers and Armourers Stores.
Coy. Stores not carried on Hand Carts.

4. ACKNOWLEDGE.

Issued at. 2/Lieut.,

24/8/17. for A/Adjutant, 9th Battalion The Suffolk Regiment.

Copy.No.1. Commanding Officer.
" " 2. 2nd-in-Command.
" " 3. Major. H. Tylden Wright.
" " 4. O.C. "A" Coy.
" " 5. O.C. "B" Coy.
" " 6. O.C. "C" Coy.
" " 7. O.C. "D" COY.
" " 8. O.C. Headquarters.
Copy.No.9. Medical Officer.
" "10. Quartermaster.
" "11. Transport Officer.
" "12. R.S.M.
" "13. War Diary.
" "14. War Diary.
" "15. Retained.
" "16. Retained.

SECRET.   Copy No.......

OPERATION ORDER No. 53.
by
Lieut-Co. F.LATHAM, D S.O. Commanding 9th Battalion The Suffolk Regt.

REF: MAPS FRANCE.
Sheet 36.B.1/40.000
Trench Maps 36.C. N.W.3 & 36.C. S.W.1.

---

1. The 6th Division is releiving the 3rd Canadian Division in the line from about N.2.b.2.0. to its junction with the 46th Division at about H.25.b.3.3 The 18th I.B. is relieving the Right Sub-Section & the 16th I.B. the left Sub-Section. The 71st I.B. will be in Divisional reserve.

2. The Battalion will move on 26th Aug: and head of Column will pass X roads P.31.d.7.9. (ref: Sheet 36.B. 1/40.000) at 8.2.a.m.

3. Transport will follow the Battalion.

4. Divisional Headquarters will open at 12 noon 25th inst. at BRAQUEMONT. Bde. Headquarters will open at 11.a.m. 26th inst at BRAQUEMONT. (L.19.a.5.3)

5. Refilling point on 25th inst. will be as usual, on 26th inst. at BRAQUEMONT CHURCH.

6. Battalion will be billetted in VAUDRICOURT on completion of move.

7. Battalion will parade on road ("A" Coy. parade ground to Q.M. Stores) in full marching order (packs, gas helmets, etc.) at 7.40.a.m. Band to carry Steel Helmets, Ammunition & Waterproof Sheets. Officers to carry Steel Helmets. In order - Headquarters, "A", DRUMS, "B", "C", "D", Transport, facing N.E., with head of Column by "A" Coy. Mess.

8. Coys. will report arrival in billets and send the No. of Billet which will be Coy. H.Q. to Orderly Room.

9. On the march the following distances will be maintained, 200 yards between Companies and between rear Company and Transport. Drums will after each halt change the Company with which they are marching - in order "C", "D", "C", "B", "A".

10. Halts will take place for 10 minutes every hour. i.e. from 50 minutes to the hour. Company Commanders will synchronize watches with A/Adjt. at 7.40.a.m.

11. Os.C. Coys. will arrange for sufficient connecting files to be sent forward of their Company to keep connection with Company in front. Os.C. Coys. should make use of their horses to ensure that connecting files are keeping connection properly.

12. Route to be followed as under :-
P.31.d.7.9. - P.22.d.0.8. Cross Roads P.22.d.2.2. - Cross Roads P.22.d.7.6. Cross Roads P.16.d. Cross Roads P.11.c. Cross Roads. P.10.b.0.8 Road junction P.5.a.4.1. Cross Roads J.36.c.2.2. - J.36.c.7.6. - K.32 Central - K.33.a.2.8.

P.T.O.

continued.

13. Os.C. Coys. will check the route by the map as they proceed so as to ensure that the connecting files are not leading them astray.

14. ACKNOWLEDGE.

Issued at............. ....2/Lieut.,

25/8/17. for A/Adjutant, 9th Battalion The Suffolk Regiment.

Copy. No. 1....Commanding Officer.
" " 2....2nd-in-Command.
" " 3....Major H. Tylden Wright.
" " 4....O.C. "A" Company.
" " 5....O.C. "B" Company.
" " 6....O.C. "C" Company.
" " 7....O.C. "D" Company.
" " 8....O.C. Headquarters.
" " 9....Medical Officer.
" " 10....Quartermaster.
" " 11....Transport Officer.
" " 12....R.S.M.
" " 13....War Diary.
" " 14....War Diary.
" " 15....Retained.
" " 16....Retained.

CONFIDENTIAL.

Headquarters,

71st Infantry Brigade.

Herewith War Diary of the Battalion under my Command for the month of September 1917.

[signature] Major. ~~Lieut-Colonel~~,

1.10.1917. Commanding 9th Battalion The Suffolk Regt.

Instructions regarding War Diaries and Intelligence Summaries are contained in F. S. Regs., Part II, and the Staff Manual respectively. Title pages will be prepared in manuscript.

WAR DIARY

or

~~INTELLIGENCE SUMMARY.~~

(Erase heading not required.)

Army Form C. 2118.

9 Suffolk Regt

BRIGADE OFFICE No. ... Date ... 71st INFANTRY BRIGADE

Vol 25

Place	Date	Hour	Summary of Events and Information	Remarks and references to Appendices
VAUDRICOURT	1/9/17		Bn in training	KH
	2/9/17		" "	KH
	3/9/17		Bn moved from VAUDRICOURT to BRAQUEMENT. O.O. No 54 attached	KH Appendix A
BRAQUEMENT	4/9/17		Bn at BRAQUEMENT until 6.15 pm, when it moved off and took over Support line	" B
			trenches from 9th Bn NORFOLKS. O.O. No 55 attached. 2/Lieut A.G. Douglas rejoined	
			Bn from F.A.	KH
TRENCHES	5/9/17		Bn in Support line trenches & providing working parties	KH
	6/9/17		" " " "	KH
	7/9/17		" " "	KH
	8/9/17		" " "	KH
	9/9/17		" " " Bn relieved 9th Bn NORFOLKS in the Front line trenches	" C
			O.O. No 56 attached. Casualties 1 OR wounded. 2/Lieut A.J. Steyt admitted	
			to F.A from 459th Field Coy R.E.	KH
	10/9/17		Bn in Front line trenches	KH
	11/9/17		" " " Casualties 4 OR wounded (3 Gasshell poisoning)	KH
	12/9/17		" " " 1 OR missing (No 19616 Pte Plummer G. D Coy)	KH

A6945 Wt. W11422/M1160 350,000 12/16 D. D. & L. Forms/C./2118/14.

259

Instructions regarding War Diaries and Intelligence Summaries are contained in F. S. Regs., Part II. and the Staff Manual respectively. Title pages will be prepared in manuscript.

WAR DIARY
or
~~INTELLIGENCE SUMMARY.~~
(Erase heading not required.)

Army Form C. 2118.

Place	Date	Hour	Summary of Events and Information	Remarks and references to Appendices
TRENCHES	13/9/17		Bn in the front line trenches. Casualties 3 OR wounded (2 Gas shell poisoning)	Appendix D
			Bn relieved by 14th Bn D.L.I. & withdrew to MAZINGARBE. O.O No 57 attached	MH
MAZINGARBE	14/9/17		Bn at MAZINGARBE. Casualties 4 OR wounded – these casualties occurred early on morning of 14th during relief. Bn relieved 1st Bn The Buffs & became Reserve Bn of the 6th Bde. O.O No 57 attached & addendum thereto.	MH " E
TRENCHES	15/9/17		Bn in Reserve.	MH
	16/9/17		"	MH
	17/9/17		"	MH
	18/9/17		Bn relieved 9th Bn Norfolks in front line trenches. O.O. No 58 attached	" F
			Maj. H. Tylden-Wright 2/1st Derbyshire Yeomanry cross posted from the Bn to the 2nd Bn Sherwood Foresters. Lieut J.A. Bramley attached to 459th Field Coy RE.	MH
	19/9/17		Bn in front line trenches. Casualties 1 OR killed 1 OR wounded	MH
	20/9/17		" " " " 2 OR killed 7 OR wounded (2 at duty)	
			These casualties are Transport personnel who were billetted at LES BREBIS and occurred by hostile shell falling in lines about 12.30 am	MH

A6945 Wt. W11422/M1160 350,000 12/16 D. D. & L. Forms/C./2118/14.

Army Form C. 2118.

Instructions regarding War Diaries and Intelligence Summaries are contained in F. S. Regs., Part II. and the Staff Manual respectively. Title pages will be prepared in manuscript.

WAR DIARY
or
~~INTELLIGENCE SUMMARY.~~
(Erase heading not required.)

Place	Date	Hour	Summary of Events and Information	Remarks and references to Appendices
TRENCHES	21/9/17		Bn. in Front line trenches. Casualties 1. OR killed 7 OR wounded (2 at duty)	RH
	22/9/17		" " " " 1 OR killed 2 OR wounded. Bn relieved	Appendix G
			by 8th Bn Sherwood Foresters & proceeded to LES BREBIS O.O. No 59 attached	
			2/Lieut. Y Almack rejoined from F.A.	RH
LES BREBIS	23/9/17		Bn moved to SOUTH MAROC & became Divisional Reserve. O.O. No. 60 attached	RH " H
S. MAROC	24/9/17		Bn in Divisional Reserve. Casualties 3 ORs wounded (1 at duty)	RH
	25/9/17		" " " & providing working parties.	RH
	26/9/17		" " " " " " 2/Lieut C H. Miller. MC.	
			reported & is taken on the strength of the Bn. Casualties 3 ORs killed 3 ORs wounded	RH
	27/9/17		Bn in Divisional Reserve, & providing working parties. Capt G M Brown	
			admitted to F.A. 2/Lieut JW Railby proceeded to DIV TRAINING COYS for duty	
			there.	RH
	28/9/17		Bn in Divisional Reserve & providing working parties. 2/Lieut A Judge proceeded	
			from Div Training Coy to HQrs RFC on probation as observer. Casualties	
			1 OR wounded	RH

A6945 Wt. W11422/M1160 350,000 12/16 D. D. & L. Forms/C./2118/14.

Army Form C. 2118.

Instructions regarding War Diaries and Intelligence Summaries are contained in F. S. Regs., Part II. and the Staff Manual respectively. Title pages will be prepared in manuscript.

WAR DIARY
or
INTELLIGENCE SUMMARY.
(Erase heading not required.)

Place	Date	Hour	Summary of Events and Information	Remarks and references to Appendices
SMAROC	29/9/17		Bn in Divisional Reserve & providing working parties. Casualties 1 OR wounded. 2 Lieut G K Crock left Bn for duty as R.T.O light tramways LES BREBIS	
	30/9/17		Bn in Divisional Reserve & providing working parties. 2 Lieut G G Cooper left Bn for duty with Divisional Sniping Coy. 2 Lieut E H Phillips wounded (at duty) 1. OR wounded	

1. 10. 17

[signature] Major ~~Lt Col~~
Commanding 9th Bn Suffolk Regt

A6945 Wt. W11422/M1160 350,000 12/16 D. D. & L. Forms/C./2118/14.

SECRET. Copy No. 16

OPERATION ORDER No. 54.
by
Lieut.Col. F.LATHAM.D.S.O. Commanding 9th Battalion The Suffolk Regt.

Reference Map.
Sheet 36.B. 1/40,000.

1. The Battalion will move to BRAQUEMONT and take over Billets vacated by 2nd Sherwood Foresters.

2. The Battalion will parade in full marching order, in column of route facing south on main road; head of column opposite Billet No. 8, in order - H.Q., Drums, "C", "D", "A", "B" at 4.45.p.m. Coys. will move at 20 yards interval.

3. Officers' Valises will be stacked outside Coy. and H.Q. Messes ready to load at 3.45.p.m. Coy. Stores, Mess Kit etc., will be stacked ready to load outside Coy. Messes at 3.45.p.m. Transport Officer will arrange accordingly.

4. Coys. will report arrival in Billets and forward number of Billet to be used as Coy. H.Q. to Orderly Room immediately on arrival.

5. An Advance Party consisting of 2/Lieut. F. Bullen, and Coy. Q.M.Sgts., and one man per platoon and 2 from H.Q., will proceed to BRAQUEMONT and report to Adjutant, 2nd Sherwood Foresters at 2.30.p.m.
Party to parade opposite "B" Coy. Officers' Mess at 1.30.p.m.

6. 2/Lieut. F. Bullen will arrange that Battalion is met by Platoon and H.Q. guides at 5.30.p.m. at the monument in NOEUX-LES-MINES.

7. Coys. will take over Billets from corresponding Companies of the 2nd Sherwood Foresters.

8. Transport Lines and Qr. Mr. Stores will move to

9. ACKNOWLEDGE.

Issued at 12.30 p.m. A.H. Phillips Lieut.,

3.9.17 A/Adjutant, 9th Battalion The Suffolk Regiment.

Copy. No. 1....Commanding Officer.
" " 2....2nd-in-Command.
" " 3....Major H. Tylden Wright.
" " 4....O.C. "A" Company.
" " 5....O.C. "B" Company.
" " 6....O.C. "C" Company.
" " 7....O.C. "D" Company.
" " 8....O.C. Headquarters.
Copy No. 9....R.S.M.
" " 10....Transport Officer.
" " 11....Quartermaster.
" " 12....Medical Officer.
" " 13....2nd Sherwood Foresters.
" " 14....Retained.
" " 15....War Diary.
" " 16....War Diary.

SECRET. 9th Battalion Suffolk Regiment. Copy No. 16
Operation Order No. 55

Ref. LOOS. 36.c.N.W., 3. 1/10,000. 3rd Sept. 1917.
LENS. 36.c.S.W., 1. 1/10,000.

1. RELIEF. The Battalion will take over the SUPPORT LINE from the 9th Norfolk Regt., on the night of the 4/5th Sept., as under :-
"A" Coy. from "B" Coy. Norfolks.
"B" Coy. from "C" Coy. Norfolks.
"C" Coy. from "A" Coy. Norfolks.
"D" Coy. from "D" Coy. Norfolks.

2. PARADE. Companies will parade at 6.15.p.m. and march in the following order - H.Q., "D" "C" "B" and "A" Coy. Interval of 200 yards between platoons. Leading Coy. not to pass LES BREBIS before 8.p.m. Connection to be kept as far as HARTS CRATER.
L.G. Limbers with Companies.
Route - LES BREBIS - MAROC (Northern edge) - HARTS CRATER - where guides will be met.

3. ADVANCE PARTIES.
Each COY. will send up by day -
1 Officer.
1 N.C.O. and 2 men per platoon.
Coy. Signallers.
HQTRS - 2/Lieut. F. Bullen.
2/Lieut. E.L. Lucas.
Provost Sergeant.
Signalling Sergeant.
6.O.R. and 2 Signallers.
The above parties will proceed separately to their destinations. They will provide guides at HARTS CRATER for the Battalion at 9.00.p.m. as follows -
Per COY :- 1 Officer and per platoon 1 guide.
HQTRS. :- 2 guides.

4. OFFICERS VALISES.
Outside Hqtrs. and Coy. Messes at 4.p.m.

5. OFFICERS TRENCH KITS.
Stacked at Hqtrs. and Coy. Messes by 4.p.m.
Mess Cart will collect them.

6. BATTALION DUMP.
This will be at HARTS CRATER. Each Coy. will leave there 1 Lce. Corporal and 10 men who will report to the PROVOST SERGEANT These parties will do all carrying for their respective Coys.

7. OUTPOST COMPANY.
While in Support one of the two front Support Coys. will be in constant readiness to Counter-Attack.
Hour of relief will be 6.p.m. daily. "B" Coy. will take on this duty and will be relieved by "C" Coy. on 5th inst.

8. TRENCH STORES.
All Trench Stores, Grenades, S.A.A., in the line will be taken over and receipts in triplicate given. A Copy will be sent to the Battalion Hqtrs. by 10.a.m. on 5th inst.
Aeroplane photos., trench maps, schemes of defense and programme of work will be taken over.

B

P.T.O.

continued.

9. DISPOSITION.
Map (1/5.000) shewing COY. dispositions will be sent to Battalion Headquarters by 10 a.m. 5th inst.

10. BOUNDARIES ON RELIEF.
Right boundary of Brigade - N.2.b.6.0. - N.2.Central - N.1.d.15.80. (old German front line just South of junction of NELSON TRENCH and NASH ALLEY) - M.6.d.75.75 (Junction of railways) - along railway to DOUBLE CRASSIER - DOUBLE CRASSIER (inclusive to 6th Divn).
Left Boundary of Brigade - Trench connecting HURRAH ALLEY with front line at point H.32.a.58.37 - HURRAH ALLEY - ENGLISH ALLEY to its junction with RAILWAY ALLEY at point G.28.d.80.25.all inclusive to 16th I.B.
Boundary between Battalions in front line - H.32.d.45.25 - N.2.a.20.90.

11. TRANSPORT.
The T.O. will take the transport lines of 2nd D.L.I. at MAZINGARBE.

12. ACKNOWLEDGE.

Issued at.......... [signature] Lieut.,

3/9/1917. A/Adjutant, 9th Battalion The Suffolk Regiment.

Copy No. 1. Commanding Officer.
" " 2. 2nd-in-Command.
" " 3. Major H. Tylden Wright.
" " 4. O.C. "A" Coy.
" " 5. O.C. "B" Coy.
" " 6. O.C. "C" Coy.
" " 7. O.C. "D" Coy.
" " 8. O.C. Headquarters.
" " 9. R.S.M.
" " 10. Transport Officer.
" " 11. Quartermaster.
" " 12. Medical Officer.
" " 13. 9th Norfolks.
" " 14. Retained.
" " 15. War Diary.
" " 16. War Diary.

SECRET. Copy No..16......

---9TH BN. SUFFOLK REGIMENT ---

O P E R A T I O N O R D E R No. 56.

1. RELIEF. The Battalion will relieve the 9th Norfolk Regiment in the left Sub-Section on 9/10th Sept.

"A" Coy.	Suffolks	will	relieve	"C"	Coy.	Norfolks.
"B" "	"	"	"	"A"	"	"
"C" "	"	"	"	"D"	"	"
"D" "	"	"	"	"B"	"	"

2. MOVE. Companies will move from their present positions at times to be notified later.

3. RATIONS. The one days reserve ration at present in HARTS CRATER will be issued to Coys. on the 9th by 4.p.m. It will be taken up with Coys. and is for consumption on the 10th. Rations for consumption on the 11th will reach Support Coys. on the morning of the 10th. Support Coys. will arrange for these rations to be carried to Front Coys. on the night of the 10th.
Rations for consumption on a certain day will arrive at the Support Coys. on the morning of the day before and will be carried by them to the Front Coys. during the same evening.
The party at HARTS CRATER will only be employed in carrying R.E. material during the evenings.

4. STORES. All Trench Stores, maps, aeroplane photos etc., will be taken over and receipts given. A list of all stores etc., will be sent to the Orderly Room by 10.a.m. the 10th inst.

5. Relief Complete will be sent to Battalion Headquarters.

6. ACKNOWLEDGE.

Issued at...6.40 p.m....... R Fitch Lieut.,

8.9.17. A/Adjutant, 9th Battalion The Suffolk Regiment.

....

Copy No. 1...C.O.
" " 2...2nd-in-Command.
" " 3...Major H. Tylden Wright.
" " 4...O.C. "A" Coy.
" " 5...O.C. "B" Coy.
" " 6...O.C. "C" Coy.
" " 7...O.C. "D" Coy.
" " 8...O.C. Headquarters.

Copy No. 9...Transport Officer.
" " 10...Quartermaster.
" " 11...R.S.M.
" " 12...Medical Officer.
" " 13...9th Norfolks.
" " 14...Retained.
" " 15...War Diary.
" " 16...War Diary.

COPY. Copy.No.16

OPERATION ORDER.No.57.

by

Lieut.Col.F.Latham D.S.O. Commanding 8th.Battalion The Suffolk Regiment.

++

1. The Battalion will be relieved in the LEFT SUB-SECTION on the night 13/14th by the 14th Battalion D.L.I.
On completion of relief Battalion will proceed to ~~LES BREBIS~~ Mazingarbe 13/14th and on 14/15 will relieve the 1st Battalion THE BUFFS and become the Reserve Battalion of the left Brigade.
O's. C. Coys will be informed which Companies of 14th. D.L.I. will relieve them as soon as possible.
Disposition as under :- 14/15TH

"C" Coy. RESERVE TRENCH (POSEN ALLEY inclusive to Northern Boundary of Brigade)
"B" Coy. GUN TRENCH.
"A" Coy. VILLAGE LINE.
"D" Coy. MAZINGARBE.
Battalion Headquarters CURZON STREET G.22.a. 90.00.

"A" Coy.	Suffolks	will	relieve	"D" Coy.	BUFFS.
"B" "	"	"	"	"B" "	"
"C" "	"	"	"	"C" "	"
"D" "	"	"	"	"A" "	"

2. All Trench Stores including petrol tins, Trench Maps, Aeroplane photo, etc., will be handed ~~and~~ taken over and receipts given and taken. Store Cards will be forwarded to the Orderly Room by 9.a.m. 14th. inst and 9.a.m. 15th. inst. respectively.

3. Sketch Map (1/5,000) shewing dispositions will be forwarded to Orderly Room by 9.a.m. 16th. inst.

4. Battalion Dump will be at POSEN Station 14/15th. onwards. Train leaves KINGSBRIDGE Station at 8.30.p.m. Rations must arrive there by 8.p.m. Transport Officer will arrange to provide the necessary animals and drag ropes.

5. Water can be obtained from tanks situated at :-
    1. TOSH ALLEY just S. of junction with RAILWAY ALLEY.
    2. TOSH ALLEY just N. of junction with RAILWAY ALLEY.
    3. 10th. AVENUE just N. of POSEN STATION.

6. O.C. "D" Coy will detail 1 man to report to Cemetery by 2.p.m. 14th.inst. He will be rationed by Brigade. No. and Name of man to be forwarded to Orderly Room by 9.a.m.13th. inst.

7. Quartermaster, and C.Q.M. Sgts. and Sgt. Dent will take over Billets in ~~LES BREBIS~~ on afternoon of 13th. CQ.M.Sgts. and Sgt. Dent will await Battalion.at ~~level crossing in LES BREBIS~~. entrance to MAZINGARBE

7a. Transport officer and Quartermaster will take over Transport Lines and Stores respectively of the 1st. THE BUFFS. on 14th. inst.

8. Relief Complete in both instances will be sent to Battalion H.Q. by B.A.B. Code.

8a. Transport officer will arrange for three limbers to be at HARTS CRATER at 4.a.m. 14th. inst to bring Trench Kit to ~~LES BREBIS~~. Mazingarbe
Further orders as regards evening move will be issued.

9. Coys and Headquarters will carry all kit across to HARTS CRATER and leave two men per Coy. in charge of same and await Transport at 4.a.m 14th. inst.

10. The Carrying parties now at HARTS CRATER will rejoin their respective Coys at LES BREBIS, and will move there under the Bn. Bombing Officer

11. ACKNOWLEDGE..

Issued at..........

S H Phillips 2/Lieut.

13. 9.17. A/Adjutant, 8th. Battalion Suffolk Regiment.

Copy. No1. Commanding Officer.
" No.2. 2nd. in. Command.
" No.3. Major. R. Tylden-Wright.
" No.4. O.C. "A" Coy.
" No.5. O.C. "B" Coy.
" NO.6. O.C. "C" Coy.
" No.7. "C" "D" Coy.
" No.8. O.C. Headquarters.
" No.9. Quartermaster.
" No.10. Transport Officer.
" No.11. Medical Officer.
" No.12. R. S. M.
" No.13. 14th. D. L. I.
" No.14. 1st. THE BUFFS.
" No.15. War Diary.
" No.16. War Diary.
" No.17. Retained.
" No.18. Retained.

....

SECRET.   Copy No....16........

Addendum to
9th Battalion Suffolk Regiment.
O P E R A T I O N   O R D E R   No. 57.

1. Companies will move off to-night in the following order - "B" "C" "A" Headquarters.
"B" Coy. will move off at 7.30.p.m. the remaining Coys. will follow at 10 minutes interval between Coys. Coys. will move by Platoons at 200 Yards interval until dusk, when they will each form a continuous line in single rank. Coys. will proceed via PHILOSOPHE.

2. Guides for "B" Coy. will be at the 16th I.B. Headquarters PREVITE CASTLE G.28.a. Those for "C" "A" and Headquarters, will be at POSEN STATION. The Officer already sent out and 2 O.R. per Coy. will await their own Coys. at Cross Roads G.20.a.35.30 and guide their Coys. to POSEN STATION.

3. Kits for Trenches and for Transport will be ready to load outside Coy. Messes at 6.p.m.

4. Lewis Guns will be ready to load at 6.30.p.m. and will be dumped at Cross Roads G.20.a.35.30 where Coys. will pick them up. One No. 1. and one No. 2. per Coy. will accompany Limber.

5. Coys. will send back to POSEN STATION to-night to fetch Kit.
From to-morrow night onward, Coys. will send their own carrying parties to carry rations from POSEN STATION to their Coys. in the Trenches.

6. Drummers will accompany the bogies for loading and off loading under orders of the Transport Officer. Mules will be provided for pulling trucks.

7. ACKNOWLEDGE.

Lieut.,

14.9.17.   A/Adjutant, 9th Battalion The Suffolk Regiment.

E

SECRET. Copy No. 16

8th. Battalion Suffolk Regiment

[illegible]

1. The Battalion will relieve the 9th. Battalion Norfolk Regiment in the Front Line Trenches tonight 18th./19th. inst.

2. "[illegible]" Coy. 8th. Suffolks will relieve "[illegible]" Coy. 9th. Norfolks. ([illegible]).
"[illegible]" Coy. 8th. Suffolks will relieve "[illegible]" Coy. 9th. Norfolks. (Centre Coy.).
"[illegible]" Coy. 8th. Suffolks will relieve "[illegible]" Coy. 9th. Norfolks. (Right Front Coy.).
"[illegible]" Coy. 8th. Suffolks will relieve "[illegible]" Coy. 9th. Norfolks. (Support Coy.)

Battalion Headquarters will be in [illegible].

Regtl. Aid Post will be by JUNCTION of [illegible] and [illegible] ALLEY.
Relief will take place in the following order [illegible].

3. Guides will be at Junction of [illegible] ALLEY and [illegible] at 6.30.p.m.

4. Head of "[illegible]" Coy. will pass Junction of [illegible] and [illegible] ALLEY at [illegible].p.m. Head of "[illegible]" Coy. will pass Junction at [illegible].p.m. Head of "[illegible]" Coy. will pass Junction at [illegible]. "[illegible]" Coy. will pass [illegible] as soon as dark [illegible].

5. Rations will be brought up by Pack Mules by overland route to about [illegible]. Headquarters Rations will be dumped at Headquarters.

6. Water will be obtained from tanks in [illegible].

7. ACKNOWLEDGE.

Issued at 2 p.m.

[signature], Captain,
18/2/17. A/Adjutant, 8th. Battalion Suffolk Regiment.

Copy. No. 1.	Commanding Officer.	Copy. No.	8.	H.Q. Headquarters.
" 2.	2nd. in Command.	"	9	Quartermaster.
" 3.	Major H. Tylden Wright.		10.	Transport Officer.
" 4.	O.C. "A" Coy.		11.	Medical Officer.
" 5.	O.C. "B" Coy.		12.	R.S.M.
" 6.	O.C. "C" Coy.		13.	9th. Norfolks.
" 7.	O.C. "D" Coy.		14.	Retained.

15 War Diary.
16 War Diary.

SECRET. Copy No. 16

9th. Battalion The Suffolk Regiment.

Operation Order No. [illegible]

1. The Battalion will be relieved in the Right Sub-Section by the 9th Battalion Sherwood Foresters on the night of [illegible]/23rd.

" " Coy 9th Foresters will relieve "A" Coy 9th Suffolks.
" " " " " " "B" " " "
" " " " " " "C" " " "
" " " " " " "D" " " "

2. One guide per Platoon and Coy Headquarters will be at Junction [illegible] and will report to 2/Lieut. [illegible] who will ensure that guides go with correct Foresters' Coy's. 2/Lieut. [illegible] will report to A/Adjutant when all Foresters' Coy's have moved up.

3. All Trench Stores, petrol tins, [illegible], etc., will be handed over and receipts obtained. [illegible] Trench Cards will be forwarded to the Orderly Room by [illegible] 23rd. inst.

4. On completion of Relief the Battalion will proceed to billets in LES BREBIS. O.C. Coy's will report " ALL IN " to Battalion Headquarters immediately on arrival.

5. An advanced party consisting of Lieut. [illegible], C.Q.M.Sgts. and [illegible] will report to Battalion Headquarters, 9th. Battalion Norfolk Regiment LES BREBIS at [illegible] inst. and take over billets from that Regiment. They will meet Coy's at the Level crossing LES BREBIS and guide them to their respective billets.

6. Officers' kits, Mess kit, etc., will be at FORT GLATZ by [illegible]. Lewis Guns, Ammunition Boxes etc., will be carried out by Coy's and dumped at FORT GLATZ to await limbers. One No. 1. and one No. 2. per Coy will be left in charge.

7. Transport Officer will arrange for [illegible] limber per Coy and 1 Limber for Headquarters to be at FORT GLATZ, at [illegible]. Also for the Lewis Gun limbers to be at same place at [illegible].

8. Relief Complete will be sent to Battalion Headquarters by B.A.B. Code.

9. ACKNOWLEDGE.

Issued at 4 p.m. [signature] Captain.,

21/ /17. A/Adjutant 9th. Battalion The Suffolk Regiment.,

....

Copy No. 1. Commanding Officer.
" " 2. 2nd In Command.
" " 3. O.C. "A" Coy.
" " 4. O.C. "B" "
" " 5. O.C. "C" "
" " 6. O.C. "D" "
" " 7. O.C. Retrs.

Copy No. [illegible] Quartermaster.
" " [illegible] Transport Officer.
" " [illegible] Medical Officer
" " [illegible]
" " 13. 9th. Sher: Foresters.
" " [illegible] Retained.
" " [illegible] Retained.

Copy No. 15... War Diary.
" " 16... War Diary.

....

S E C R E T.

To................

Reference B.O. No.59 Para..2. for 2/Lieut. J.V. Tailby read 2/Lieut. F. Bullen.

"B" Coy. 8th Foresters will relieve "A" Coy. 9th Suffolks.
"D" " " " " " "B" " " "
"A" " " " " " "C" " " "
"C" " " " " " "D" " " "

"A" "B" and "C" Coy. will each send two guides per Coy. to junction CHALK PIT ALLEY - TOSH ALLEY at 8.15.p.m.

"D" Coy. will send two guides to junction LOOS TRENCH - RAILWAY ALLEY at same time.

Foresters' Companies will come up in the following order:-

"C" - "A" - "D" - "B".

....

Captain,

22/9/17. A/Adjutant 9th Battalion The Suffolk Regiment.

SECRET. Copy No. 15

9th Battalion The Suffolk Regiment.

Operation Order No. 60.

---

1. On the night 23/24th inst. the Battalion will move from LES BREBIS to SOUTH MAROC and will be in Divisional Reserve.

2. The Battalion will move in the following order H.Q., "B" "C" "D" "A". "A" Coy. moving off from the level crossing LES BREBIS at 8.p.m. Coys. will move of at 200 yards interval.

3. An advance Party consisting of 2/Lieut. E.L. Lucas and 2 N.C.Os. per Coy. and Headquarters will report to Town Major, MAROC, M.2.a.15.05. at 2.p.m. 23rd inst., they will meet at level crossing 1.30.p.m. ~~and guides Coys and Head~~ 1. N.C.O. per Coy. and Headquarters will return to Companies and guide Companies and Headquarters to Billets in SOUTH MAROC.

4. Kit, Cooking Utensils, etc., accompanying Battalion will be stacked outside Coy. and Headquarter Messes ready to load at 7.p.m. Kit, etc. for Transport will be at same places ready to load at 7.30.p.m.

5. Transport Officer will arrange Transport for above. Lewis Guns and Drums will be carried by Platoons.

6. Transport Lines and Quartermaster's Stores will remain as at present.

7. Water tanks are located in the new area as follows :-

M.11.b.60.40.
M.10.d.45.05½.
M.12.a.80.60.
M. 2.d.70.60.
M. 2.b.97.13.
Wells. M.17.b.30.05.
M.17.a.30.70.
M.16.b.80.90.
M.11.d.80.45.
M.11.c.35.40.

Water drawn from any of the above locations should be chlorinated before use.

8. Main Brigade Grenade Stores are located at :-

M.11.d.7.3.
M.10.d.7.1.
M.18.a.2.6.
M.17.a.7.7.

9. Advanced Dressing Station is at M.11.a.6.1. (on light railway). Advanced R.E. Dump is at M.12.b.7.0.

10. ACKNOWLEDGE.

Issued at 12 noon. W Hitch Captain,

23.9.17. A/Adjutant, 9th Battalion The Suffolk Regiment.

P.T.O.

continued.

Copy No. 1....Commanding Officer.
" No. 2....2nd-in-Command.
" No. 3....O.C. "A" Company.
" No. 4....O.C. "B" Company.
" No. 5....O.C. "C" Company.
" No. 6....O.C. "D" Company.
" No. 7....O.C. Headquarters.
" No. 8....Quartermaster.
" No. 9....Transport Officer.
" No. 10....Medical Officer.
" No. 11....R.S.M.
" No. 12....Retained.
" No. 13....Retained.
" No. 14....War Diary.
" No. 15....War Diary.

ORDERLY ROOM
No. 1633
Date.
9th SUFFOLK REGT.

Headquarters,

7*st Infantry Brigade.

Herewith War Diary of the Battalion under my Command for the month of October 1917.

[signature] Lieut-Colonel.,

1.11.1917. Commanding 9th Battalion The Suffolk Regt.

Instructions regarding War Diaries and Intelligence Summaries are contained in F. S. Regs., Part II, and the Staff Manual respectively. Title pages will be prepared in manuscript.

WAR DIARY
or
INTELLIGENCE SUMMARY.
(Erase heading not required.)

Army Form C. 2118.

9 Suffolk R
Vol 26

Place	Date	Hour	Summary of Events and Information	Remarks and references to Appendices
MAROC	1.10.17		Bn in Divisional Reserve & providing working parties. Casualties 2 ORs wounded. Bn relieved by the 1st Bn Leicestershire Regt & withdrew to VAUDRICOURT. O.O. No 61 attached	WH Appendix "A"
VAUDRICOURT	2.10.17		Bn in Rest. Casualties 1 OR wounded. 2/Lieut G. F. Bryant proceeded to Div. Depot Bn to relieve 2/Lieut J.V. Railby.	WH
	3.10.17		Bn in training. 2/Lieut J.V. Railby rejoined Bn from Div. Depot Bn.	WH
	4.10.17		" " 2/Lieut J.V. Railby proceeded to take up duties as O.C. Bde Lewis Gun School	WH
	5.10.17		Bn in training. 2/Lieut H Almack admitted to F.A. sick	WH
	6.10.17		" "	WH
	7.10.17		" "	WH
	8.10.17		" " Bn relieved 14th Bn D.L.I. in the support line trenches. O.O. No 62 attached.	WH Appendix "B"
TRENCHES	9.10.17		Bn in Support line trenches. Bn relieved the 2nd Bn D.L.I. in the Front line trenches. O.O. No 62 attached	WH " "B"

A6945 Wt. W11422/M1160 350,000 12/16 D. D. & L. Forms/C./2118/14.

269

Instructions regarding War Diaries and Intelligence Summaries are contained in F. S. Regs., Part II. and the Staff Manual respectively. Title pages will be prepared in manuscript.

WAR DIARY
or
INTELLIGENCE SUMMARY.
(Erase heading not required.)

Army Form C. 2118.

Place	Date	Hour	Summary of Events and Information	Remarks and references to Appendices
TRENCHES	10.10.17		Bn in Front line trenches. 2 Lieut E.L. Lucas proceeded to England for 6 months duty in that country	WH
	11.10.17		Bn in Front line trenches. 2/Lieut A.H. Stoyle rejoined Bn from FA through 15th I.B.D.	WH
	12.10.17		Bn in Front line trenches.	WH
	13.10.17		" " " Bn relieved by the 1st Bn Leicestershire Regt & withdrew to Support line trenches. O.O. No 63 attached	WH Appendix C
	14.10.17		Bn in Support line trenches	WH
	15.10.17		" " "	WH
	16.10.17		" " " Bn relieved by 1st Bn West Yorkshire Regt & proceeded to relieve 1st Bn K.S.L.I. in the Front line trenches. O.O. No 64 attached. Casualties 1 O.R. wounded.	WH Appendix D
	17.10.17		Bn in Front line trenches.	WH
	18.10.17		" " " Casualties 2 O.Rs killed. 11. O.Rs wounded (1. Accidentally 4 at duty).	WH

A6945 Wt. W11422/M1160 350,000 12/16 D. D. & L. Forms/C./2118/14.

Instructions regarding War Diaries and Intelligence Summaries are contained in F. S. Regs., Part II. and the Staff Manual respectively. Title pages will be prepared in manuscript.

WAR DIARY
or
INTELLIGENCE SUMMARY.
(Erase heading not required.)

Army Form C. 2118.

Place	Date	Hour	Summary of Events and Information	Remarks and references to Appendices
TRENCHES	19.10.17		Bn in Front line trenches. Bn was subjected to a very heavy bombardment	
			Casualties 2/Lieut R F Packer killed 2 Lieuts C C Dew + C Sneesby	
			wounded 2/Lieut F Goatcher wounded WH 2/Lieut C H Miller wounded (at duty). 6 ORs killed 25 ORs	
			wounded (3 at duty) 1 OR missing 'B' Coy relieved 'C' Coy in the	
			firing line 'D' was unable to relieve 'A' Coy until night 20/21st OO No 65	
			attached WH	Appendix E
	20.10.17		Bn in Front line trenches. 2 Lieuts S T Marchant & A C J Taylor joined	
			from 3rd Bn Norfolk Regt + are taken on the strength of the Bn WH	
	21.10.17		Bn in Front line trenches. Casualties 2 ORs wounded. Bn relieved	
			by 8th Bn N.Fs + withdrew to BULLY GRENAY. O.O. 66 attached WH	" F
BULLY GRENAY	22.10.17		Bn marched to NOEUX-LES-MINES + entrained for LILLERS marching from	
			thence to AUCHY AU BOIS. O O No 66 attached. WH	" F
AUCHY-AU-BOIS	23.10.17		Bn in training. 2/Lieut G K Cock rejoined Bn from Light Railways	
			LES BREBIS. WH	
	24.10.17		Bn in training WH	
	25.10.17		" " 2/Lieut G K Cock admitted to F A sick WH	

A6945 Wt. W11422/M1160 350,000 12/16 D. D. & L. Forms/C./2118/14.

Instructions regarding War Diaries and Intelligence Summaries are contained in F. S. Regs., Part II. and the Staff Manual respectively. Title pages will be prepared in manuscript.

Army Form C. 2118.

WAR DIARY
or
INTELLIGENCE SUMMARY.
(Erase heading not required.)

Place	Date	Hour	Summary of Events and Information	Remarks and references to Appendices
AUCHY AU BOIS	26.10.17		Bn in training	DH
	27.10.17		" "	DH
	28.10.17		" "	DH
	29.10.17		Bn moved by route march to LATHIEULOYE O.O No 67 attached	DH Appendix G
	30.10.17		Bn moved by route march to DENIER & BERLENCOURT O.O No 68 attached	" H
			2 Lieut. F.D. Down reported & is taken on the strength of the Bn	DH
	31.10.17		Bn in training. 2 Lieut. G. Catcher died of wounds	
			Drafts	" I

1.11.17

[signature] Lt. Col
Commanding 9th Bn Suffolk Regt

A6945 Wt. W11422/M1160 350,000 12/16 D. D. & L. Forms/C./2118/14.

SECRET. Copy.No. 15

9th.Battalion The Suffolk Regiment.

Operation Order No.81.

++

Ref: Map FRANCE Sheet 36.B.

1. The Battalion will be relieved from S.MAROC by the 1st Battalion Leicestershire Regiment., on the night of 1st/2nd October.

2. On Relief the Battalion will proceed to Billets in VAUDRICOURT, Busses or Lorries will be at LES BREBIS Church at 3.a.m.

3. Working parties will be found tonight as per Working Party Table of todays date, but all parties must be back in S.MAROC by 2.a.m. O.C. Coy's will report to Battalion Headquarters as soon as they are ready to move off.

4. Transport Lines and Quartermaster Stores will remain as at present.

5. An Advance Party consisting of 2/Lieut.F.Bullen and 1 full rank N.C.O. per Company and Headquarters will parade at the Orderly Room at 12.30.p.m. and proceed to VAUDRICOURT where they will report to the Town Major at 3.p.m.

6. All officers Kit, Mess Kit, Cooking utensils etc., will be stacked at Ration Dump ready to load at 9.45.p.m.

7. Transport officer will arrange for 1 Limber per Coy and 1 Limber for Headquarters to be at above place at that hour, also for Lewis Gun Limbers to be at above place at 1.30.a.m.

8. 2/Lieut.C.H.Miller M.C. will be at LES BREBIS Church at 3.a.m. and superintend the embussing of the Battalion.

9. Acknowledge.

Issued at. 11.15 am.

Captain.,

1/10/17. A/Adjutant 9th.Battalion The Suffolk Regiment.,

. . . .

Copy.No.1. C.O.	Copy.No.9. Transport Officer.
" " 2. O.C. "A" Coy.	" "10. Medical Officer.
" " 3. O.C. "B" Coy.	" "11. R.S.M.
" " 4. O.C. "C" Coy.	" " 12. 1st Leicestershires.
" " 5. O.C. "D" Coy.	" " 13. Retained.
" " 6. 2nd.In Command.	" " 14. Retained.
" " 7. O.C. Headquarters.	" " 15. War Diary.
" " 8. Quartermaster.	" " 16. War Diary.

!-!

SECRET. Copy No. 15

9th Battalion The Suffolk Regiment.
Operation Order No. 62.

---

1. The Battalion will relieve 14th Battalion D.L.I. in Support Line Trenches as under on the night of 8/9th October 1917.

"A" Coy. in Reserve Trench.
"B" Coy. in NASH ALLEY.
"C" Coy. in Reserve Trench.
"D" Coy. in Old Reserve Trench (M.6.d.50.80.)
H.Q. in BUGS ALLEY (N.1.a.05.10.)

2. Busses will be available to convey the Battalion from X.4.a.9.1. to LES BREBIS Church. The Battalion will parade in the following order with Head of Column by "B" Coy Mess :- H.Q. "A" "C" "B" and "D" Coy. ready to move off at 6.15.p.m. 8th inst.

3. Os.C. Coys. will detail 1 Officer per Coy and 1 N.C.O. per platoon and 2/Lieut. C.H.Miller.M.C. and 1 N.C.O. for Headquarters to be at HARTS CRATER at 5.p.m. 8th inst. as advance party. Guides of 14th D.L.I. will conduct them to Company trenches. This party ~~will~~ will parade at the Orderly Room at 2.p.m. 8th inst. ready to proceed.

4. On completion of relief the Battalion will be under orders of the B.G.C. 16th I.B.

5. On night of 9/10th the Battalion will relieve 2nd Batt: D.L.I. in the Right Sub-Section of the AUGUSTE Section as under :-

"A" Coy. COBB Trench.
"B" Coy. Front Line (Left.)
"C" Coy. CATAPULT Trench.
"D" Coy. Front Line (Right.)
H.Q. N.7.b.70.80.

The 1st Leicestershires will move into Support Trenches.

6. On completion of relief boundaries will be as under :-

(a) Southern Boundary between 71st and 16th Inf. Bdes. CANTEEN ALLEY (incl. to 16th I.B.) as far as N.8.a.50.45 thence to junction of CONGRESS and CONTRACT (N.7.a.95.35.) thence along trench to N.7.a.9.5. (trench incl. to 16th I.B.) - Road junction N.12.b. 05.75. thence along road to CITE ST.PIERRE Church - N.11.a.85.75 - along DOUBLE CRASSIER.

(b) Inter-Battalion Boundary - CITE ST. AUGUSTE Railway.

(c) Northern Boundary between 71st I.B. and Right Brigade 46th Divn. N.2.b.5.8.- N.2.a.22.90. (NUN'S ALLEY) - H.31.c.7.4.-H.31.c.2.7. -SCOTS ALLEY (excl.) - G.36.b.3.1. - ENGLISH ALLEY (incl.)- G.29.d.7.1. - G.26.c.7.9.

7. Relief complete in each case will be reported to Battalion Hqtrs. by B.A.B. Code.

8. All Trench Stores, aeroplane photos, etc., will be taken over and receipts given. Receipted Store Cards to be forwarded to Battalion H.Q. by 10.a.m. 9th and 10th inst. respectively.

9. Officers Kit, Mess Kit, etc., going to trenches will be stacked outside H.Q. and Coy H.Q. at 5.30.p.m.
Kit, etc., going to Transport Lines will be stacked ready to load outside H.Q. and Coy H.Q. at 4.p.m.
Transport Officer will arrange accordingly.

P. T. O.

B

Continued.

10. Lewis Guns, Ammunition Boxes, etc., will be taken with Coys.

11. BOMB STORES. 1. HARTS CRATER - Main Dump.
2. LOOS G.36.d.2.4.
3. COUNTER DUMP at railhead N.7.a.5.7.
4. NA POO DUMP M.1.d.85.50.
5. INNISKILLEN FORT in LOOS.

12. WATER. HARTS CRATER.
HARRISONS CRATER.
Junction of NETLEY TRENCH and NASH ALLEY.

13. RATION DUMP. HARTS CRATER, by Horse Transport.

14. ADVANCED DRESSING STATION - St. PATRICKS, LOOS.

15. On the 8th inst. Rations for 9th inst. will be carried by Coys. On 8th inst. Transport Officer will arrange to bring rations for consumption on 10th inst. to HARTS CRATER and hand same over to R.S.M. and Coys. will arrange to send down on day of 9th inst. for the rations for consumption on 10th inst. On 9th inst. Rations for consumption on 11th inst. will be brought by Trams to N.7.a.4.6., pushed by Drummers (or by Transport to M.12.b.9.7.)

16. On night of 8/9th inst., R.S.M. and 2 orderlies will remain at HARTS CRATER and take over rations from Transport Officer.

17. ACKNOWLEDGE.

Issued at 1.10 am.... [signature] Captain,

8.10.17. A/Adjutant, 9th Battalion The Suffolk Regiment.

Copy. No. 1.	C.O.	
" " 2.	O.C. "A" Coy.	
" " 3.	O.C. "B" Coy.	
" " 4.	O.C. "C" Coy.	
" " 5.	O.C. "D" Coy.	
" " 6.	O.C. H.Q.	
" " 7.	2nd-in-Command.	
" " 8.	Quartermaster.	
Copy. No. 9.	Transport Officer.	
" " 10.	R.S.M.	
" " 11.	Medical Offr.	
" " 12.	2nd D.L.I.	
" " 13.	14th D.L.I.	
" " 14.	Retained.	
" " 15.	War Diary.	
" " 16.	War Diary.	

SECRET. Copy No. 15.

9th Battalion The Suffolk Regiment.
Operation Order No. 63.

1. The Battalion will be relieved in the Right Sub-Section of the AUGUSTE Section by the 1st Leicestershire Regt. on the night of 13/14th October as under :-

"C" Coy. 1st Leicestershires will relieve "A" Coy. 9th Suffolks.
"B" " " " " " "B" " " "
"D" " " " " " "C" " " "
"A" " " " " " "D" " " "

2. On completion of relief, the Battalion will withdraw to Brigade Support as under :-

"A" Coy. NASH ALLEY.
"B" Coy, RESERVE TRENCH (LEFT).
"C" Coy, RESERVE TRENCH (RIGHT).
"D" Coy, OLD RESERVE TRENCH (M.6.d.50.80).
Bn. H.Q. BUGS ALLEY (N.1.a.95.10).

3. Guides, 4 per Coy, will be at following places at times stated, to conduct Coys. of relieving Battalion :-

"A" Coy. at junction NERO & CATAPULT at 5.30.p.m. to meet "C" Coy. 1st Leicestershires. proceed via CATAPULT - EASTER to COBB.
"B" Coy. at junction NESTOR - CATAPULT at 6.15.p.m. to meet "B" Coy. 1st Leicestershires. Proceed via NESTOR to front line.
"C" Coy. will be relieved about 4.p.m. by "D" Coy 1st Leicestershires. No Guides required. "D" Coy. 1st Leicestershires will follow "C" Coy, 1st Leicestershires.
"D" Coy, at junction CATAPULT - EASTER & CONGRESS at 6.p.m. to meet "A" Coy. 1st Leicestershires. proceed via EASTER & CARFAX to front line.

Each Guide will have a memo: signed by O.C. Coy. stating his own Coy. and that of the relieving Battalion.

4. "A" & "B" Coys. will send an advance party to reconnoitre the line to be taken over. The Officer i/c of "A" Coy, party will send back guides to junction of CATAPULT - NERO (N.1.c.78.80) to meet Coy. The Officer i/c of "B" Coy. party will send back guides to meet Coy at junction CATAPULT - NESTOR (N.1.c.90.58).

5. All trench stores, Maps, Aeroplane photos, Petrol Tins, Gum Boots, etc., will be handed over and receipts obtained. Three Trench Store Cards are attached, one for return to Orderly Room by 10.a.m. 13th inst., one to be handed over and one for return to Orderly Room (receipted) by 10.a.m. 14th inst.

6. Reliefs complete will be notified to Battalion Headquarters by B.A.B. Code, both on relief by 1st Leicestershires and when "All in" in Support system.

7. Rations for consumption on the 14th inst. will reach Coys. during the day of 13th inst. They will be issued and carried out on the man.

Each Coy. will detail 8 men with full kit to report to Battn. Headquarters by 4.30.p.m., latest, on 13th inst. These men will then proceed to dump and assist the N.C.O. and 6 men per Coy. already there to carry rations for consumption on 15th inst. to Coy. positions in Support. Care should be taken that men selected should know way to their new Coy. Headquarters by the Duckboard track. They will await their Coys. there.

Ration Dump will be on LENS-BETHUNE road at junction with DUCKBOARD track (leading to BUGS ALLEY & NASH ALLEY).

8. Os.C. Coys. and Headquarters will render a strength return to Orderly Room daily by 6.p.m. showing every Officer, N.C.O., and man with them in trenches. This return must be up to time.

9. The Duckboard track from LENS-BETHUNE road to NASH ALLEY is not to be used by daylight.

P.T.O.

CONTINUED.

10. The Companies in NASH ALLEY and OLD RESERVE TRENCH are available for
    1. Reinforcing Reserve Line.
    2. Delivering a Counter Attack should enemy obtain a footing in Reserve Line.

    Os.C. "A" and "D" Coys, will arrange that all approaches both by trench and overland are reconnoitred by officers and N.C.Os.
    In all probability "A" Coy. would move to that portion of Reserve Line between CATAPULT-EASTER trench junction to junction CARFAX - DOUGLAS trench junction.
    "D" Coy. to that portion of CATAPULT between NERO and CONGRESS.

11. In case of alarm, working parties found by Battalion, will man the Reserve Line - N.1.b.71.95 - N.1.b.99.80 - N.1.b.78.40 - N.1.d.90.58 - N.1.d.80.52 - N.7.b.20.90 - N.2.c.43.08 - N.8.a.65.87 - N.8.a.65.45.

12. ACKNOWLEDGE.

Issued at 9.45 pm. Captain,

12.10.17. A/Adjutant, 9th Battalion The Suffolk Regiment.

Copy No. 1....Commanding Officer.
" " 2....2nd in Command.
" " 3....O.C. "A" Coy.
" " 4....O.C. "B" Coy.
" " 5....O.C. "C" Coy.
" " 6....O.C. "D" Coy.
" " 7....O.C. Headquarters.
" " 8....Transport Officer.
" " 9....Quartermaster.
" " 10....Medical Officer.
" " 11....R.S.M.
" " 12....1st Leicestershires.
" " 13....Retained.
" " 14....Retained.
" " 16....War Diary.
" " 17....War Diary.

SECRET. Copy No. 15

9th Battalion The Suffolk Regiment.
Operation Order No. 64.

---

1. On the night of 16/17th October, the Battalion will be relieved in the Support Line AUGUSTE Section by 1st Bn. West Yorks Regt., 18th Inf. Bde., and will thereafter proceed to relieve 1st Bn. K.S.L.I., 16th Inf. Bde. in the left Sub-section EMILE Section as under :-

"C" Coy. 9th Suffolks will relieve "A" Coy. 1st K.S.L.I. (Right front Coy
"A" Coy. plus half platoon "D" Coy. 9th Suffolks will relieve "D" Coy. 1st K.S.L.I. (left front Coy.)
"B" Coy. 9th Suffolks will relieve "C" Coy 1st K.S.L.I. (Right Support Coy)
"D" Coy. less ½ platoon 9th Suffolks will relieve "B" Coy. 1st K.S.L.I. (left Support Coy.)

2. Guides on the scale of 3 per Coy. and 2 for Battn. Headquarters will be at the junc; of NARWHAL & COUNTER TRENCHES (N.7.a.90.65) Coys. will arrive at this point as far as possible in the following order "A", "C", "B", "D" Coy. Headquarters will move off at a time to be notified later.

3. Os.C. Coys. will detail one Officer and 2 N.C.Os. to proceed to their positions in advance and take over stores from the 1st Bn. K.S.L.I. in daylight. Signalling Officer will detail operators & linesmen to proceed in advance. Linesmen to go over lines in daylight.

4. Trench Stores, Maps, Aeroplane Photos, Prtrol Tins & <u>Gum Boots</u> will be handed over to 1st Bn. West Yorks Regt. & taken over from the 1st K.S.L.I receipts being given in each case. Receipted Trench Store Cards being forwarded to Orderly Room by 10.a.m. 17th inst.

5. Disposition Maps 1/5,000 will be forwarded to Battn. Headquarters by 12 noon 17th inst.

6 Relief complete in left Sub-section will be forwarded to Battn. Hd. Qtrs. by B.A.B. Code.

P.T.O.

Continued.

7. WATER SUPPLY.- (a) at Brigade Headquarters.
(b) Junction of CATAPULT & CONGRESS TRENCH.
(c) M.12.a.85.50.
(d) M.12.a.28.20.
(e) LENS HOSPITAL N.7.c.10.70.

8. RATION ROUTES.-
Route for Transport - LES BREBIS - GRENAY along FOSSE 11 Road - to CITE ST PIERRE M.17.a.25.85 thence to M.12.a.85.57 where rations will be dumped; transport returning via M.12.a.30.85 - M.11.Central - M.10.d.40.10 along FOSSE 11 Road.

9. SALVAGE.- Coys. are responsible for clearing their areas of all Salvage and sending it back to Battn.Headquarters.

10. ACKNOWLEDGE.

Issued at 11.55 a.m.
16.10.17.

[signature] Captain,
A/Adjutant. 9th Battalion The Suffolk Regiment.

Copy No. 1. Commanding Officer.	Copy No. 9. R.S.M.
" " 2. O.C. "A" Coy.	" " 10. 1st Bn. K.S.L.I.
" " 3, O.C. "B" Coy.	" " 11, 1st Bn. West Yorks Regt.
" " 4. O.C. "C" Coy.	" " 12, Retained.
" " 5, O.C. "D" Coy.	" " 13. Retained.
" " 6. O.C. Headquarters.	" " 14. War Diary.
" " 7, Quartermaster.	" " 15. War Diary.
" " 8. Medical Officer.	

SECRET. Copy No..... 11

9th Battalion The Suffolk Regiment.
Operation Order No. 68.

---

1. Tonight (19/20th inst.) the following reliefs will take place :-

"D" Coy. will relieve "A" Coy.
"B" Coy. " " "C" Coy.

"A" Coy. will leave one ½ platoon in CONNECTION TRENCH under the orders of O.C. "D" Coy.

2. On completion of relief "A" Coy. will withdraw to Left Support and "C" Coy. to Right Support.

3. All details of relief to be arranged direct between Os.C. Coys. concerned. Relief to take place as soon after dark as possible.

4. Os.C. "B" & "D" Coys. will hand over all details of carrying parties, working parties, etc., "C" Coy. will find the 10.p.m. relief for the 3rd Australian Tunneling Coy. All information regarding patrols and front line posts to be most carefully handed over by front line Coys.

5. Coys. will send small advance parties to take over stores, etc.

6. Relief complete to be reported by B.A.B. Code.

7. ACKNOWLEDGE.

Issued at.......... W. Fitch Captain,

19.10.17. A/Adjutant, 9th Battalion The Suffolk Regiment.

Copy No. 1..C.O.
" " 2..O.C. "A" Coy.
" " 3..O.C. "B" Coy.
" " 4..O.C. "C" Coy.
" " 5..O.C. "D" Coy.
" " 6..O.C. Headquarters.
Copy No. 7..R.S.M.
" " 8..Medical Offr.
" " 9..Retained.
" " 10..Retained.
" " 11..War Diary. ✓
" " 12..War Diary.

E

SECRET.

Copy No....15....

9th Battalion The Suffolk Regiment.
Operation Order No. 66.

Ref: maps HAZEBROUCK 5 A 1/100.000.
LENS 1/10.000.

20.10.17.

1. The 6th Div: is being relieved by the 11th Div: The 71st I.B. being relieved by the 34th I.B. on 20th/21st and 21st/22nd Oct.

2. On the night 21st/22nd inst. the Battalion will be relieved from the front line system by the 8th Battalion Northumberland Fusiliers.
"Y" Coy. Fusiliers will relieve "A" Coy. 9th Suffolks (Left Support).
"X" " " " " "B" " " " (Right Front)
"Z" " " " " "C" " " " (Right Support),
"W" " " " " "D" " " " (Left Front).

3. On completion of relief, the Battalion will withdraw to billets in BULLY GRENAY.

4. An advance party consisting of Lt. & Qr. Mr. R. Starling, C.Q.M.Sgts. and Sgt. Dent, will report to the TOWN MAJOR, BULLY GRENAY at 2.p.m. 21st inst. They will meet Coys. and Headquarters at M.1.d.65.32 and guide them to their billets.

5. On the 22nd inst., the Battalion, less transport and Q.M. Stores, will move by rail from NOEUX-LES-MINES to LILLERS and will march thence to billets in "B" Sub-area, ST HILAIRE.

6. Transport will move by road straight through to their new billets. The whole of the Bde. Transport moving as one column under Command of the Senior Officer. The strictest march discipline will be observed by Transport during the coming move. Special points to be watched are:- No overloading, no unauthorized personnel with Regtl. Transport.
Battalion Transport will not move from their present lines before 22nd inst. Q.M. Stores will move with Transport.

7. The following will hold themselves in readiness to proceed at short notice to "B" Sub-area, ST HILAIRE, as an advance party and report to TOWN MAJOR, WESTREHEM. - 2/Lieut. F. Bullen, C.Q.M.Sgts. and Sgt. Dent.
It is hoped that a bus will be available on the morning of the 22nd inst. to convey the above advance party. Further orders will be issued.

8. Details, i.e. Bde. Storemen, etc., will rejoin their Coys. as soon after relief as possible.

9. All trench stores, maps, aeroplane photos. Defence Schemes, etc., will be handed over. Trench Cards will be forwarded to Orderly Room by 10.a.m. 21st inst. and receipted cards by 10.a.m. 22nd inst.

10. Relief complete to be reported to Battalion Headquarters by "Your S.U.501 received at #.

11. Officers Kit, Mess Kit, Coy. Stores, etc., will be carried down to the CINEMA, ST PIERRE, M.12.a.25.30, to be there by 7.p.m. Transport Officer will arrange for 1 Limber for Headquarters and ½ Limber per Coy. to be at the CINEMA at that hour.

12. Transport Officer will arrange for Lewis Gun Limber to be at the CINEMA at 12.30.a.m. Lewis Guns will be dumped there by Coys. going out, ~~2~~ TWO Nos. 1 per Coy. being left in charge.

13. ACKNOWLEDGE.

Issued at...11.0 p.m....

W. Fitch
Captain,

20.10.17.

A/Adjutant, 9th Battalion The Suffolk Regiment.

P.T.O.

Copy No. 1...Commanding Officer.
" " 2...O.C. "A" Coy.
" " 3...O.C. "B" Coy.
" " 4...O.C. "C" Coy.
" " 5...O.C. "D" Coy.
" " 6...O.C. Headquarters.
" " 7...R.S.M.
" " 8...Transport Officer.
" " 9...Quartermaster.
" " 10...Medical Officer.
" " 11...8th Battn Northumberland Fusiliers.
" " 12...Retained.
" " 13...Retained.
" " 14...War Diary.
" " 15...War Diary.

SECRET. Copy No........ 15

9th Battalion The Suffolk Regiment.
Operation Order No. 67.

Ref. Sheet 36 B Ed b 1/40.000.
HAZEBROUCK 5A 1/100.000.
LENS Sheet 11. 1/100.000.

1. On the 29th inst. the Battalion will move from AUCHY-AU-BOIS to billets in LA THIEULOYE by the following route NEDONCHELLE - BAILLEUL-LES-PERNES - AUMERVAL - PERNES - FAUX VALHUON - LA THIEULOYE.

2. The Battalion will parade in full marching order in column of route ready to move off at 9.10.a.m., with head of column by "D" Coy. Mess. Order of March - Drums, H.Q., "D", "B", "C", "A".
Dress for dismounted Officers - Full marching Order.
Dress for mounted Officers - Skeleton Order.

3. An advance party consisting of 2/Lieut. S.H. Phillips and Sgt. Dent, will report to the Staff Capt. at 71st I.B. H.Q. at 7.a.m. A bus will convey them to new billeting area.

4. An advance party of C.Q.M.Sgts. and 1 O.R. per Coy. will parade at the Orderly Room at 8.30.a.m. with bicycles and will report to 2/Lieut. S.H. Phillips on arrival at LA THIEULOYE.

5. Officers' Valises will be stacked at Q.M. Stores ready to load at 8.a.m. Officers' Mess Kit will be stacked ready to load outside Coy. and H.Q. Messes at 8.a.m. Blankets will be rolled in bundles of ten, carefully labelled and stacked outside Q.M. Stores ready to load at 7.a.m.

6. Haversack ration will be carried.

7. A Lorry will report to the Q.M. Stores at 7.a.m. and will return for a second journey to convey surplus Kit of the Battalion and 9th Norfolk Regiment.

8. Transport will accompany the Battalion.

9. Refilling point for 29.10.17 will be at the Church LA THIEULOYE at 4.p.m. Supply wagons will dump supplies for 30th inst. in Quartermasters Stores before proceeding to refilling point. After refilling they will return to their units and march with them on the following day. Refilling point for 30th inst. will be notified later.

10. All Latrine Buckets will be returned to Q.M. Stores before Coys. and H.Q. leave their present billets.

11. ACKNOWLEDGE.

Issued at....4 am....

[signature] Captain,

29.10.17. A/Adjutant, 9th Battalion The Suffolk Regiment.

Copy No. 1..Commanding Officer.	Copy No. 9..Transport Officer.
" " 2..2nd-inCommand.	" " 10..Quartermaster.
" " 3 O.C. "A" Coy.	" " 11..Medical Officer.
" " 4 O.C. "B" Coy.	" " 12..71st Inf. Bde.
" " 5 O.C. "C" Coy.	" " 13..Retained.
" " 6 O.C. "D" Coy.	" " 14..Retained.
" " 7 O.C. O.C. Headquarters.	" " 15. War Diary.
" " 8 R.S.M.	" " 16. War Diary.

SECRET. Copy No. 15

9th Battalion The Suffolk Regiment.
Operation Order No. 68.

Ref. Sheet 36 B Ed 6 1/40.000.
Sheet 51 C. 1/40.000.
LENS 11. 1/100.000.

1. On the 30th inst. the Battalion will move from LA THIEULOYE to billets in BARLENCOURT and DENIER by the following route - BAILLEUL AUX CORNAILLES - AVERDOINGT - MAIZIERES - SARS LES BOIS - BARLENCOURT and DERNIER.

2. The Battalion will parade in full marching order in column of route head of column by South Eastern house of village on "B" Coy. road., (N.30.d.9.6) ready to move off at 8.a.m. Order of march - Drums, H.Qtrs., "B", "A", "D", "C", Transport.
Dress for Officers will be as for to-day. O.C. "C" Coy. will detail a Rear party of 1 Officer and 2 N.C.Os.

3. Haversack rations will be carried.

4. Officers' Valises will be stacked at Q.M. Stores ready to load at 7.a.m. Officers' Mess Kit will be stacked outside Coy. and H.Q. Messes ready to load at 7.a.m. Blankets will be stacked at Q.M. Stores at 7.a.m.

5. An advance party consisting of 2/Lieut. S.H. Phillips and Sgt. Dent will report to the Staff. Capt. at the Church at 8.30.a.m.

6. An advance party consisting of C.Q.M.Sgts. and 1. N.C.O. for Transport will report to Orderly Room at 7.30.a.m., and proceed to new billeting area, reporting to 2/Lieut. S.H. Phillips on arrival.

7. A Lorry will report to Q.M. Stores at 7.a.m. and will return for a second journey to convey surplus Kit of the Battalion and 9th Norfolk Regiment. Quartermaster will detail a responsible N.C.O. to return with this Lorry and ensure that all Kit left behind is brought intto the new area.

8. There will be no refilling on 30th October.

9. ACKNOWLEDGE.

Issued at 9.10 p.m. Captain,

29.10.17. A/Adjutant, 9th Battalion The Suffolk Regiment.

Copy No. 1. Commanding Officer.	Copy No. 9. Transport Officer.
" " 2. 2nd-in-Command.	" " 10. Quartermaster.
" " 3. O.C. "A" Coy.	" " 11. Medical Officer.
" " 4. O.C. "B" Coy.	" " 12. 71st Inf. Bde.
" " 5. O.C. "C" Coy.	" " 13. Retained.
" " 6. O.C. "D" Coy.	" " 14. Retained.
" " 7. O.C. Headquarters.	" " 15. War Diary.
" " 8. R.S.M.	" " 16. War Diary.

Appendix I

DRAFTS.

7.10.17.	11 O.Rs.	joined D.D.Bn.	4.10.17.
12.10.17.	6 "	" "	6.10.17.
15.10.17.	1 "	From 15th I.B.D.	
20.10.17.	3 "	joined D.D.Bn.	17.10.17.
30.10.17.	2 "	From 15th I.B.D.	

W. Fitch Captain,

A/Adjutant, 9th Battalion The Suffolk Rgt.

Rank.	Name.	Remarks.
Lieut.Col.	F. Latham. D.S.O.	Commanding.
Captain.	G.K. Moseley.	
Captain.	R. England. M.C.	O.C. "D" Coy.
A/Captain.	L. Wilmot-Johnson.	O.C. "C" Coy.
A/Captain.	W.F. Fitch. M.C.	A/Adjutant.
Lieut.	H.E. Falkner.	
Lieut. (A/Capt.)	R.B. Christophers.	O.C. "A" Coy.
Lieut.	G.F. Bryant.	
Lieut.	A.G. Douglas.	
2/Lieut.	F.D. Down.	
2/Lieut.	A.H. Stoyle.	
2/Lieut.	G. Hopkins.	
2/Lieut. (A/Capt.)	C.V. Canning.	O.C. "B" Coy.
2/Lieut.	F. Bullen.	Bomb. Officer.
2/Lieut.	E.W.N. Tayler.	
2/Lieut.	C.H. Miller. M.C.	L.G.O.
2/Lieut.	R.E. Cook.	
2/Lieut.	E.L. Turner.	Bn. Sig: Officer.
2/Lieut.	W.J. Futter.	
2/Lieut.	J.A. Simmons.	
2/Lieut.	W.A. Bridewell.	
2/Lieut.	S.H. Phillips.	Ass. Adjt.
2/Lieut.	G.M.T. Head.	
2/Lieut.	S.T. Marchant.	
2/Lieut.	A.C.J. Taylor.	
Capt. & Qr.Mr.	R. Starling.	Quartermaster.

ATTACHED.

Rank.	Name.	Remarks.
Major.	W.R. Whitson (2nd H.L.I.)	2nd-in-Command.
Captain.	V.E. Lloyd. (R.A.M.C.)	Medical Officer.
Lieut.	J.V. Lee. (2/1st R.E.K.Yeo.)	Trans: Offr:
Captain.	E.V. Blackburne. C.F.	C.of E. Chaplain.

CONFIDENTIAL.

Headquarters,
71st Inf. Bde.

War Diary for November 1917
herewith please.
Delay regretted.

S. Latham Lt Col.
Comd'g. 9th Bn. Suffolk Regt.

1/12/17

Instructions regarding War Diaries and Intelligence Summaries are contained in F. S. Regs., Part II, and the Staff Manual respectively. Title pages will be prepared in manuscript.

WAR DIARY
or
INTELLIGENCE SUMMARY.
(Erase heading not required.)

Army Form C. 2118.

9 Suffolk Regt
7/6
Vol 27

Place	Date	Hour	Summary of Events and Information	Remarks and references to Appendices
DENIER & BERLENCOURT	1.11.17		Bn in training	KH
	2.11.17		"	KH
	3.11.17		" Capt. C.K. Moseley admitted to F.A. sick.	KH
	4.11.17		"	KH
	5.11.17		"	KH
	6.11.17		" Lieut. C.J. Bryant left Bn to report to Divisional Wing for duty	KH
	7.11.17		" Reinforcements 7 ORs	KH
	8.11.17		"	KH
	9.11.17		"	KH
	10.11.17		" Capt. C.K. Moseley rejoined Bn from F.A.	KH
	11.11.17		"	KH
	12.11.17		" Reinforcements 5 ORs	KH
	13.11.17		" Regt Transport left Bn to proceed to unknown destination	
			O.O. No. 69 att'd. KH	Appendix II
	14.11.17		Lieut. C.J. Bryant rejoined Bn from Divisional Wing.	KH

A6945 Wt. W11422/M1160 350,000 12/16 D. D. & L. Forms/C./2118/14.

Instructions regarding War Diaries and Intelligence Summaries are contained in F. S. Regs., Part II. and the Staff Manual respectively. Title pages will be prepared in manuscript.

WAR DIARY
or
INTELLIGENCE SUMMARY.

(Erase heading not required.)

Army Form C. 2118.

Place	Date	Hour	Summary of Events and Information	Remarks and references to Appendices
DENIER & BERLENCOURT	15.11.17		Bn left DENIER, marched to FREVENT and entrained. Detrained at PERONNE and marched to hutments in MOISLAINS. O.O. No 70 attd. KH	Appendix B
MOISLAINS	16.11.17		Bn in hutments during the day. During the evening the Bn moved by route march to BOIS DESSART where it was billeted under canvas.	KH
BOIS DESSART	17.11.17		Bn under canvas & is issued with additional special equipment.	KH
	18.11.17		" " " "	KH
	19.11.17		" " " " Bn moved to positions of assembly in conjunction with Tanks preparatory to attack on HINDENBURG LINE north of BEAUCAMP: O.O. No 71 attd. KH	Appendix C
TRENCHES	20.11.17		Bn formed up in "Tank formation" (appendix D) at positions of assembly immediately in rear of the Tanks, of which there were two sections working with the Bn. (appendix E) Assembly point being in rear of our then Support line from ARGYLE Rd to BARRICADE Rd. 'A' Coy was formed up in one wave across the front allotted the Bn. 'D' Coy in two waves in rear of 'A' Coy and the Right section of Tanks and 'B' Coy in two waves in rear of 'A' Coy and the left section of Tanks. 'C' Coy had half a Coy	D E

A6945 Wt. W11422/M1160 350,000 12/16 D. D. & L. Forms/C./2118/14.

Army Form C. 2118.

9 Suffolk Regt.

Vol

Instructions regarding War Diaries and Intelligence Summaries are contained in F. S. Regs., Part II. and the Staff Manual respectively. Title pages will be prepared in manuscript.

WAR DIARY
or
INTELLIGENCE SUMMARY.
(*Erase heading not required.*)

Place	Date	Hour	Summary of Events and Information	Remarks and references to Appendices
TRENCHES	20.11.17		in rear of D Coy and half in rear of B Coy, in one wave, acting as Bn. support. Assembly was complete at about 1 am. and men wrapped themselves in blankets and slept in their positions. Zero hour was at 6.20 am. Tanks & Bn. moved forward at 6.10 am. and our Artillery barrage opened at zero. Bn. moved off in Lines of platoon column until through our own wire & within 200 yds of PLUSH TR. when platoons swung out into extended order. Some trouble was experienced from the Tanks not keeping direction until past PLUSH TR. Of the Right section two of the Tanks were out of action shortly after Zero, and the third lost direction leaving D Coy to get through the HINDENBURG wire, through the ordinary gaps made by the enemy. Enemy retaliatory barrage was weak but concentrated. A portion of D Coy was caught in the shell-fire and sustained several casualties. 'A' Coy dealt with PLUSH TR. successfully and Tanks and remainder of Bn passed through to attack the main HINDENBURG LINE. At 9.5 am messages were received that the Bn objectives had been captured, enemy resistance had been feeble + casualties slight. Coys were in touch with both	

A6945 Wt. W11422/M1160 350,000 12/16 D. D. & L. Forms/C./2118/14.

Instructions regarding War Diaries and Intelligence Summaries are contained in F. S. Regs., Part II. and the Staff Manual respectively. Title pages will be prepared in manuscript.

WAR DIARY
or
INTELLIGENCE SUMMARY.
(Erase heading not required.)

Army Form C. 2118.

Place	Date	Hour	Summary of Events and Information	Remarks and references to Appendices
TRENCHES	20-11-17		flank Bns. The Commanding Officer established Bn. HQ in the original enemy first line immediately after objectives had been captured.	
			Lieut G F Bryant who was commanding 'C' Coy then got into touch with 'B' Coy Tanks and moved his half Coy to the NE to follow the Tanks in and through MARCOING. 2/Lieut C. Hopkins went in advance to reconnoitre the country & find 2/Lieut A J C Taylor who was in command of the other half Coy. He proceeded to about L22 a 4.4. (MARCOING Sheet 57C N.E. 4. Ed 5A 1:10.000) and returning met the complete Coy in the valley about L 21. d, 2/Lieut A J C Taylor having joined Lieut Bryant from the Railway in L 21 c. The Coy moved forward in Artillery formation to a point about L. 21. d 80 70. where they were sniped at from their left front. The Coy extended to open order and advanced to the cross roads at L22 a 60. 63, then turned E. and attacked the village. Enemy resistance here was practically nil. 2/Lieut A J C Taylor & one platoon were detailed to remain in the vicinity of the Church to mop up some dug-outs & cellars. 2/Lieut C. Hopkins went in advance with	

A6945 Wt. W11422/M1160 350,000 12/16 D. D. & L. Forms/C./2118/14.

Army Form C. 2118.

Instructions regarding War Diaries and Intelligence Summaries are contained in F. S. Regs., Part II. and the Staff Manual respectively. Title pages will be prepared in manuscript.

WAR DIARY
or
INTELLIGENCE SUMMARY.
(Erase heading not required.)

Place	Date	Hour	Summary of Events and Information	Remarks and references to Appendices
TRENCHES	20.11.17		a platoon and the remainder of the Coy followed in close support, & pushed through to the Canal bridges & held them until the 29th Division had passed through. 'C' Coy with Tanks were the first troops to enter village, and passed through, mopping up as they went, to their objectives. Casualties in village one OR killed and one OR wounded. The Coy captured about 30 prisoners including one officer, and the papers of an enemy Divisional office. The Coy reported back to the Bn in the HINDENBURG FRONT LINE SYSTEM about 3.30 pm. Bn remained in the captured trenches and consolidated. Prisoners captured by the Bn amounted to about 150 including 3 officers, and 3 machine guns were also captured.	
			Casualties 8 ORs killed. 3 Offrs wounded (2/Lieut E.W.H. Taylor 2/Lieut W.A. Bridewell + 2/Lieut G.M.T. Head) 56 ORs wounded.	
			O.O. No 71 attd.	WH Appendix E
	21.11.17		Bn consolidated captured trenches	WH
	22.11.17		Bn moved to HINDENBURG SUPPORT SYSTEM. O.O No 72 attd	WH " F

A6945 Wt. W11422/M1160 350,000 12/16 D. D. & L. Forms/C./2118/14.

Instructions regarding War Diaries and Intelligence Summaries are contained in F. S. Regs., Part II, and the Staff Manual respectively. Title pages will be prepared in manuscript.

WAR DIARY
or
INTELLIGENCE SUMMARY.
(Erase heading not required.)

Army Form C. 2118.

Place	Date	Hour	Summary of Events and Information	Remarks and references to Appendices
TRENCHES	23.11.17		Bn in Reserve	NH
	24.11.17		"	NH
	25.11.17		"	NH
	26.11.17		" Bn moved to front line trenches O.O. No. 73 attd. NH	Appendix G
	27.11.17		Bn in front line trenches Casualties 1 OR wounded	NH
	28.11.17		" " Casualties 9 ORs wounded. Reinforcements 2 Offs 119	OR. NH
	29.11.17		" " Casualties 1 OR killed 1 OR wounded.	NH
	30.11.17		" " Casualties 1 Off + 24 ORs killed 2 Offrs + 12 ORs	
			wounded. (1 Off killed Major W.R. Whitson. 2 Offrs wounded Lieut C.J.	
			Bryant + 2Lieut A.J.C. Taylor) Enemy attacked a post held by C	
			Coy + post withdrew, but was afterwards re established. Enemy	
			attacked British line on our right flank and penetrating to GOUZEAUCOURT	
			compelled Regt. Transport to evacuate their lines	NH

[signature] Lt Col
Commanding 9th Bn Suffolk Regt

A6945 Wt. W11422/M1160 350,000 12/16 D. D. & L. Forms/C./2118/14.

SECRET. Copy No....#15....

9th Battalion The Suffolk Regt.
Operation Order No. 69.

Ref Sheet 51c.
1/40,000
& LENS 1/100,000.

1. The 71st Inf. Bde. Transport Group, including all riding horses will move to-night 13/14th ~~XXXXXX~~ November under the orders of the B.T.O.

2. Battalion Transport will pass GRAND RULLECOURT road junction O.15.a.98.98 (Sheet 51c) at 5.18.p.m.

3. Baggage and Supply Wagons will move with Unit's Transport.

4. The Battalion will refill as usual today. There will be a second refilling for the Brigade Transport Group and personnel at the Church LIENCOURT at 1.p.m.

5. An Advance Billeting party consisting of L.C.Stevenson & McLeod (Transpt) will meet a representative of the 6th Division at the Church ORVILLE at 2.p.m. today This Party will alsoact as guides to the Transport and will meet the Transport at HALLOY.

6. Cookers will proceed with Battalion Transport, but Camp Kettles will be left.

7. Officers Valises will be stacked outside Coy and H.Q. Messes ready to load at 2.p.m.
Only such Officers Mess Kit as is absolutely necessary will be retained, the remainder being stacked outside Coy ~~XXXXX~~ and Hqtr Messes ready to load at 2.p.m.

8. ACKNOWLEDGE.

Issued at 10.10am W Fitch Captain,

13.11.17. A/Adjutant, 9th Battalion The Suffolk Regiment.

Copy No.		
" "	1.	Commanding Officer.
" "	2.	2nd-in-Command.
" "	3.	O.C. "A" Coy.
" "	4	O.C. "B" Coy.
" "	5.	O.C. "C" Coy.
" "	6.	O.C. "D" Coy.
" "	7.	O.C. Headquarters.
" "	8.	71st Inf. Bde.
" "	9.	R.S.M.
" "	10.	Transport Officer.
" "	11.	Quartemaster.
" "	12.	Medical Officer.
" "	13.	Retained.
" "	14.	Retained.
" "	15.	War Diary.
" "	16.	War Diary.

H

SECRET. Copy No....16.....

9th Battalion The Suffolk Regiment.
Operation Order No. 70.

Ref. Map Sheet 51c.

1. The 71st Infantry Brigade is moving by rail to the Northern Training area on 15th November. The Battalion will move by rail from FREVENT.

2. On arrival at Detraining Station, Battalion will proceed by march route to billets.

3. Battalion will parade in column of route in full marching order ready to move off at 11.a.m. Head of column by "D" Coy's Mess BERLENCOURT, facing S.W. Order of march - Drums, H.Qtrs., "B", "D", "C", "A".

4. 2/Lieut. C.H. Miller.M.C. will report to entraining officer (2/Lieut. J.V. Tailby) at FREVENT Station at 1.p.m. He will report to the A/Adjutant before proceeding. Immediately on arrival at Detraining Station, he will report to the Detraining ~~XXX~~ Officer (Lieut. H.E.Hayne.)

5. Officers concerned will obtain certificates from the inhabitants certifying that there are no claims against the Battalion, or that they have been settled. Certificates to be handed to the A/Adjutant on parade at 11.a.m.

6. Blankets will be rolled in bundles of TEN and carefully labelled. "B", "C", & "D" Coys. will stack their's ready to load at the FORGE, BERLENCOURT by 9.30.a.m. "A" Coy. at Coy. H.Qtrs. by 9.30.a.m. and Headquarters at H.Qtrs. Mess by 9.30.a.m.

7. Officers Kit, Mess Kit, Coy. Boxes, Dixies, etc., will be stacked ready to load at same places and same time as in para. 6.

8. "B" & "C" Coy. Handcarts will parade EMPTY with their Coys. On arrival at entraining station, wheels will immediately be detached and carts moved into trucks of Coys. concerned. Handcarts of Headquarters and "A" Coy. will be sent to H.Qtrs. by 9.30.a.m.

9. 40 men to each coach.

10. Breakfast at 7.30.a.m. Unconsumed portion of day's rations will be carried on the men. Battalion will not arrive at billets until about midnight 15/16th inst.

11. ACKNOWLEDGE.

Issued at 11 p.m.......... R. Fitch Captain,

14.11.17. A/Adjutant, 9th Battalion The Suffolk Regiment.

Copy No. 1. Commanding Officer.	Copy No. 9. R.S.M.
" " 2. 2nd-in-Command.	" " 10. Transport Officer.
" " 3. O.C. "A" Coy.	" " 11. Quartermaster.
" " 4. O.C. "B" Coy.	" " 12. Medical Officer.
" " 5. O.C. "C" Coy.	" " 13. Retained.
" " 6. O.C. "D" Coy.	" " 14. Retained.
" " 7. O.C. Headquarters.	" " 15. War Diary.
~~" " 8. 71st Inf. Bde.~~	" " 16. War Diary.

8

SECRET. Copy No..........

9th Battalion The Suffolk Regiment.
Operation Order No. 71.

Ref. 57c N.E. 4 1/10.000.
57c S.E. 2 1/10.000. BEAUCAMP 1/10.000.
Parts of 57c N.E. and S.E.

1. The 71st Inf. Bde. on Z day will attack enemy's line N.N.E. of BEAUCAMP being a portion of an attack on a large scale and which is being launched in the form of a surprise.

2. The 9th Suffolk Regt., on the right and 1st Leicestershire Regt. on the left of Bde. Sector of attack will capture 1st system of the 1st Objective which is the HINDENBURG Front Line system, consisting of a front line and immediate support line.

3. FIRST PHASE - FIRST OBJECTIVE.
The 9th Suffolk Regt., will attack and capture Front Line L.31.d 14.28 to L.31.c.04.43 and Immediate Support Line L.31.d.30,53 to L.31.c.33.83 and also enemy advanced outpost line (PLUSH Trench) R.1.c.77.70 to Q.6.b.54.24.

The 1st Leicestershires will capture corresponding trenches on West and the 16th I.Bde.(8th Bedfordshire Regt.) will capture trenches on the East.

4. FIRST OBJECTIVE.
The 9th Norfolk Regt., will pass through and capture RIBECOURT with ½ Bn. 2nd Sherwood Foresters on their Eastern side connecting with troops of 16th I.Bde.

5. 2nd OBJECTIVE.
HINDENBURG Support Line System = 11th Essex Regt., on left and ½ Bn. Sherwood Foresters on Right.
All attacks will be in conjunction with Tanks, which will precede the various lines of attacking troops.

6. COY. ATTACK AREAS.
"A" Coy. will follow behind tanks on Battalion Frontage and Mop up PLUSH Trench obtaining touch with own troops to either flank.
"D" Company will work with right tank section and capture and hold No. 1 Area.
"B" Company will work with left tank section and capture and hold No. 2. Area.
"C" Company will work in support to Battalion attack with ½ Coy. working in support to each of the attacking companies.
The whole attack will take place in accordance with training through which the Battalion has recently been placed.

"D" Coy. will bomb down O.G.2. to L.31.d.30.55 until touch with ..8th BEDFORDSHIRE Regt., is obtained.
"C" Coy. will bomb down O.G.1 to L.31.d.14,28 until touch with ..8th BEDFORDSHIRE Regt. is obtained.

7.(a) In case either Flank Regt. (right or left) does not succeed in obtaining their objectives a defensive flank will be made on the threatened flank. In no case will any portion of trench once captured be evacuated, all men must know that other troops will unceasingly be coming up from the rear.

(b) Any Shell hole M.Gs. met with between PLUSH and HINDENBURG front system will be dealt with by "B" and "D" Coys. on their way past but in no case will any man of "B" and "D" Coy. go down a dug-out - this will be the duty of Support Company (i.e. "C" Coy.)

(c) On reaching objective Os.Commanding "B" and "D" Coys. will each send out Battle outposts consisting of Lewis Guns (and two riflemen with each gun).

(d) O.C."D" Coy.will detail a party of 1 N.C.O and 6 men to establish touch with the..2nd BEDFORDSHIRE.....Regt., (16.I.B.) Post to be at about L.31.d.30.55. East of the Road.

(e) All Postswill be Platoon Posts and not "individual" Posts so that control can be maintained.

(f) When objective has been gained platoon posts will be formed and in no case will any post be made within 20 yards from an existing Road so as not to impede future traffic.

(g) Each Commander will re-organise his Company platoon or section immediately he has gained his objective, after which Os.C.Coys. will arrange for a Counter-Attack Platoon.

8. After Foresters and Norfolks have passed through and taken 1st Objective "A" and "B" Coys.will form a portion of the Brigade Reserve and will only be moved on orders received from the B.G.C. Brigade.

9. Each Platoon Commander next to and immediately in rear of a Main Body Tank will march by Prismatic Compass - bearing °Magnetic and will bring his compass ready set for night marching to be checked by Adjutant at 1.p.m. 19th inst. If a Tank is noticed to be losing the general line of direction the Platoon Commander concerned will at once signal to Tank by waving his hand so that Tank gets on to its proper bearing.

10. 1 Sub-Section of 71st M.G.Company will be employed with Battalion, and is to be used as Guns of opportunity and for the defence of the Objectives gained and will move to O.G.1 with Left Support ½ Company.

11. 1 Stokes Mortar and team of 71st T.M.Battery will be employed to overcome any resisting points and will move to O.G.1 with ~~Right~~ LEFT Support ½ Company.

1 L.Cpl. and 10 men already detailed will carry Stokes Ammunition for this gun and will remain with gun. This N.C.O and 10 men will parade at Orderly Room at 11.a.m. 19th inst., in Fighting Order complete with light packs and 1 blanket and will then proceed to join T.M.Battery and move to position of assembly on Y day with T.M. team.

12. Battalion Headquarters until Battalion Objective is taken will be in dug-out at R.7.c.05.75 where reports will be sent. Battalion Headquarters will later move into VALLEY TRENCH (O.G.1) just East of ARGYLE ROAD at a point and time to be notified after objective has been captured. Os.C.Companies will be notified when Battalion Headquarters is about to move.

13. With a view to exploiting success as soon as the 2nd Objective of the Brigade has been taken (THE "BROWN LINE") "C" Coy. will proceed to MARCOING in order to Support the TANKS of "B" Battalion Tank Corps in securing the bridges at L.23.a.65.00, L.23.a.40.85 and L.23.b.30.80.

("A" Coy. of 1st K.S.L.I is also going forward with the same object in view)

It will cover its advance by patrols and its left flank will be covered by M.G.Fire from the HINDENBURG SUPPORT LINE ~~XXXXXX~~ by the 2 sections M.G.C. advancing with 2nd Sherwood Foresters and 11th Essex.

Its advance will be by bounds first to the road Junction at L.22.a.05.10., the Company of the 1st K.S.L.I advancing to the road junction at L.22.d.30.50. The advance will then be pushed through MARCOING to the bridges and touch will be gained with the Tanks which have been sent on and the bridges held until the arrival of the 29th Division which may be expected in an hour or less.

The 20th Division is also pushing forward troops to the road junction at L.22.d.30.50.

14. Battalion Station Call will be " O.Q.19. "
No.1 Runner Post at Q.12.a.60.25.
No.2 " " at Q. 6.d.20.05.

Battalion will have a trench telephone line to Brigade Headquarters

Fullerphone communication <u>only</u> to be used before ZERO, after ZERO D.111s may be used.

15. (a) <u>AFTER ZERO</u>:-
Brigade code call will be K.F.Q. Battalion code call will be K.F.I.

(b) No.3 Runner Post at Q. 6.b.50.25.
Brigade forward station at L.31.c.10.40. Battalion wire will be run from Bn.Hdqtrs.to Bde.Forward Station.

(c) As soon as 1st Objective is captured Brigade forward station will move forward to the vicinity of L.25.d.50.50.
No.4 Runner Post at L.31.c.10.40.
No.5 in MOLE TRENCH L.31.a.70.30.

(d) Brigade visual stations will be at Q.11.d. near BROKEN TRENCH, near BOAR COPSE (Q.6.c) and at L.31.c.10.40.

(e) When Brigade Headquarters advances it will move to the vicinity L.31.c.10.40.

16. <u>"MOPPING UP" AREAS</u>.:-
After the objectives of the Battalion are taken Companies are responsible for areas as under :-
<u>"A" COY.</u>
PLUSH TRENCH
from Q.6.b.55.20 to R.1.c.60.80.,and the area in front of it up to VALLEY TRENCH bounded on the WEST by ARGYLE ROAD and on the EAST by a line from R.1.c.60.80 to L.31.c.99.20.

<u>"B" COY.</u>
The area bounded by the four points L.31.c.00.40 - L.31.a.5.5.- L.31.a.90.25.- L.31.c.3.3.

<u>"D" COY.</u>
The area bounded by the four points L.31.c.3.3 - L.31.d.1.3.- L.31.b.6.2 - L.31.a.90.25.

~~15~~ 17 Positions of Dumps will be issued later.

~~16.~~ 18. ACKNOWLEDGE.

Issued at 8.45 am

W Fitch Captain,

19/11/1917. A/Adjutant., 9th Battalion The Suffolk Regt.

Copy No.1.	Commanding Officer.
" " 2.	O.C."A" Coy.
" " 3.	O.C. "B" Coy.
" " 4.	O.C. "C" Coy.
" " 5.	O.C. "D" Coy.
" " 6.	71st Infantry Brigade.
" " 7.	Retained.
" " 8.	Retained.
" " 9.	War Diary.
" "10.	War Diary.

NOT TO BE TAKEN INTO FRONT TRENCHES.

****

INFANTRY AND TANK OPERATIONS.

1. GENERAL PRINCIPLES.

1. The difference in the conditions under which the attack is launched necessitates quite different tactics from those which are suitable in the case of an attack under a creeping barrage.

2. The main differences in conditions are :-

(a) The supporting artillery is for the most part unregistered.

(b) The enemy's wire is not destroyed along the whole front so as to be passable everywhere but only crushed down to form practicable passages at certain points.

(c) The enemy's trenches and defences, particularly in the case of the front system, have not been subjected to a preliminary bombardment and are more or less intact.

(d) The enemy has not had his moral shaken by continuous heavy shelling nor by harassing fire preventing his receiving supplies and food regularly.

On the other hand it is to be hoped that the attack would take him by surprise with the result that :-

(e) His defences would only be normally manned and the garrison not fully on the alert.

(f) There would be no special concentration of guns to meet an attack so that the hostile barrage would not be likely to be nearly so intense as that met with in normal offensive operations.

(g) The sudden appearance of line of advancing infantry preceded by lines of tanks might quite well produce a momentary panic.

3. The effect of these conditions is :-

(a) That our artillery must lift off the successive objectives whilst the infantry is still at a considerable distance from them. Therefore the garrison of the defences will have time after the artillery lifts and before the infantry drops into the trench to be assaulted, in which to man the defences and open fire.

(b) That the assaulting troops, whether they advance in lines or in columns, must pass through the wire in columns at a few definite points. These constitute defiles on which the enemy could concentrate his fire and in which the attacking infantry would offer a vulnerable target.

(c) That the assaulting infantry does not strike the whole of an objective in one wave simultaneously along its whole front.

4. 3 (a) Is to a certain extent compensated for by the fire which the tanks can maintain as they advance but the infantry must be prepared to supplement this by their own fire.

It is important to push on to the assault without a check and not to lose distance on the tanks. Losses in crossing a fire-swept area are in proportion to the time taken in crossing it. Failure to arrive close on the heels of the tanks means loss of the benefit of the panic and confusion caused by them.

At the same time the volume and accuracy of the enemy's fire can be reduced by our own covering fire. Covering fire can be

maintained/

maintained without delaying the advance if the advance is carried out by alternate rushes, one body of troops, e.g. one section, covering with its fire the movement of another.

Riflemen and even moreso Lewis guns cannot produce their most effective fire when they are on the move. Therefore they should move quickly from one fire position to another.

5. To meet 3 (b) infantry once committed to a passage through the wire should get through at its best speed. It should not be committed to the wire until it is apparent that it can go straight through without a check, it should make the fullest use of the breadth of the gap, and if compelled to check in the wire should extend and lie down in the space between two belts.

Whilst one body of infantry is passing through the wire covering fire by the infantry remaining on our side of the wire is of increased importance.

Bunching at either end of a passage through the wire or checking in it are both particularly dangerous.

If the infantry closes up on the tank it is following it will have to halt to wait till it has a clear passage through the wire or go through slowly behind the tank. Therefore the tank is started 50 to 100 yards ahead of the infantry and this distance should be kept.

The best time for the first infantry to begin the passage of the wire is when the tank it is following has reached the trench it is to attack.

6. To meet the situation in 3 (c) the tanks move along the trenches from the point at which they strike them and infantry must follow close after them to take advantage of the panic they cause and to catch the defenders when they are keeping down in the trench to avoid the fire of the tank.

If this is done little opposition should be met with in the process of clearing up but if the enemy is given time to recover after the tank has passed the operation of clearing a trench may degenerate into bombing up it in the face of opposition which is slow and uncertain in its results.

Every tank clearing a trench should be accompanies by bombers in the trench and whenever possible by men moving along the top. The duty of the bombers is to clear dug-outs and shelters and to kill or capture a beaten enemy. Opposition if met with can be best dealt with by the men moving along the top, using their rifles. Quite a small number of men will suffice for this latter duty but enough men must work along inside the trench to allow of thorough cleaning up without dropping back behind the tank as it moves along, i.e. there must be enough men moving along the bottom in a section of trench to allow of small parties being dropped where necessary whilst the remainder keep following up the tank.

7. Lewis-guns are not of much use in the bottom of a deep trench, nor when moving steadily along behind a tank.

8. Each body of infantry must know what its task is and must not imagine that it is merely to follow a particular tank.

If one of the main-body tanks of a section breaks down the advanced guard tank of the same section takes its place and takes on its duties.

Infantry, however, once through the wire must not wait if its tank has broken down but must carry on with its allotted task.

9. Quick initiative and thorough control of his command are specially necessary for each platoon and section commander in these tactics.

11. GENERAL LINES OF AN ATTACK.

ASSEMBLY. 1. A tank section usually forms up for attack with the advanced guard tank about 100 yards in advance of the main-body tanks and with the latter abreast of one another and about 50 yards apart.

The infantry may either be formed up, before the advance, in attack formation behind its tanks or may be assembled in the open or in trenches in front of the assembly place of the tanks and join in behind the latter as they pass.

ATTACK FORMATION. (See diagram A.) 2. The three tanks of a section move off together but the right tank moves slower than the left hand tank at first to allow the latter to gain 50 to 100 yards advance on it.

The infantry will be formed in waves of platoons in two lines with the inner flanks of platoons covering off their own tanks.

Platoons detailed as "Stops" will form the first wave, those detailed as "Trench Clearers" the second wave. Behind these again will move the support companies in any suitable formation.

The Lewis-gun and rifle sections of the "Stop" platoons should form the first line of the first wave as they represent the fire-power of the platoon. As a rule the Lewis-gun section will be best placed on the outer flank.

The order of the sections in trench clearing platoons cannot be definitely laid down. A suggested arrangement is as follows :- The Lewis-gun section is placed on the inner flank of the rear line and the bombing section on the inner flank of the front line. These two sections pass through the wire first, the bombing section on the left and the Lewis-gun section on the right. The Lewis-gun section can then be got into position at once on the parados to cover the movement of subsequent sections and platoons through the wire, and the bombing section can drop into the trench to follow up the tank. The rifle-grenade section follows the bombers into the trench, the rifle-section should follow the Lewis-gun section and if possible keep along the top on the far side of the trench, following up the tank.

The question of the relative position of sections in trench-clearing platoons depends upon the order in which they are required.

ACTION OF THE TANKS. 3. The tanks should maintain their formation until they reach the wire of the main line. The right hand main-body tank must not incline inwards to follow the left hand tank too soon but should rather make a slight detour to the right to allow more time for the infantry following the left hand tank to get through the wire in front of it. The right hand tank must allow at least the clearers of the left hand platoon to precede it.

ACTION OF THE INFANTRY. 4. When the left-hand main-body tank reaches the wire the "Stops" following it should rush up to the best fire position on our side of the wire from which to cover the advance of their own trench clearing platoon.

The/

The trench cleaners should lie down until they see that they will have a clear passage through the wire and then move quickly after their tank. They should time their advance so that the leading sections enter the passage through the wire about when the tank is astride of the trench.

If the left hand trench "Stops" have a good fire position they should remain where they are until the right hand tank and its trench-clearers have passed through the wire. If their position is not good they should try and get through in front of the right hand tank and take up a better position on the other side.

The action of the right hand infantry in crossing each belt of wire will be similar to that already described for the left hand infantry.

Diagram A.

Normal Attack Formation.

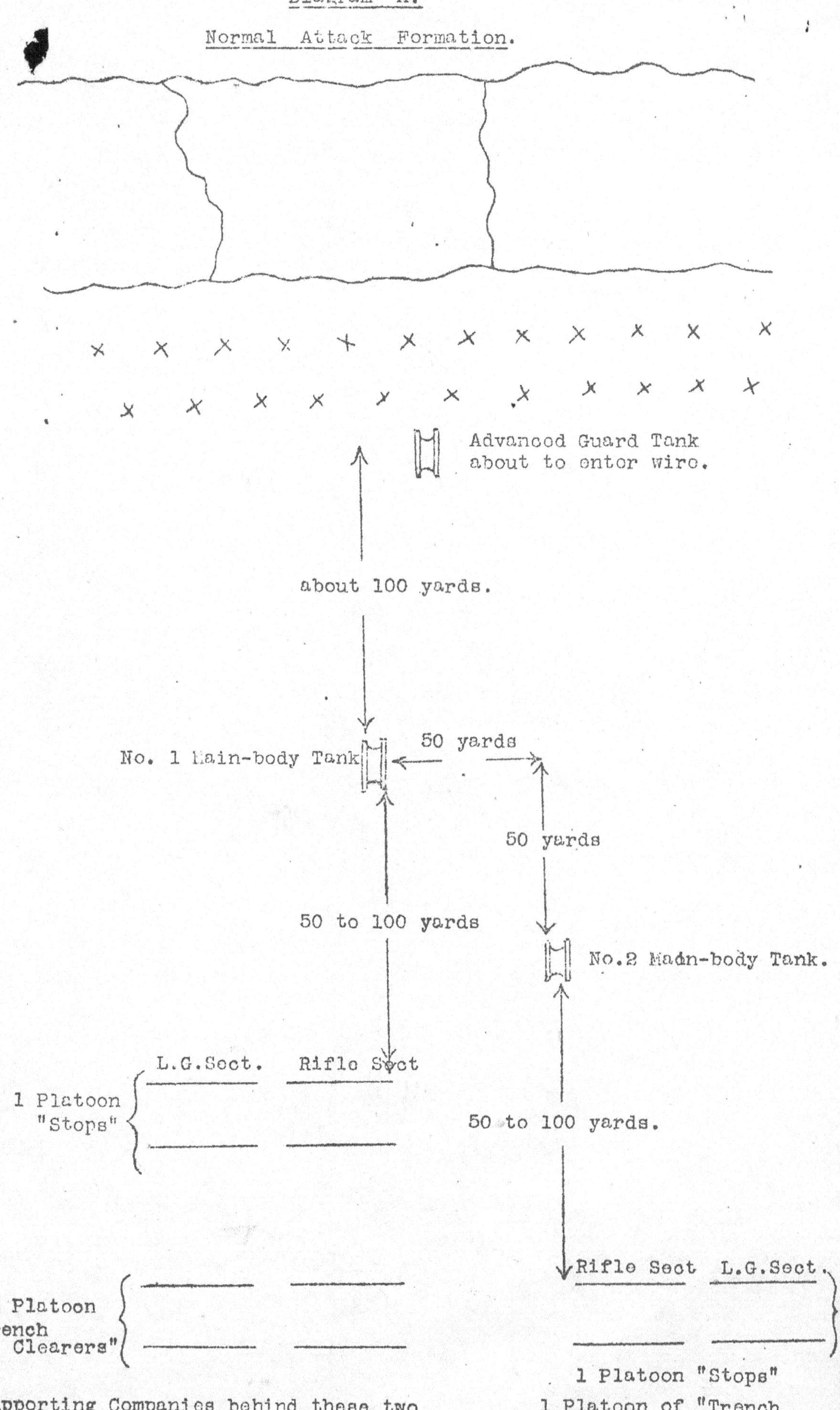

Supporting Companies behind these two companies in any suitable formation.

1 Platoon of "Trench Clearers" behind.

Diagram B.

Position when No.1 M.B. Tank is in the wire.

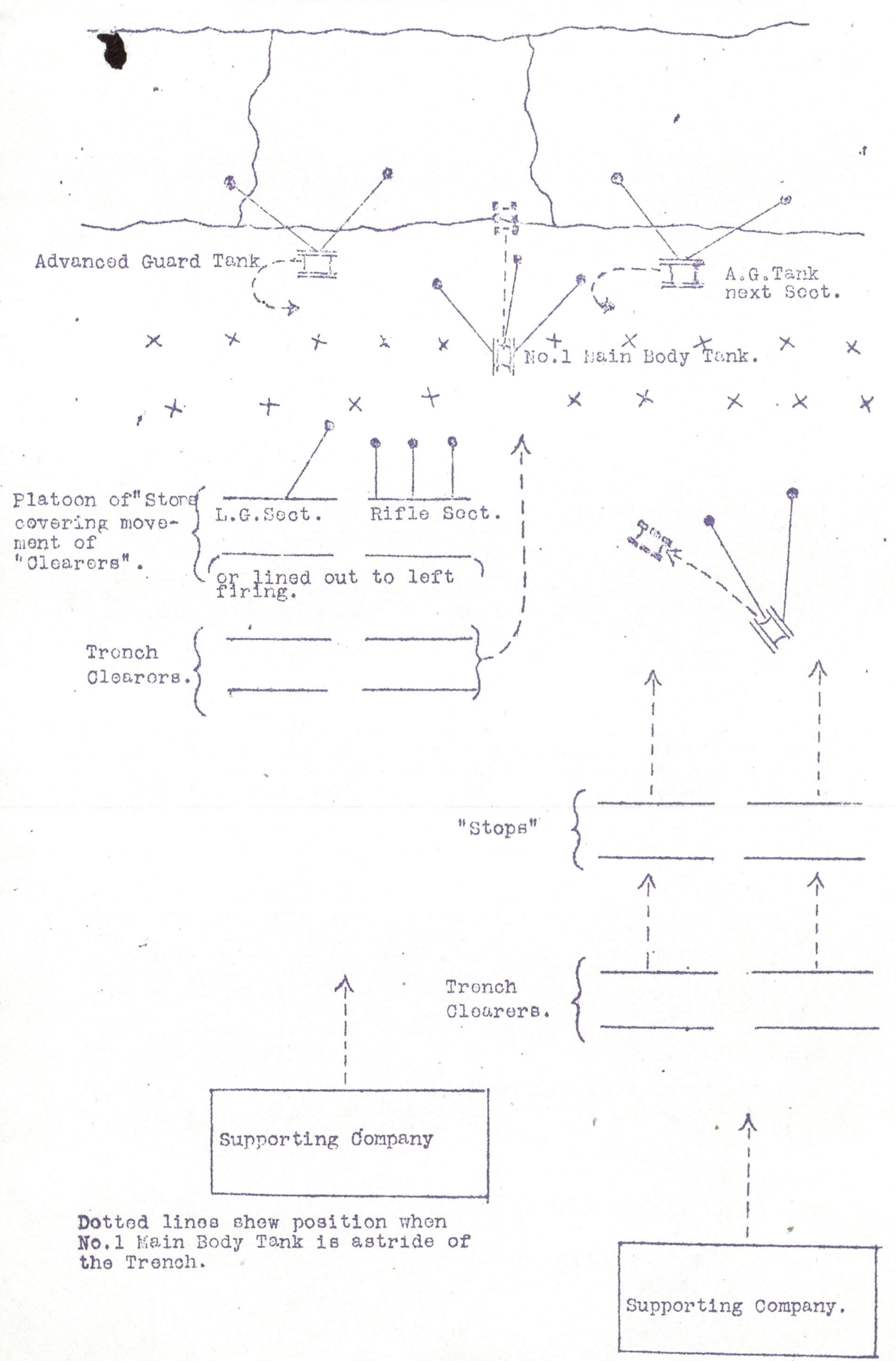

Dotted lines shew position when No.1 Main Body Tank is astride of the Trench.

S E C R E T.

TRAINING NOTE

TANK AND INFANTRY OPERATIONS

WITHOUT METHODICAL ARTILLERY PREPARATION.

1. SECRECY.

This training note is published for general information and instruction. Its contents, however, must be kept secret, as the knowledge of the tactics laid down in it might prove of value to the enemy.

2. INFANTRY TANK BATTLE.

Where surprise is essential, occasion may arise when it is advisable to launch an attack at such short notice that it is not possible to prepare it methodically by artillery: in this case it may be found feasible to use Tanks instead. Under these circumstances, no wire cutting being possible, the Tanks will have to lead the Infantry through the enemy's wire and protect them during their attack.

3. TANK SECTION ATTACK AREAS. (Diagram 1.)

Given the objective to be attacked, the first thing to do is to divide it into a series of ' Tank Section Attack Areas ! These areas should generally include a tactical point, for if these are captured, it should not be difficult to clean up the trenches between them. If the objectives is part of a system of trenches, the area selected should if possible be free of communication trenches, for if these are deep and broad the Tank may experience serious trouble in crossing them. Thus in diagram 1. the area A"B"C"D. would be more suitable than E"F"G"H, or B"F"G"H, because A"B"C"D. contains fewer communication trenches, that is obstacles to the Tank's progress.

4. TANK ECHELONS.

The Tanks operating against each separate objective should constitute one Tank Echelon. This Echelon should be divided into two waves or lines - the Advanced Tanks and the Main Body. The strength of the Advanced Tanks will vary, but normally it may be taken at one third of the total Tanks employed against any one objective. If possible, Tank Companies should be kept intact and not split up over two or more objectives.

5. DUTY OF ADVANCED TANK.

The Duty of the Advanced Tank is to proceed slightly ahead of the Main Body and threaten the enemy and keep down his fire whilst the Main Body followed by the Infantry advance on and cross the enemy's wire and trenches. Once this duty is finished, the Advanced Tank will become a reserve to the Main Body, and render it, if required, immediate assistance.

6. DUTY OF THE TANK MAIN BODY.

The duty of the Main Body is to place the Infantry through the wire and to assist and protect them whilst capturing the objectives.

7. AREA OF OPERATIONS OF TANK MAIN BODY AND ADVANCED GUARD.

The Area of Operations of the Main Body is the objective itself, that of the Advanced Tank the ground immediately in front of the objective and, generally speaking, on our side of the trench to be captured.

8. NUMBER OF TANKS TO FRONTAGES.

The proportion of Tanks to be employed on any one front will depend more on the numbers of tactical points this front contains than on its extent. As a rough rule the allotment of Tanks to any one front may be calculated at one to every 100 to 200 yards of frontage.

9. TANK FORMATION OF ATTACK.

The Tank Unit of attack will be a section of 3 Tanks which will work together, one acting as the advanced Tank and Two as the Main Body Tanks. If one of the Main Body Tanks break down, the Advanced Tank will replace it and lead the Infantry on.

The formation of attack should be one which will permit of Tanks in Section of threes being launched at definite tactical points, rather than one in line equally distributed along the whole frontage; for the object of the Tanks is to penetrate the objective at several points, place the Infantry through at these points and then protect the Infantry as they work down the trenches.

Briefly the object of the Tank is to break the enemy's line and then assist the Infantry to envelop the unbroken portions of it.

10. ALLOTMENT OF INFANTRY TO TANKS.

Normally the Infantry will only follow the Main Body. The number allotted to operate with each Tank will depend on the strength of the objective to be attacked and the nature and situation of the lines of approach leading up to it. In most cases it will not be advisable to allot more than one platoon (36 to 40 men) to follow immediately each Tank; as the path crushed down throughthe wire by the two tracks of the Tank will only permit of men moving along them in single file, and any crowding at the point of penetration may result in unnecessary casualties.

This allotment of one platoon per Tank does not prevent several other platoons following on behind and making use of the paths created. If the enemy's fire is not heavy, it should generally be feasible to traverse one path by four platoons without undue delay. Hurried crossings must, however, be avoided, for, if the leading men catch their feet in the crushed down wire and pull it up, delay to those in rear will result.

11. FORMATION OF THE INFANTRY. (See diagram 2).

In order to facilitate the approach, Infantry should be organised in Section single files. These single files can advance either in small Platoon columns of four single files abreast, or in two of two abreast, or singly. They can also be rapidly formed into line should it be necessary for them to use their rifles. Whoever is at the head of the file is automatically file leader. This system enables command to be maintained during the approach and is most suitable when working with Tanks, as eventually single files have to be formed to cross the enemy's wire.

12. ORGANISATION OF THE INFANTRY FORMATION. (See diagram 3).

The Infantry for each Trench Objective should be organised in three waves or lines.

1. Trench cleaners.
2. Trench stops.
3. Supports.

Their duties will be as follows :-

1. To operate with Tanks and clear the trenches.
2. To form 'Stops' in the trenches at various points and to improve paths through the wire. To mark

these paths by means of flags so that those following may see where gaps exist. To place ladders in the captured trench, to prepare the parados for rapid exit.

3. To support (1) and (2) and form an Infantry Advanced Guard on the further side of the trench to protect the advance of the next Echelon.

Diagram 3 gives diagramatically the formation suggested for a Company of Tanks and two Battalion of Infantry.

13. ORGANISATION OF A TRENCH CLEANING PLATOON.

The Trench Cleaning Platoon should be organised on the lines laid down in S.S.143, the bombers (1 section) alone entering the trench, the remaining three sections working with the Tank along the Trench in the open.

14. FORMING UP FOR ATTACK. (See diagram3)

Tanks and Infantry will usually have to form up during hours of darkness, consequently if noise and confusion are to be prevented the most complete preparation for their assembly must be undertaken, and all falling in and movements must be reduced to a simple drill,

The preparation will consist in marking out the exact places where Tank and Infantry will stand and in taping and preparing routes to the places of assembly (Starting Point) and forward from them.

Diagram 3 shows a method of forming up a Company for the attack : A,B,C,D, are the advanced Tanks, E.F., G.H., I.J., and K.L. those of the Main Body. Immediately behind these are placed 8 platoons each on a file frontage, that is two sections in single file side by side, and two in a similar formation behind them, these 8 Platoons form the Trench Cleaners. At 50 yards distance behind the Trench Cleaners come 8 more Platoons in similar formation, these are the Trench Stops. Behind these, at whatever distance considered necessary, is drawn up the supports in two lines, consisting of 8 platoons each as shown in Diagram 3.

15. MOVEMENT FORWARD.

The movement forward will usually take place at dawn, the whole echelon moving off together, the Advanced Tanks slightly ahead. Zero hour must be selected at a time which will permit of the Tank Drivers seeing their way.

16. THE ATTACK. (See Diagrams4 and 5).

The Advanced Tanks will cross straight overthe enemy's wire and swing to the left and move along the enemy's trench close to the parapet. They will not cross the trench until the Main Body Tanks and the Infantry are over.

The Main Body Tanks will traverse the enemy's trench at the same spot, so as to economise in the use of fascines. One will move down the fire trench and the other proceed forward to the support trench, where if necessary, it will cast its fascine and cross over, then turn and work down the support trench to the left.

Diagrams 4 and 5 illustrate the action of two tanks clearing a trench.

Once a Tank Section Attack Area is cleared, the Advanced and Main Body Tanks should move forward and join those of the next echelon, which will probably by this time have gone through. By so doing each Echelon will be reinforced as the battle proceeds. Infantry will not accompany these Tanks in this move.

Once the Infantry have been well placed in the enemy's trenches by the Tanks, they must depend on themselves to do all minor cleaning up work, as the number of Tanks available will seldom permit of Tanks remaining with them throughout an entire operation.

Should a Tank break down, the Infantry must press on by themselves: their security will depend on so doing.

17. RALLYING.

If Tanks have been ordered to rally, so that they may re-organise for further operations, Infantry must release them from their protective duties at the earliest moment, for delay in doing so may cause failure in the plan of attack.

18. PRECAUTIONS IN CROSSING WIRE.

Tanks working in threes should cross the wire at the same spot, or if this is not feasible, at intervals of not less than 100 yards. The reason for this is that it has been found that if two Tanks cross the wire at a less interval, the second Tank crossing sometimes loosens the wire crushed down by the first and partially closes the gap first made.

Infantry should keep from 25 to 50 paces behind the Tank as it enters the wire, so as not to get entangled in any trailing strands. Crowding round the Tank must be guarded against and also hurried progress along paths made, for otherwise loops of wire may be pulled up by the men's feet and the advance of those in rear delayed.

19. TANK FASCINES.

Every fighting Tank will carry a Tank fascine. This consists of a large bundle of brushwood about 4ft. 6in. in diameter. It is used to fill in wide trenches and so enable the Tank to cross them.

Whenever a Tank fascine is used, the Tank Commander will have a red and yellow flag thrown out of the Tank, if he is unable to fix it in the ground. All Infantry, and especially those of the Trench Stopping party, must be warned to look out for these flags and when they find one, to stick it into the parapet three paces away to the right or left of the Tank fascine. The flag must not be placed immediately opposite the fascine, otherwise the next Tank crossing will either knock it over or have to send a man out to remove it.

20. TRAINING.

The training of Infantry and Tanks will be carried out on the above lines, the following points being observed :-

(i) Exercises should be very simple.

(ii) The Assembly prior to the Attack and the attack between Infantry and a Section of three Tanks should be worked out as a drill and practised until it becomes automatic.

(iii) All attacking units should practise at least one Assembly at night.

(iv) Frequent practice in crossing wire which Tanks have crushed down should be carried out.

(v) Means of dealing with unexpected hostile machine guns should be carefully thought out by both Infantry and Tank Commanders and, if possible, practised during training.

--------ooo------------

DIAGRAM 1

SUPPORT LINE

FIRE LINE

A B C D E F G H

DIRECTION OF TANK ADVANCE

D

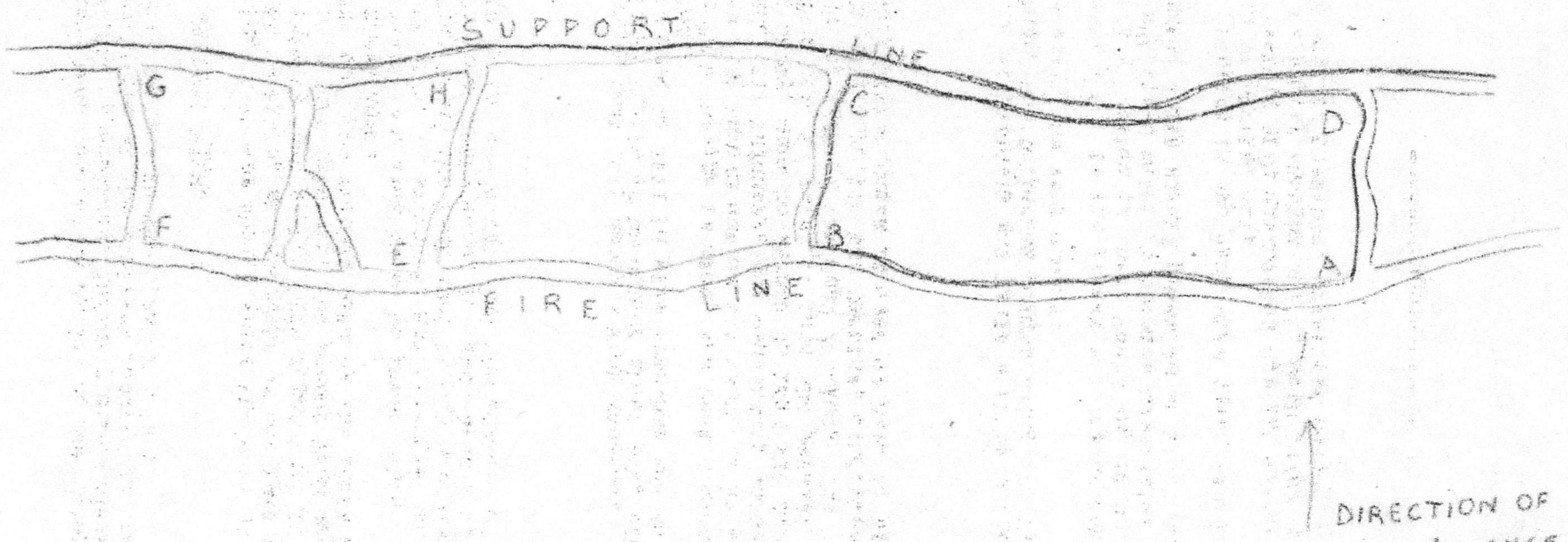

DIAGRAM 2

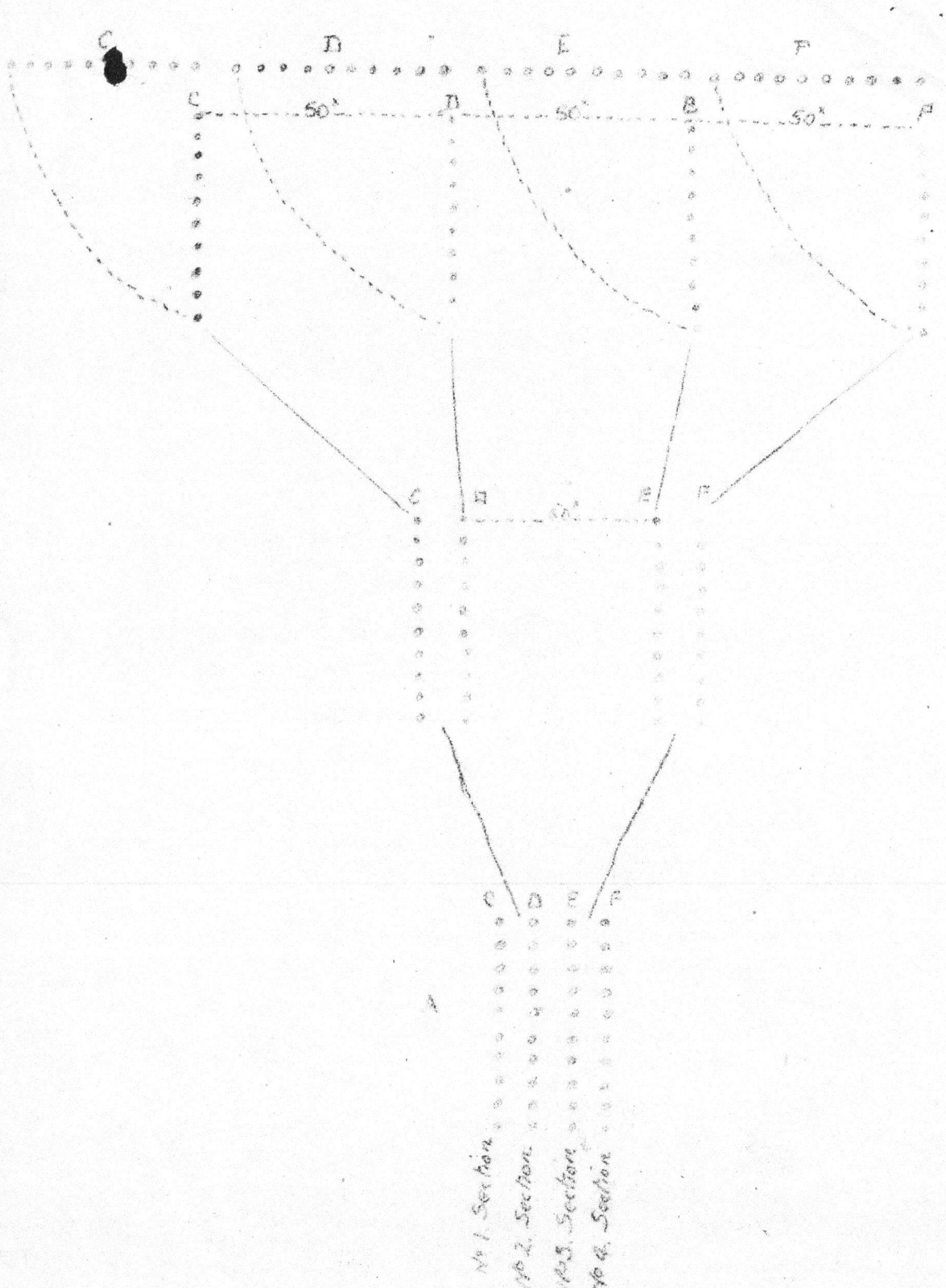

C D E & F are each a Section in single file.
A is a complete Platoon of four Sections in single file
The intervals between files & single files may be whatever is required

DIAGRAM 3

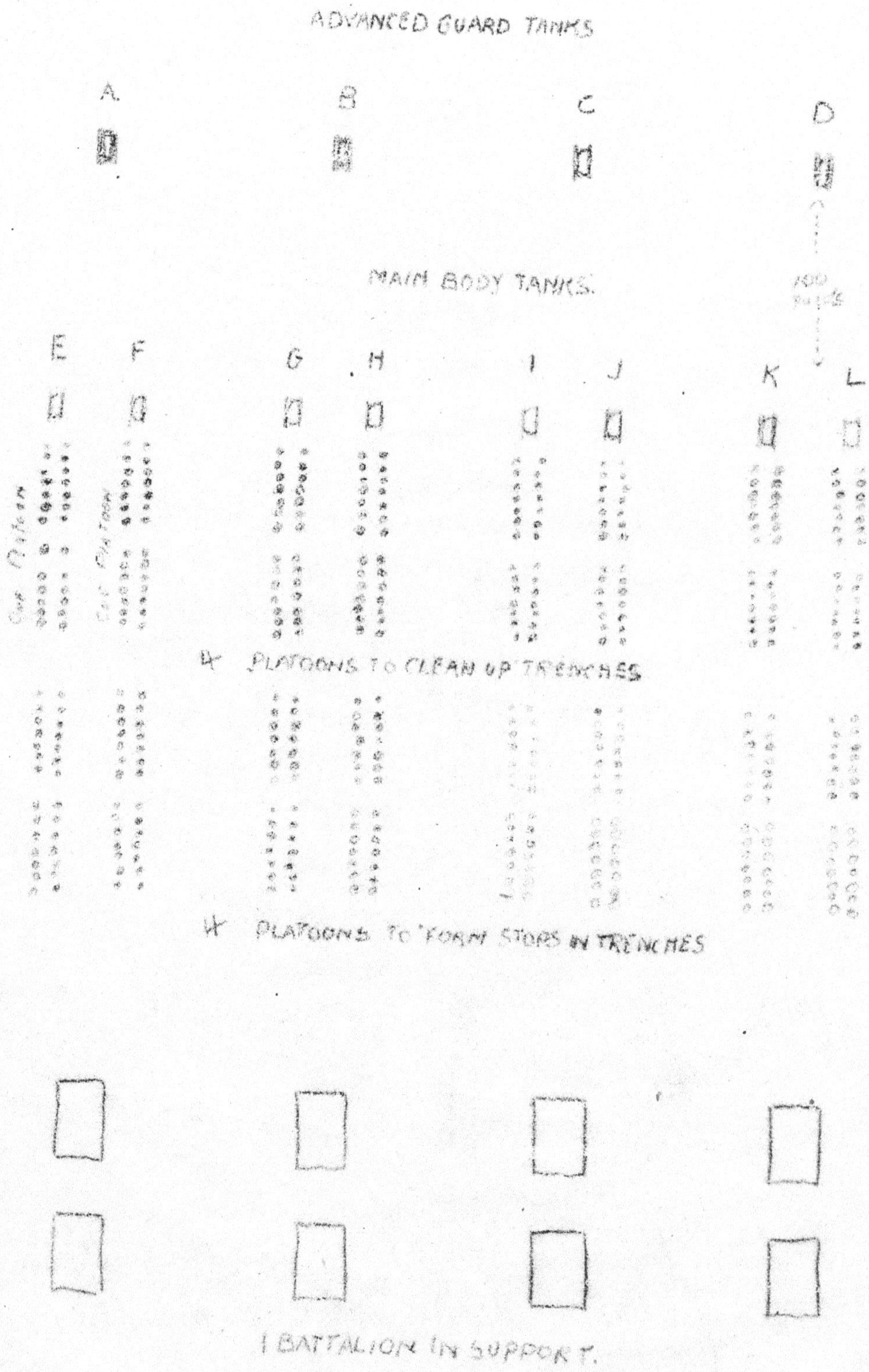

ADVANCED GUARD TANKS

A. B C D

100 yards

MAIN BODY TANKS.

E F G H I J K L

Coy Platoon

Coy Platoon

4 PLATOONS TO CLEAN UP TRENCHES

4 PLATOONS TO FORM STOPS IN TRENCHES

1 BATTALION IN SUPPORT.

DIAGRAM 4.

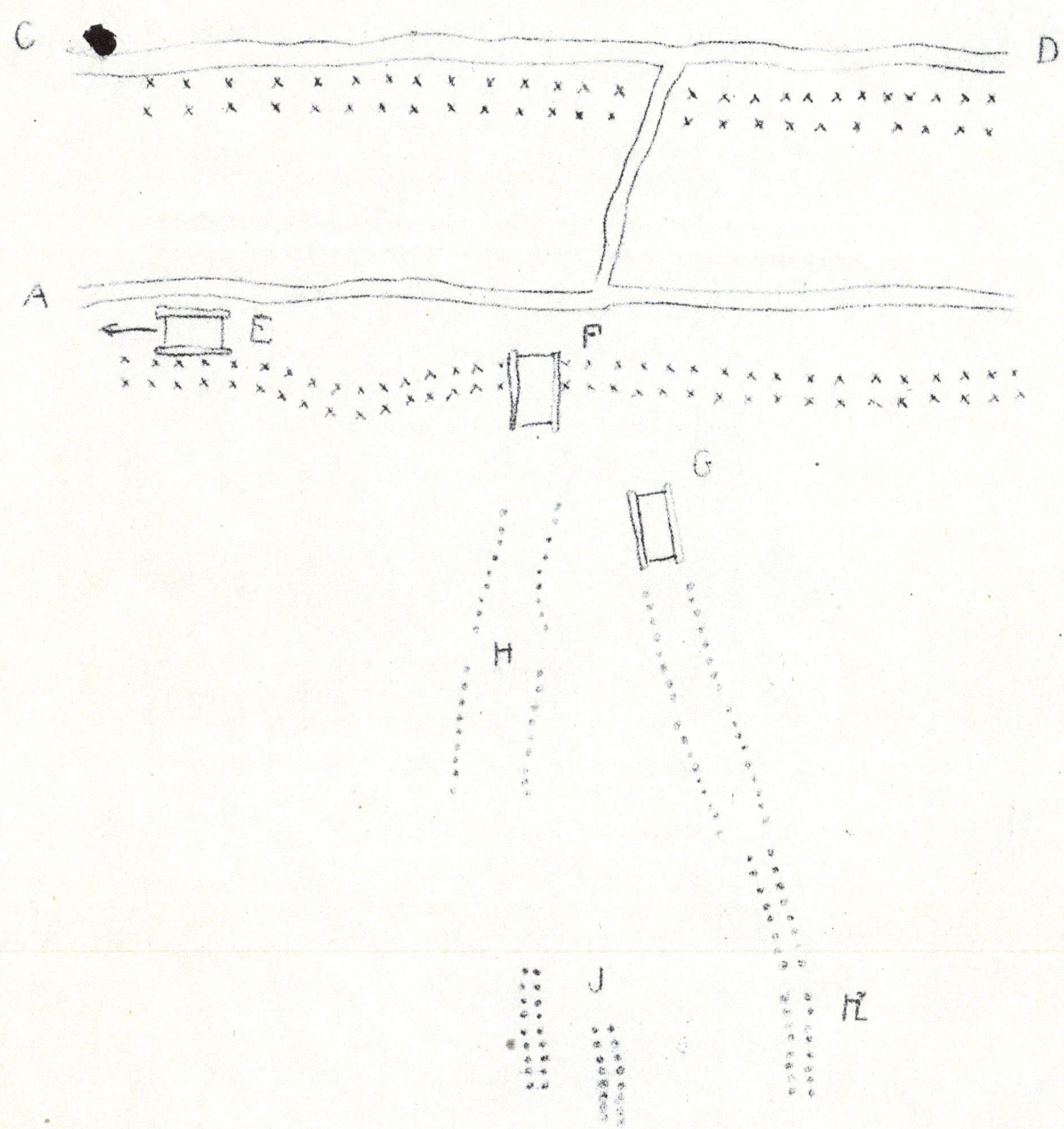

AB - FIRE TRENCH
CD = SUPPORT TRENCH
E - ADVANCED GUARD TANK
F&G - MAIN BODY TANKS
H&I - TRENCH CLEANERS (1 PLATOON EACH)
J&K - TRENCH STOPS (1 PLATOON EACH)
L&M - SUPPORTS (2 PLATOONS EACH)

L

M

DIAGRAM 5.

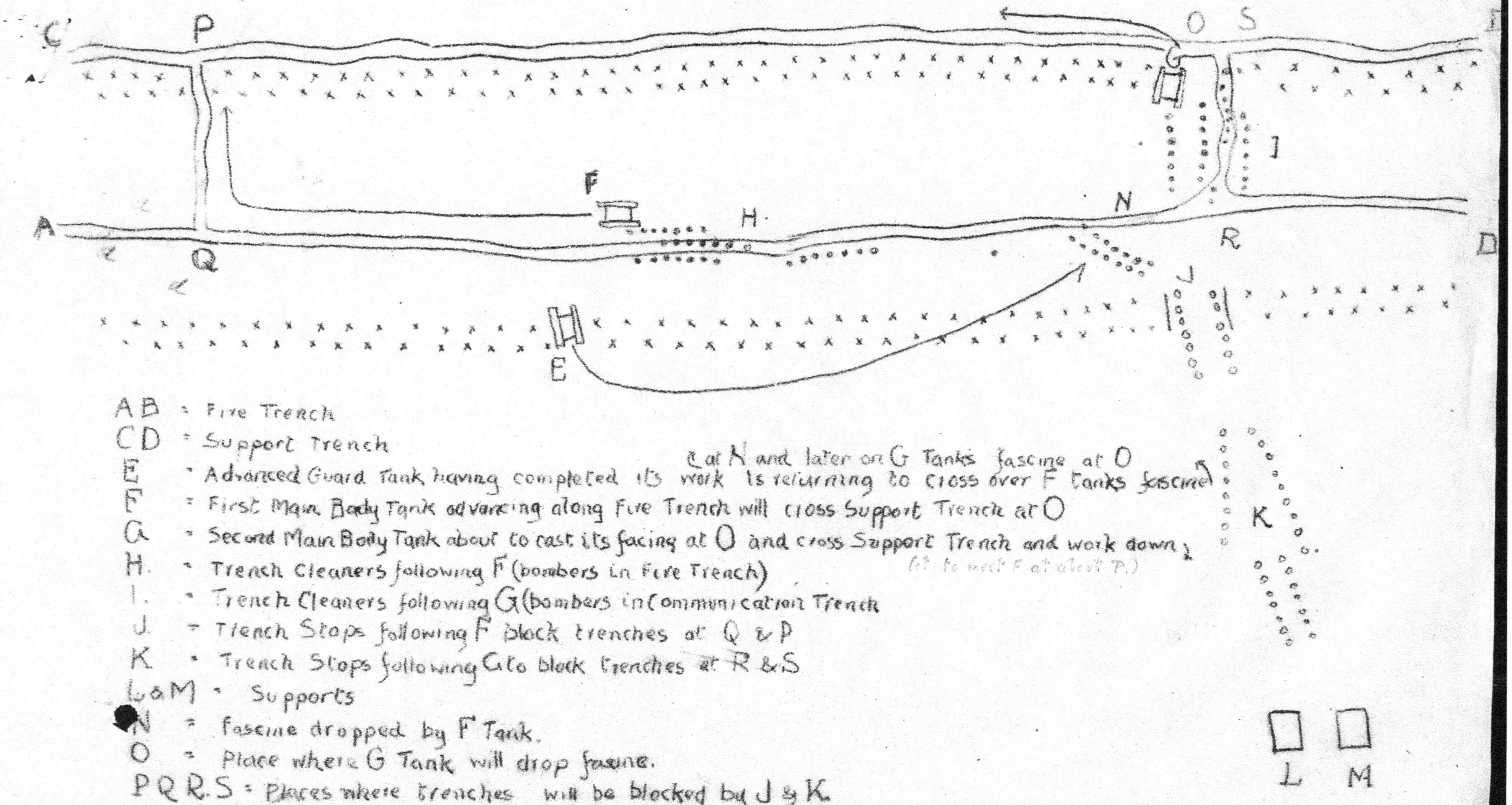

AB = Fire Trench
CD = Support Trench
E = Advanced Guard Tank having completed its work is returning to cross over F tanks fascine (at N and later on G Tanks fascine at O)
F = First Main Body Tank advancing along Fire Trench will cross Support Trench at O
G = Second Main Body Tank about to cast its facing at O and cross Support Trench and work down; (it to meet F at about P.)
H. = Trench Cleaners following F (bombers in Fire Trench)
I. = Trench Cleaners following G (bombers in Communication Trench
J. = Trench Stops following F block trenches at Q & P
K = Trench Stops following G to block trenches at R & S
L & M = Supports
N = fascine dropped by F Tank.
O = Place where G Tank will drop fascine.
P Q R. S = Places where trenches will be blocked by J & K.

SECRET.

O.C. " " Company.

Herewith tracing shewing the actual names and numbers of the tanks which you will follow. The numbers and names will be painted on. The tracing shews the positions each tank will take up.

Captain,

18.11.17. A/Adjutant, 9th Battalion The Suffolk Regiment.

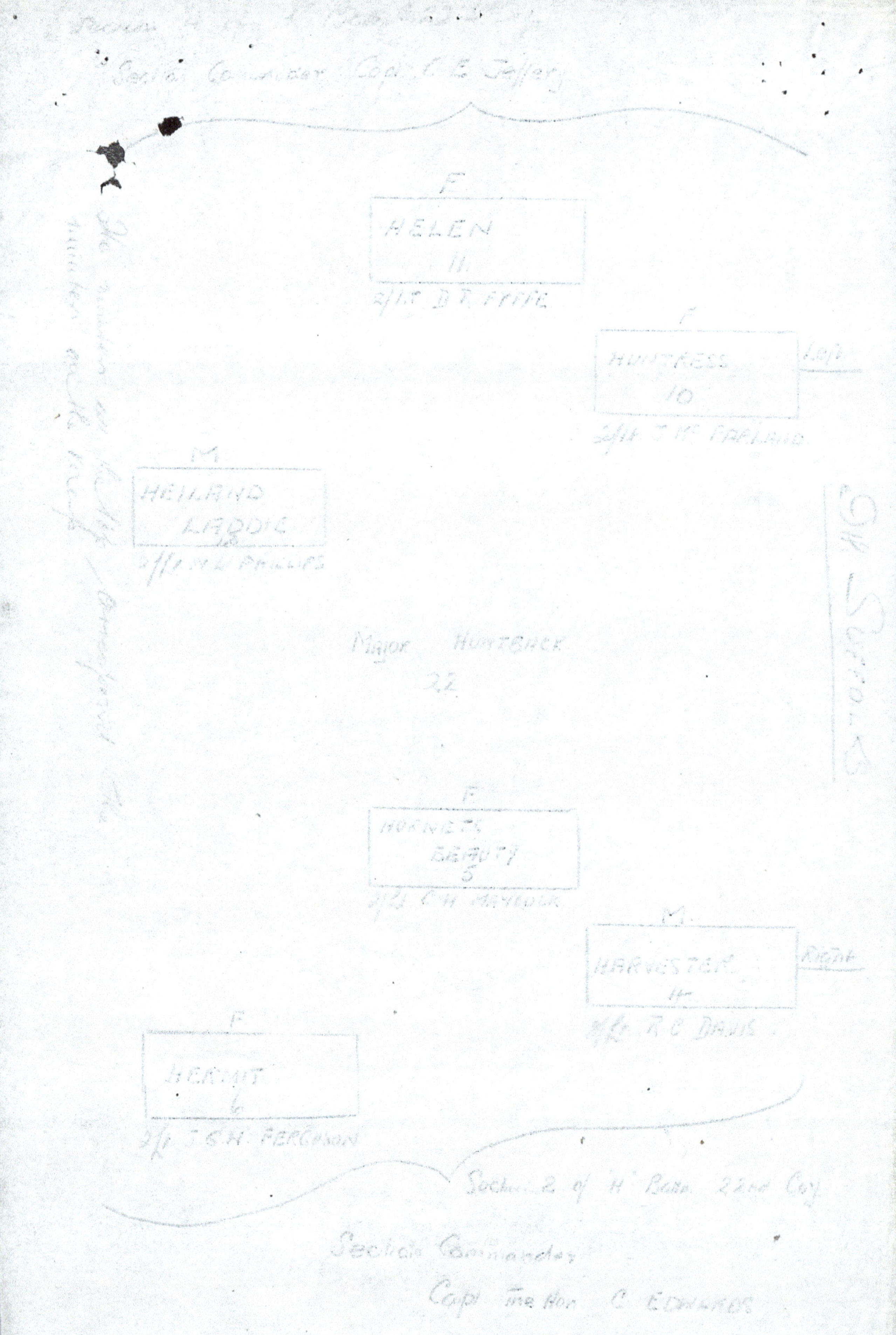

Section Commander Capt C E Jeffery

F

HELEN
11

2/Lt D R FYFFE

F

HUNTRESS
10

2/Lt J McFARLAND

Left

M

HEILAND LADDIE
12

2/Lt N L PHILLIPS

Major HUNTBACK
22

9th Suffolks

F

HORNETS BEAUTY
5

2/Lt C H MAYCOCK

M

HARVESTER
14

2/Lt R C DAVIS

Right

F

HERMIT
6

2/Lt J G H FERGUSON

Section 2 of 'H' Batt. 22nd Coy

Section Commander
Capt The Hon C EDWARDS

SECRET. Copy No. 2

9th Battalion The Suffolk Regiment.
Operation Order No. 72.

---

1. The Battalion will move to-day to the HINDENBURG SUPPORT SYSTEM. Left flank will be FORK AVENUE. Right flank will be old [illegible]h I.B. boundary (COUILLET WOOD).

2. "D" Coy. will be on the right of the Northern line of the SUPPORT SYSTEM and "B" Coy. on the left. "C" Coy. will be on the right of the Southern line of the system, and "A" Coy. on the left.

3. The line is not occupied at present.

4. All movement will be by platoons.

5. Os.C, Coys. will report "All in" to Battalion H.Qtrs. as soon as Coys. are in.

6. Coys. will move off about 1.30.p.m. Battalion H.Qtrs. will be in the Southern line of the system. Place will be notified later.

7. ACKNOWLEDGE.

Issued at.......... [signature] Captain,

22.11.17. A/Adjutant, 9th Battalion The Suffolk Regiment.

Copy. No.	1..Commanding Officer.	Copy No.	7..	Transport Officer.
" "	2..O.C. "A" Coy.	" "	8..	71st Inf. Bde.
" "	3..O.C. "B" Coy.	" "	9..	Retained.
" "	4..O.C. "C" Coy.	" "	10..	Retained.
" "	5..O.C. "D" Coy.	" "	11..	War Diary.
" "	6..O.C. Headquarters.	" "	12..	War Diary.

SECRET. Copy No.........13

9th Battalion The Suffolk Regiment.
Operation Order No. 73.

---

1. The Battalion will relieve the 2nd Battalion YORK & LANCS. in the front line system to-night 26/27th. Nov.

"A" Coy. 9th Suffolks will relieve	"C" Coy. 2nd Y & L.
"B" " " " "	"B" " " "
"C" " " " "	"A" " " "
"D" " " " "	"D" " " "

2. "A" Coy. will be the front line Coy. holding post at & in neighbourhood of L.5.c.21.31, where there will be half a Coy. under an Officer. Coy. H.Qrs. in Sandpit.
"B" Coy. will hold right portion of trench forming main line of resistance. "C" Coy. will be on the left, and "D" Coy. in the centre. Battalion H.Qtrs. will be at L.10.d.10.25.
R.A.P. will be at Battalion H.Qtrs.

3. Water Cart will come up nightly with rations to Battalion H.Qtrs. Coys. will arrange to fill their water tins from Cart which will then return to Transport.

4. All water bottles will be filled before moving off this evening. Water tins will be taken up empty.

5. It is to be carefully impressed on all ranks that the enemy at RUMILLY RIDGE can observe all movement & smoke above trenches. Men are not allowed out of trenches by day except on duty. The invariable result of smoke or movement is shelling. Except on duty no soldiers are to go into NOYELLES.

6. Os.C. Coys. will arrange for one guide per Coy. to be at Battalion H.Qtrs. at 2.15.p.m. to-day to guide advance parties of relieving unit to their respective Coys.

7. Battalion will move off in following order "A", "C", "B", "D", & H.Qtrs., & will pass Battalion H.Qtrs. moving by platoons at 50 paces interval. Head of "A" Coy. to pass Battalion H.Qtrs. at 6.p.m. Os.C. Coys. will be at the head of Coys.

8. Guides from 2nd Battalion YORK & LANCS. (1 per Platoon) will join Battalion en route.

9. Relief complete will be reported to Battalion H.Qtrs. by "Your S.U. 96 received."

10. ACKNOWLEDGE.

Issued at............. W. Fitch Captain,

26.11.17. A/Adjutant, 9th Battalion The Suffolk Regiment.

Copy No. 1..Commanding Officer. Copy No. 8..71st Inf. Bde.
" " 2..O.C. "A" Coy. " " 9..2nd Bn. York & Lancs.
" " 3..O.C. "B" Coy. " " 10..Retained.
" " 4..O.C. "C" Coy. " " 11..Retained.
" " 5..O.C. "D" Coy. " " 12..War Diary.
" " 6..O.C. Headquarters. " " 13..War Diary.
" " 7..Transport Officer.

"A" Form.

Army Form C. 2121.
(In pads of 100.)

MESSAGES AND SIGNALS.

No. of Message..............

Prefix............Code.............m | Words. | Charge. | This message is on a/c of: | Recd. at.........m.

Office of Origin and Service Instructions.

C Boy

Sent
At..............m.
To..............
By..............

.... Service.

(Signature of "Franking Officer.")

Date........
From..........
By..........

TO 9th Suffolks.

Sender's Number.	Day of Month.	In reply to Number.	AAA
* G.O/304.	20.		

Wire from 6th Division timed 4-20 pm begins AAA Divisional Commander congratulates all ranks on the fact that the Division has captured all objectives taken 16 officers 700 O.Rs. prisoners including two Battalion Commanders AAA This is the best bag for the day three guns have also been captured AAA Ends AAA The B.G.C adds his congratulations on the very successful issue of the days fight AAA Added all Units

From 71 I B
Place
Time

The above may be forwarded as now corrected. (Z) [illegible] Wayman Capt.

Censor. Signature of Addressor or person authorised to telegraph in his name.

* This line should be erased if not required.

(3198.) Wt. W 12952/M1294. 375,000 Pads. 1/17. H. W. & V., Ld. (E. 818.)

S650.

D.A.G.
G.H.Q.
3rd Echelon.

I enclosed the WAR DIARY of the 9th Bn, The Norfolk Regt. for November 1917.

[illegible]
Lt-col
Comdg 9 Norf. Rgt.

16-12-17.

9th Battalion The Suffolk Regiment.

NOMINAL ROLL OF OFFICERS OF THE ABOVE BATTALION DECEMBER 1917.

Rank.	Name.	Coy.	Gazetted.	Remarks.
Lt.Col.	F. Latham.D.S.O.	H.Q.	2[illegible]. [illegible].16.	Comdg.
Captain.	P.L. Scudamore.	"A"	17. 5.15.	O.C. Div. Coy.
Captain.	G.M. Brown.	"A"	2.10.15.	Hos.
Captain.	G.K. Moseley.	"C"	4. 6.16.	
Captain.	C. Atherton.D.S.O.	H.Q.	14. [illegible].16.	Adjutant.
Captain.	R. England.M.C.	"D"	4.10.16.	O.C. "D" Coy.
Captain.	L. Wilmot-Johnson.	"C"	8. 6.17.	O.C. "C" Coy.
Captain.	W.F. Fitch.M.C.	H.Q.	8. [illegible].17.	A/Adjutant.
Captain.	C.V. Canning.	"B"	[illegible]. 8.1[illegible].	O.C. "B" Coy.
Lieut.	J.C. Rowbotham.	"A"	4. 1.17.	B.T.O.
Lieut.	H.L. Hayne.	H.Q.	1. 4.17.	B.I.O.
Lieut.	H.E. Falkner.	"B"	1. 7.17.	
Lieut.	A.G. Douglas.	"D"	1. 7.17.	
Lieut.	F.D. Down.	"B"	1. 7.17.	
2/Lieut.	H. Williamson.	"C"	26. 7.15.	
2/Lieut.	A.H. Stoyle.	"B"	15.11.15.	
2/Lieut.	G. Hopkins.	"C"	5. 6.16.	
2/Lieut.	F. Bullen.	"C"	7. 7.16.	Bomb.Offr.
2/Lieut.	H. Almack.	"A"	7. 7.16.	
2/Lieut.	J.V. Tebby.	"B"	25. [illegible].16.	
2/Lieut.	C.H. Miller.M.C.	H.Q.	5.11.16.	B.I.G.O.
2/Lieut.	J.H. Somerville.	"D"	25.4.17.	L.G.O.
2/Lieut.	R.E. Cook.	"A"	25. 4.17.	
2/Lieut.	E.L. Turner.	"C"	25. 4.17.	Sig.Offr.
2/Lieut.	W.J. Futter.	"B"	26. 4.17.	
2/Lieut.	H. Simons.	"D"	26. 4.17.	
2/Lieut.	J.A. Bromley.	"D"	26. 4.17.	
2/Lieut.	J.A. Simmons.	"A"	26. 4.17.	
2/Lieut.	G.[illegible] Harvey.	"B"	26. 4.17.	
2/Lieut.	G.G. Cooper.	"B"	30. 5.17.	
2/Lieut.	S.H. Phillips.	"C"	30. 5.17.	
2/Lieut.	S.H. Habershon.	"C"	25. 7.17.	
2/Lieut.	S.T. Marchant.	"A"	29. 8.17.	
Captain & Qr. Mr.	R. Starling.	"B"	10. [illegible].17.	Quartermaster.

ATTACHED.

Rank.	Name.	Coy.	Gazetted.	Remarks.
~~Major.~~	~~T.B. Hall. (Norfolk Regt.)~~	~~H.Q.~~		~~[illegible] Command.~~
Captain.	V.E. Lloyd. (R.A.M.C.)	H.Q.	14. 8.16.	Medical Offr.
Lieut.	J.V. Lee. (3/1st R.E.K.Yeo.)	"C"	2. 5.16.	Trans.Offr.
Captain.	E.V. Blackburne (C of E.).	"C"	28. 5.16.	Chaplain.

CONFIDENTIAL.

Headquarters,

71st Infantry Brigade.

Herewith War Diary of the Battalion under my Command for the month of December 1917.

[signature] Lieut-Colonel.,

1.1.18. Commanding 9th Battalion The Suffolk Regiment.

Instructions regarding War Diaries and Intelligence Summaries are contained in F. S. Regs., Part II. and the Staff Manual respectively. Title pages will be prepared in manuscript.

WAR DIARY
or
INTELLIGENCE SUMMARY.
(Erase heading not required.)

9 Suffolks

Army Form C. 2118.

Vol 28

Place	Date	Hour	Summary of Events and Information	Remarks and references to Appendices
TRENCHES	1.12.17		Bn in front line trenches moderate bombardment. Bn relieved by the 9th Bn Norfolk Regt + withdrew to support where all Coys were in Reserve line. Casualties 1 OR killed 3 ORs wounded. O.O. No 75 attd. Lieut A.P. Gardham transferred to 2nd Bn.	See appendix I. RH
	2.12.17		Bn in Support. 'C' + B Coy heavily shelled. Work on trenches digging + wiring. Casualties 1 OR killed + 2 ORs wounded.	RH
	3.12.17		Right flank threatened by enemy attacking MARCOING. 'C' Coy swung round to face S.E. + dig in in front of road (PREMY CHAPEL – NINE WOOD) in support to 2nd Sherwood Foresters. 'B' Coy in communication trench in Reserve. Work on making new line.	RH
	4.12.17		Bn in Support. Casualties 4 ORs wounded. 2/Lieut W.J. Tutter admitted F.A. N.Y.D.N.	RH
	5.12.17		Bn withdrew at 4 am leaving A + B Coy as Outpost line. O.O. No 76 attd. 'C' + 'D' relieved by one Coy of 9th Bn Norfolk Regt + withdrew to Bde support (as counter attacking Bn)	See appendix II. RH
	6.12.17		'A' + 'B' Coys rejoined Bn in support at 3 am. 'D' Coy working on front line wiring. Casualties 3 ORs wounded.	RH

A6945 Wt. W11422/M1160 350,000 12/16 D. D. & L. Forms/C./2118/14.

Instructions regarding War Diaries and Intelligence Summaries are contained in F. S. Regs., Part II. and the Staff Manual respectively. Title pages will be prepared in manuscript.

WAR DIARY
or
INTELLIGENCE SUMMARY.
(*Erase heading not required.*)

Army Form C. 2118.

Place	Date	Hour	Summary of Events and Information	Remarks and references to Appendices
TRENCHES	7.12.17		Bn in support & providing working parties. Casualties 9 ORs wounded	KH
	8.12.17		" " " " A/Capt R. B. Christophers	
			wounded and one OR wounded (Gas shell)	KH
	9.12.17		Bn in support & providing working parties Casualties 2 ORs. wounded.	KH
	10.12.17		" " " 2/Lieut Williamson & 3 ORs joined Bn	KH
	11.12.17		" " "	KH
	12.12.17		" " " Bn relieved by 9th Bn R.W.Fs	See appendix II
			O.O. No 77 attd.	KH
ETRICOURT	13.12.17		Bn at rest in ETRICOURT. 2/Lieut J. M. Somerville admitted to F.A. sick Major T. B. Hall cross-posted to Bn from 2nd Bn Sherwood Foresters with effect from 13.12.17 as 2nd in Com.	KH
	14.12.17		Bn moved by busses to BAILLEULMONT. O.O. No 78 attd.	KH See appendix IV
BAILLEULMONT	15.12.17		Bn resting. Reinforcements 2 ORs.	KH
	16.12.17		" Major W. R. Elliston joined Bn from England.	KH
	17.12.17		Bn Training	KH
	18.12.17		do Capt & Adjt C. Allerton D.S.O. rejoined Bn from England.	
			Reinforcements 3 ORs	KH

A6945 Wt. W11422/M1160 350,000 12/16 D. D. & L. Forms/C./2118/14.

Instructions regarding War Diaries and Intelligence Summaries are contained in F. S. Regs., Part. II. and the Staff Manual respectively. Title pages will be prepared in manuscript.

WAR DIARY
or
INTELLIGENCE SUMMARY.
(Erase heading not required.)

Army Form C. 2118.

Place	Date	Hour	Summary of Events and Information	Remarks and references to Appendices
BAILLEULMONT.	19/12/17		Battalion Training 2/Lt. S.E. CLARKE Joined Bn.	fa
"	20/12/17		do. 2/Lt. J.W. HARDING Joined Bn.	fa.
"	21/12/17		do	fa
"	22/12/17		do	fa
"	23/12/17		do 2/Lt. J.A. BLANCH. and 2 O.R. Joined Bn.	fa
"	24/12/17		do 2/Lt. S.T. MARCHANT and 2/Lt. H. WILLIAMSON left Bn. to join 7th Bn. Suffolk Regt.	
			Lt. COL. F. LATHAM. D.S.O., 2/Lt. H.L. FRAMPTON and No. 16186 CM. A. SARGENT. mentioned in Sir DOUGLAS	
			HAIG's despatches.	fa
"	25/12/17		do. The Commanding Officer visited all Companies and wished the men good	fa
"	26/12/17		do luck for the coming year. Gifts were received from the following	fa
"	27/12/17		do Queen Alexandra's Field force fund. Lady Cadogan and committee of	fa
"	28/12/17		do N.W. Suffolk conservatives Lord Francis Hervey. Divisional Fancies	fa
"	29/12/17		do and Cards of Good wishes from Major M.F. Heigham and Capt. H.C. Stanford.	fa
"	30/12/17		do	fa
"	31/12/17		do.	fa.

F. Latham Lt Col.
Commanding 9th (S) Bn. Suffolk Regt.

A6945 Wt. W11422/M1160 350,000 12/16 D. D. & L. Forms/C./2118/14.

Appendix I.

SECRET.

Ref. attached Operation Order No. 75. Cancel para. 3 & substitute.

Os [illegible]. Coys. will send down 2 N.C.Os at once to report to Bn. H.Qtrs. They will proceed to reconnoitre the positions at present occupied by the Norfolks.

After reconnoitring "A". "C" & "D" Coys. will await their Coys. at L.10.c.68.72. "B" Coy. will rejoin their Coy. & guide the Coy. down after relief. We are taking up position of Norfolk Coys. letter for letter Coy.

[signature]

Captain,

1.12.17. A/Adjutant, 9th Battalion The Suffolk Regiment.

Appendix I.

Copy No. 11

SECRET.

9th Battalion The Suffolk Regiment.
Operation Order. No. 75.

---

1. The Battalion will be relieved in the front line system by the 9th Bn. Norfolk Regt. to-night 1st/2nd Dec. commencing at dusk.

"A" Coy. Norfolks will relieve "A" Coy. Suffolks.
"B" " " " " "B" " "
"C" " " " " "C" " "
"D" " " " " "D" " "

2. On completion of relief, Bn. will take over positions at present occupied by the 9th Norfolks. Bn. H.Qtrs. will be at L.15.b.80.25.

3. Os.C. Coys. will send down 1 Officer & 1 N.C.O. per Coy. to report to Bn. H.Qtrs. at 2.p.m. They will proceed to reconnoitre the Norfolks positions & will await their Coys. at Bn. H.Qtrs. & guide them to their new positions. Coy. runners will guide their Coys. as far as Bn. H.Qtrs.

4. Platoon guides of "A", "C" & "D" Coys. will await Norfolks Coys. at country road junction L.10.c.68.72. Guides will report to 2/Lieut. R.E. Cook at this point at 4.45.p.m. Platoon guides of "B" Coy. will await Coy. Norfolks at junction of track & tramway at L.10.d.72.01. on Eastern edge of Wood at 4.45.p.m.

5. Of the special equipment held by Coys. for the recent operations, Ground flares will be handed over on Bn. dump. Tools, Grenades, additional S.A.A., Very Lights, Sandbags, S.O S. Grenades will be handed over on Coy. dumps.

6. Receipted lists of Trench Stores handed over will be forwarded to Bn. H.Qtrs. by 10.a.m. 2nd. inst.

7. Great care is to be observed in handing over all posts.

8. Relief complete will be reported to Bn. H.Qtrs. by "Your S.U.280 received" . "All in" will be reported to Bn. H.Qtrs. immediately Coys are in the new positions.

9. ACKNOWLEDGE.

Issued at.........

W Fletcher Captain,

1.12.17. A/Adjutant, 9th Battalion The Suffolk Regiment.

Copy No. 1..Commanding Officer.
" " 2. O.C. "A" Coy.
" " 3..O.C. "B" Coy.
" " 4..O.C. "C" Coy.
" " 5..O.C. "D" Coy.
" " 6..71st Infantry Brigade.
" " 7..Medical Officer.
" " 8..9th Norfolks.
" " 9..Retained.
" " 10..Retained.
" " 11..War Diary.
" " 12.. War Diary.

Appendix I

SECRET. 9th Battalion The Suffolk Regt. Copy No....9...

Operation Order No. 76.

---

1. The Bde. is withdrawing to-night to HINDENBURG Support System. Right boundary L.27.d.5.4. Left boundary STATION AVENUE leading from L.25.b.3.6. to L.21.a.7.9. An outpost line is being taken up from L.34.d.8.0. to L.8.b.2.8. "B" Coy. will hold portion L.28.a.3.8. to road junction L.22.a.0.Q. "A" Coy. will hold from L.22.a.0.1. to PREMY CHAPEL L.15.d.6.8.
Os.C. Coys. will hold the outpost line by 5 posts per Coy.
O.C. "C" Coy. will send one Lewis Gun Section complete to report to O.C. "B" Coy. at once. O.C. "D" Coy. will likewise send one Lewis Gun Section complete to report to O.C. "A" Coy. at once.
The outpost line will be held until the morning of 6th December. Instructions regarding its withdrawal will be issued later.
Os.C. Coys. will gain touch with outpost Coys. on their flanks.
One Section 71st M.G. Coy. under Lieut. M. SPROATS. will report to Capt. CANNING at L.22.a.0.1. at once.
(a) At 3.a.m. 5th inst. 1st Leicestershire Regt. will withdraw from its present position & occupy FORK AVENUE from L.21.c.8.4. Northwards.
(b) At 3.a.m. Outpost Coy. Foresters & Norfolks will withdraw & pass through the front & support lines to HINDENBURG Support System.
(c) At 3.30.a.m. Two Bns. holding Front Line will withdraw through Reserve line to HINDENBURG Support System. Norfolks L.27.a.2.8. to L.20.d.1.8. Foresters L.27.d.5.4. to L.27.a.2.8.
(d) At 4.a.m. Suffolks less two Coys. will withdraw through new Outpost Line to FORK AVENUE from L.27.a.6.1. to L.21.c.8.4, connecting on the right with the Foresters & on the left with the Leicestershires.

Coys. of 18th I.B. N. of CANTHING withdraw at 3.a.m. and 3.15.a.m. Coys. in Reserve Line withdraw at 3.30.a.m.

Os.C. Coys. will ensure that all N.C.Os. are aware of the troops that are withdrawing through them.

All flares S.O.S. Grenades, Tools, Ammunition & Grenades will be taken back to new positions by Coys. concerned.

Rations & R.E. Material will be dumped at L.20.d.4.3.

"D" Coy. will be on the left & "C" Coy. on the right on new line.

Os.C. Outpost Coys. will report by Orderly immediately they have taken up position, sending sketch 1:10.000.

ACKNOWLEDGE.

Issued at 9.p.m.

W. Fitch
Captain,

4.12.17. A/Adjutant, 9th Battalion The Suffolk Regiment.

Copy No. 1..Commanding Officer.
2..O.C. "A" Coy.
" " 3..O.C. "B" Coy.
" " 4..O.C. "C" Coy.
" " 5..O.C. "D" Coy.
" " 6..Medical Officer.
" " 7..Retained.
" " 8..Retained.
" " 9..War Diary.
" " 10..War Diary.

Appendix II

SECRET. Copy No. 14

9th Battalion The Suffolk Regiment.
Operation No. 77.

---

1. The Bn. will be relieved in the line on the night 12/13th Dec. by the 9th Bn. Royal Welsh Fusiliers.

2. On completion of relief, Bn. will move to billets in ETRICOURT. Coys. will proceed independently, maintaining 200 yards interval on the march as far as EQUANCOURT, where Coys. may close. Route :- L.25.d.32.30 - TRESCAULT - METZ - EQUANCOURT - ETRICOURT. Box Respirators will be worn the "Alert" position as far as ETRICOURT.

3. Representatives of 9th R.W.F. will visit Coys. before dawn on the morning of the 12th Dec.

4. An advance party consisting of 2/Lieut. S.H. PHILLIPS, C.Q.M.Sgts. & Sgt. DENT, will report to the Staff Capt. at Area Commandants Office at ETRICOURT at 2.p.m. 12th Dec. and will meet Coys. & H.Qtrs. at North Eastern entrance to ETRICOURT.

5. Following Stores, etc., will be handed over & receipts obtained. Receipted lists being forwarded to Orderly Room by 10.a.m. 13th inst. Surplus pack saddlery sets, Petrol Tins, Crates - water tin, Tarpaulins, Tents, Stoves oil drum, Grenades, S.O.S. grenades, Trench Maps, aeroplane photos, S.A.A. surplus to that of the man's establishment, Trench Shelters by those Coys. in possession, etc. Os.C. Coys. will forward to Bn. H.Qtrs. list of stores to be handed over by 6.a.m. 12th Dec.

6. All hedging gloves in possession of Coys. will be forwarded to Bn. H.Qtrs. by 6.a.m. 12th inst.

7. Transport Officer will arrange for one limber per Coy. & one for H.Qtrs. to be at about L.25.c.4.3. by 6.p.m. Coys. will load their Lewis Guns, L.G. & Bombing equipment, Officers Mess Kit, etc. at that point when passing. Transport Officer will also arrange for Cookers, Water Carts & Officers Mess Carts to proceed to ETRICOURT with rations.

8. Relief complete will be reported to Bn. H.Qtrs. by "Your S.U.51 received." Os.C. Coys. will report "all in" immediately on arrival at ETRICOURT.

9. Instructions regarding which Lr Coy. will relieve Coys., Time of relief, guides, etc., will be issued later.

10. Transport lines will be handed over on the 13th inst.

11. ACKNOWLEDGE.

Issued at 12.15 a.m. W Fritch Captain,

12.12.17. A/Adjutant, 9th Battalion The Suffolk Regiment.

Copy No. 1..Commanding Officer.
" " 2..O.C. "A" Coy.
" " 3..O.C. "B" Coy.
" " 4..O.C. "C" Coy.
" " 5..O.C. "D" Coy.
" " 6..Transport Officer.
" " 7..Quartermaster.
" " 8..9th Bn. Royal Welsh Fusiliers.

Copy No. 9..71st Infantry Brigade.
" " 10..2/Lieut. S.H. Phillips.
" " 11..Medical Officer.
" " 12..Retained.
" " 13..Retained.
" " 14..War Diary.
" " 15..War Diary.

Appendix III.

SECRET. Copy No. 15.

9th Battalion The Suffolk Regiment.
Addendum to Operation Order No. 77.

---

1. 2/Lieut. C.H. Miller.M.C. & 1 Sgt. per Coy. will form rear party & will collect all stragglers & march them in a formed body, they will move in rear of Battalion & not approach closer than 200 yards to rear Coy., until EQUANCOURT has been passed. With the exception that when Battalion reaches its Cookers, S. of HAVRINCOURT WOOD, all stragglers will join their Coys, & get their hot food.

Os.C. Coys. will at once submit the name of the Sgt. detailed, by telephone, as follows - "Ref. your S.U.33. Sgt. (Name)". These Sgts. will report to 2/Lieut. C.H. Miller.M.C. at cross roads L.25.d.3.3. (MARCOING Sheet) as their Coy. marches by.

2. Cookers will be awaiting Coys. at Southern exit of that portion of HAVRINCOURT WOOD through which the road to METZ passes. Coys. will fall out independently when they meet their Cookers & issue the hot food.

3. "D" Coy. R.W.F. will take over from "A" Coy. Suffolks.
"B" " " " " " " "B" " "
"A" " " " " " " "C" " "
"C" " " " " " " "D" " "

4. R.W.F. Coys. consist of 3 Platoons.
"B", "C" & "D" Coys. will each send 3 guides to cross-roads L.32.a.2.3. to be there at 6.30.p.m. & guide R.W.F. Coys. to their positions.

"A" Coy. will send 3 guides to road junction L.25.d.30.05 by 6.45.p.m. & will guide "D" Coy. R.W.F. "D" Coy. R.W.F. is coming up by ARGYLE Rd. Os.C. Coys. will ensure that their guides know the way from rendez-vous to their Coy. area, & if need be, will send guides under an Officer at dusk to the rendez-vous, these guides with Officer then coming back to Coy. over the route that they will take later, when guiding the R.W.F. Coys.

Os.C. Coys. will give their guides a paper stating which Coy. R.W.F's they are to guide.

M.O. will arrange for 1 guide to be at Bn. H.Qtrs. at 7.p.m. to await & guide R.A.P. personnel R.W.F. from Bn. H.Qtrs. to R.A.P.

O.C. H.Qtrs. will arrange for 2 guides to be at cross-roads L.32.a.2.3. at 6.30.p.m. to guide R.W.F. H.Qtrs.

[signature] Captain,

12.12.17. A/Adjutant, 9th Battalion The Suffolk Regiment.

Copy No. 1..Commanding Officer.
" " 2..O.C. "A" Coy.
" " 3..O.C. "B" Coy.
" " 4..O.C. "C" Coy.
" " 5..O.C. "D" Coy.
" " 6..Transport Officer.
" " 7..Quartermaster.
" " 8..9th Bn. Royal Welsh Fusiliers.

Copy No. 9..71st Infantry Brigade.
" " 10..2/Lieut. S.H. Phillips.
" " 11..Medical Officer.
" " 12..Retained.
" " 13..Retained.
" " 14..War Diary.
" " 15..War Diary.

SECRET. Copy No. 12.

9th. Battalion The Suffolk Regiment.

Operation Order No. 78.

Ref. Sheet 57.C. 1/40,000.
[illegible]

---

1. The 71st Inf. Bde Group will move by bus on the 14th Decr. Buses will be at the Southern entrance of MANANCOURT on the [illegible]-MANANCOURT road facing north at 11.30 a.m.

2. Transport will move by road. Orders as regards starting point, hour of start, and route will be issued later.

3. An advance party consisting of 2/Lieut. S.N. Phillips, C.Q.M.S. of "B" Coy, C.Q.M. Sgt of "D" Coy and Sgt [illegible] will report at Town Major's office ETRICOURT at 8 a.m. from whence they will be conveyed by bus to destination. They will report to the Staff Captain at destination and will await Battalion. They will also arrange to meet Regimental Transport on arrival at destination.

4. 2/Lieut. C.H. Miller M.C. and 2/Lieut R.E. Cook will report to Brigade Intelligence Officer at head of Bus Column, V.13.a.9.0, at 11.15 a.m. tomorrow and will be allotted buses Nos. 37-88. They will superintend embussing of Battalion. 2/Lieut. C.H. Miller M.C. will obtain embussing strength of the Battalion from A/Adjutant before proceeding.

5. Battalion will parade in full marching order in close column of Coy's on ground to N.E. of Battalion camp facing N.E. at 9.30 a.m. Battalion will move off in the Brigade column by the following route:- Camp V.3. - ETRICOURT - MANANCOURT. Men will carry one blanket each.

6. Officers Valises, Mess Kit, Coy Stores etc., will be stacked outside Quartermaster's Stores ready to load by 7.30 a.m. All bicycles will proceed by road with Transport.

7. Rations for consumption on 14th. inst will be carried on the man. Rations for consumption on 15th. inst will be carried on Supply Wagons and issued on arrival at destination.

8. One lorry will report at Town Major's office ETRICOURT at 8 a.m. tomorrow. Quartermaster will arrange to have this lorry met and guided to Quartermaster's Stores.

9. ACKNOWLEDGE.

Issued at.......[illegible].......

[signature] Captain.

13/12/17. A/Adjutant 9th Battalion The Suffolk Regiment.

-:-:-:-:-:-:-:-:-:-:-:-:-:-:-:-:-:-:-

Copy No. 1. H.Q.
" " 2. O.C. "A" Coy.
" " 3. O.C. "B" Coy.
" " 4. O.C. "C" Coy.
" " 5. O.C. "D" Coy.
" " 6. [illegible] H.Q.
" " 7. 71st I.B.

Copy No. 8. M.O.
" " 9. Qr Mr.
" " 10. T.O.
" " 11. R.S.M.
" " 12. War Diary.
" " 13. War Diary.
" " 14. Retained.

....

Appendix IV

Nominal Roll of Officers who were actually with the Battalion on 31.12.1917.

Lieut.Col.	F. Latham.D.S.O.
Major.	W.R. Elliston.
Captain & Adjutant.	C. Allerton.D.S.O.
Captain.	R. England.M.C.
Captain.	L. Wilmot-Johnson.
Captain.	C.V. Canning.
Lieut.	H.E. Falkner.
Lieut.	A.G. Douglas.
2/Lieut.	A.H. Stoyle.
2/Lieut.	F. Bullen.
2/Lieut.	H. Almack.
2/Lieut.	J.A. Blanch.
2/Lieut.	J.W. Harding.
2/Lieut.	C.H. Miller.M.C.
2/Lieut.	R.E. Cook.
2/Lieut.	J.A. Simmons.
2/Lieut.	G.W. Harvey.
2/Lieut.	S.H. Habershon.
Captain & Qr. Mr.	R. Starling.

ATTACHED.

Captain.	V.E. Lloyd. (R.A.M.C.)	Medical Officer.
Captain.	E.V. Blackburne. (C. of E.)	Chaplain.

9th Battalion The Suffolk Regiment.

Nominal Roll of Officers who were actually borne on the strength of the above Battalion on 31.12.1917.

Lieut. Col. F. Latham.D.S.O.

Major. W.R. Elliston.

Captain. P.L. Scudamore.
Captain. G.M. Brown.
Captain. G.K. Moseley.
Captain & Adjutant C. Allerton.D.S.O.
Captain. R. England.M.C.
Captain. L. Wilmot-Johnson.
Captain. W.F. Fitch.M.C.
Captain. C.V. Canning.

Lieut. J.C. Rowbotham.
Lieut. H.L. Hayne.
Lieut. H.E. Falkner.
Lieut. A.G. Douglas
Lieut. F.D. Down.

2/Lieut. A.H. Stoyle.
2/Lieut. G. Hopkins.
2/Lieut. F. Bullen.
2/Lieut. H. Almack.
2/Lieut. J.V. Tailby.
2/Lieut. J.A. Blanch.
2/Lieut. J.W. Harding.
2/Lieut. C.H. Miller.M.C.
2/Lieut. J.M. Somerville.
2/Lieut. R.E. Cook.
2/Lieut. E.L. Turner.
2/Lieut. W.J. Futter.
2/Lieut. H. Simmons.
2/Lieut. J.A. Bramley.
2/Lieut. G.W. Harvey. ← 2/Lieut. J.A. Simmons.
2/Lieut. G.G. Cooper.
2/Lieut. S.H. Phillips.
2/Lieut. S.E. Clarke. ← 2/Lieut. S.H. Habershon.

Captain & Qr.Mr. R. Starling.

ATTACHED.

Major. T.B. Hall. 2nd-in-Command.
(Norfolk Regiment.)
Captain. V.E. Lloyd. Medical Officer.
(R.A.M.C.)
Lieut. J.V. Lee. Transport Officer.
(2/1st R.E.K.Yeo.)
Captain. E.V. Blackburne. Chaplain.
(C. of E.)

CONFIDENTIAL.

Headquarters,
71st Infantry Btigade.

Herewith Original War Diary of the Battalion under my Command for the month of January 1918.

Latham,
Lieut.Colonel,
1.2.1918. Commanding 9th Battalion The Suffolk Regiment.

Instructions regarding War Diaries and Intelligence Summaries are contained in F. S. Regs., Par. II. and the Staff Manual respectively. Title pages will be prepared in manuscript.

WAR DIARY
or
INTELLIGENCE SUMMARY.
(Erase heading not required.)

Army Form C. 2118.

9 Suffolk R
Vol 29

Place	Date	Hour	Summary of Events and Information	Remarks and references to Appendices
BAILLEULMONT	1/1/18.		Battn training. Bn proceeded by route march to COURCELLES LE COMTE. 0079 attached	[illegible]
CAMP A. COURCELLES	2/1/18		do. Capt (T. LT/COL) F. LATHAM. DSO. awarded BREVET MAJORITY for distinguished service in the field	
			2/LT G. F. FRANKLIN joined Battalion.	[illegible]
do	3/1/18.		do. Following officers were awarded military cross for distinguished service in the field	
			T/CAPT C. V. CANNING 2/LT (T/LT) J. V. LEE. No 9006. Sgt [illegible] HURLE awarded meritorious	
			Service medal in recognition of services rendered during the present war	[illegible]
do	4/1/18		do. 8 OR joined Bn.	[illegible]
do	5/1/18		do G.O.C. Brigade inspected Companies by platoons as follows. C Coy marching order	
			D Coy drill order B Coy fighting order A Coy kit inspection	[illegible]
do	6/1/18		do Divisional commander presented medal ribbon to W.O. NCOs & men of the	
			Brigade. Brigade formed up on 1st Leicesters parade ground at 10.15 AM	
			No 13695. L/CPL F. PARR received military medal ribbon and 40575 Pte R TAYLOR	
			a gallantry card. Brigade afterwards marched past by Battalions	[illegible]
do	7/1/18		do	
do	8/1/18		do 2/Lieuts P. C. DEW and W. B. SAPEY joined Battalion	[illegible]
do	9/1/18.		do Corps Commander visited Battalion on Battn Parade ground.	[illegible]

A6945 Wt. W11422/M1160 350,000 12/16 D. D. & L. Forms/C./2118/14.

299

Instructions regarding War Diaries and Intelligence Summaries are contained in F. S. Regs., Part. II. and the Staff Manual respectively. Title pages will be prepared in manuscript.

WAR DIARY
or
INTELLIGENCE SUMMARY.
(*Erase heading not required.*)

Army Form C. 2118.

Place	Date	Hour	Summary of Events and Information	Remarks and references to Appendices
CAMP 4 COURCELLES	10/1/18		Battn training 2/Lt. W.B. SAPEY admitted F.A. Major W.R. ELLISTON ½ Bn left Bn for temporary attachment at 1st Battn [illegible]	[illegible]
do	11/1/18		do Lieut T.C.H. WOODS 4th Bn joined Battn. C.Q.M.S. joined Bn from Base	[illegible]
do	12/1/18		do	[illegible]
do	13/1/18		do	[illegible]
do	14/1/18		do	[illegible]
do	15/1/18		do	[illegible]
do	16/1/18		do 27 O.R. joined Battalion	[illegible]
do	17/1/18		do Bn proceeded by route march to FREMICOURT O.O. 80 attached	[illegible]
FREMICOURT	18/1/18		do Bn relieved the 1/4 Seaforth Highlanders in the trenches, O.O. 81 and disposition map attached.	[illegible]
Trenches	19/1/18		Battn in trenches Casualties one O.R. killed one wounded	[illegible]
"	20/1/18		do	[illegible]
"	21/1/18		do	[illegible]
"	22/1/18	[illegible]	do	
	22/1/18		do Battalion relieved in trenches by 9th Norfolks O.O. 82 attached	[illegible]
LEBUCQUIERE	23/1/18		Battn at rest working parties from A. B and C Coys supplied by Col. F. Latham DSO. western aeroplane course	[illegible]
	24/1/18		do	[illegible]

A6945 Wt. W11422/M1160 35,000 12/16 D. D. & L. Forms/C./2118/14.

Instructions regarding War Diaries and Intelligence Summaries are contained in F. S. Regs., Part II. and the Staff Manual respectively. Title pages will be prepared in manuscript.

WAR DIARY
or
INTELLIGENCE SUMMARY.
(Erase heading not required.)

Army Form C. 2118.

Place	Date	Hour	Summary of Events and Information	Remarks and references to Appendices
LEBUCQUIERE	25/1/18		Batt at rest. Working parties found by Royl Engrs (?) and who were relieved by 8th Bedfords. See OO 53 attached.	[illegible]
"	26/1/18		" Batt found working party of 450 men	[illegible]
"	27/1/18		" Batt found " " " 450.	[illegible]
"	28/1/18		" Batt " " " 250. Lt Col J. Latham DSO returned from aeroplane course	[illegible]
"	29/1/18		" Batt " " " 200. The Officers of the Battn had a	[illegible]
"	29/1/18 (?)		farewell dinner as Batt is to be disbanded in the near future owing to shortage	[illegible]
"	3		of man power. Letters from Divisional and Brigade Commanders were read out by the	[illegible]
			Commanding Officer. Roll of Officers who were present is attached.	
"	30/1/18		Batt at rest. Batt found working parties of 200 men	[illegible]
"	31/1/18		do do do	[illegible]

1/2/18

J. Latham Lieut Col
Commanding 9th Suffolk Regt

A6945 Wt. W11422/M1160 350,000 12/16 D. D. & L. Forms/C./2118/14.

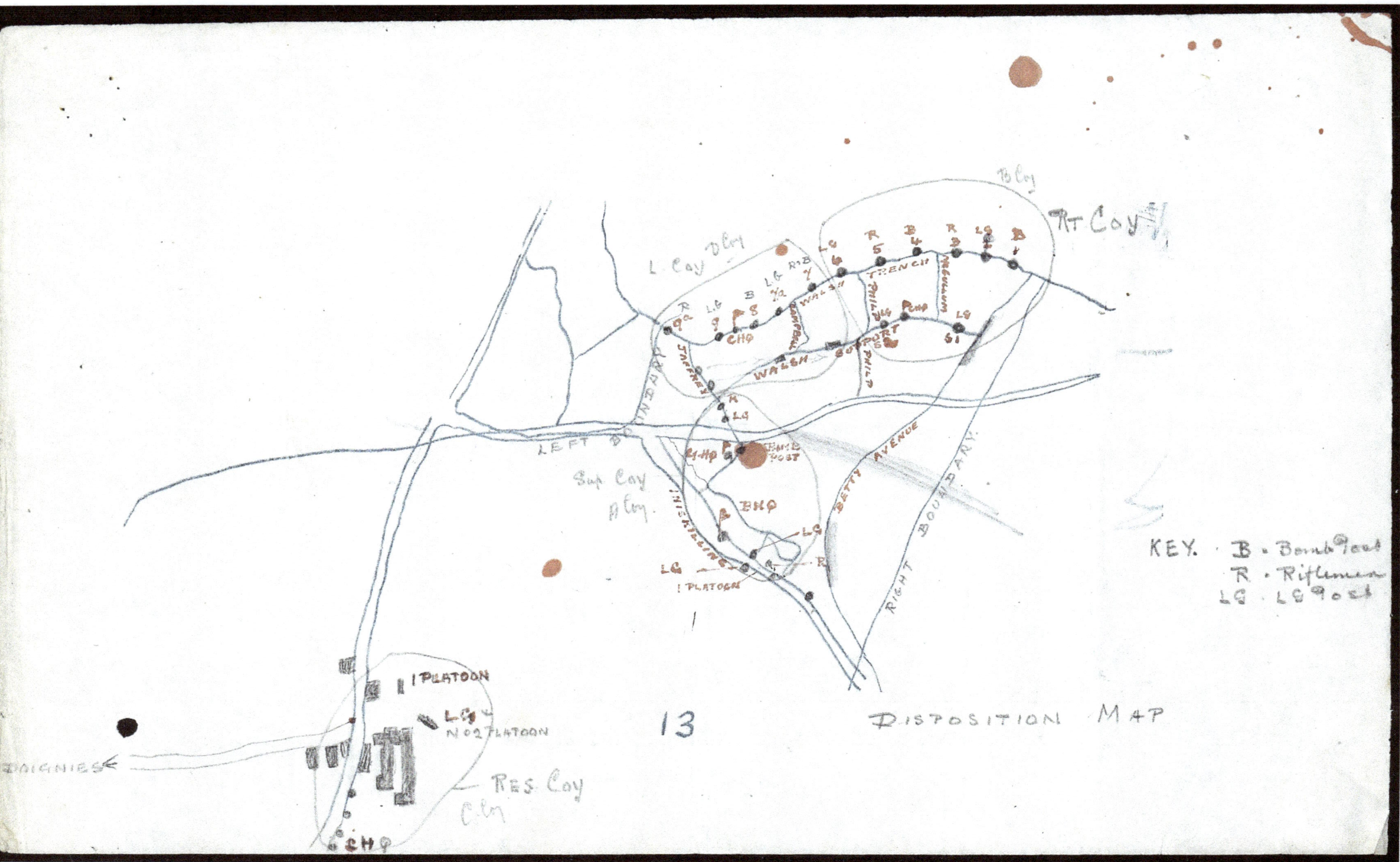

Rt Coy
B Coy
L Coy
D Coy
Sup Coy
A Coy
Res Coy
C Coy
TRENCH
MCGULLUM
PHILIPS
WALSH
CAMPBELL
SUPPORT
JAFFREY
CHQ
BHQ
LEFT BOUNDARY
RIGHT BOUNDARY
BETTY AVENUE
INISKILLING
1 PLATOON
No 2 PLATOON
DOIGNIES
13
DISPOSITION MAP
KEY. B · Bomb Post
R · Riflemen
LG · LG Post

SECRET Copy No....15....

9th Battalion The Suffolk Regiment,
Operation Order No. 80.

Ref: Map 57.C. 1/40.000.

1. To-morrow 17th inst. the Battalion will move by Route March from its present area to FREMICOURT via ACHIET-LE-GRAND, BIHUCOURT, BAPAUME, FREMICOURT. Order of march - ~~DRUMS~~, HEADQUARTERS, "C", DRUMS, "A", "B" & "D" Coys. Coys. will move at 100 yds. interval. Transport will move with Battalion divided into two portions. Intervals of 100 yds. to be maintained. The Battalion will be formed up on Battalion parade Ground ready to move at 7.20.a.m. Transport will form up under orders of Transport Officer.

2. 2/Lieut. F. Bullen will be in charge of rear party.

3. An Advance party consisting of 2/Lieut. S.H. Phillips, C.Q.M.Sgts. and Sgt. Dent for Headquarters, will parade with bicycles outside Orderly Room at 7.15.a.m. and will report to Headquarters, 8th Argyle & Sutherland Highlanders at 9.30.a.m. and will meet Battalion at Road Junction I.19.c.5.1.

4. Officers' Valises, Mess Kits, Orderly Room Boxes, Band packs, H.Q. Stores, Rations and Dixies will be ready to load at 6.30.a.m.

5. Blankets and Coy. Stores will be stacked inside Q.M. Stores by 6.15.a.m.

6. Os.C. Coys., Headquarters and Transport, will forward certificates to Adjutant stating that all Huts, etc., have been left clean.

7. Attention of all concerned is directed to 6th Divisional Orders on March Discipline.

8. ACKNOWLEDGE.

Issued at....6.45 pm....

G. Allerton, Captain,

16.1.18. Adjutant, 9th Battalion The Suffolk Regiment.

Copy No. 1...Commanding Officer.
" " 2...2nd-in-Command.
" " 3...O.C. "A" Company.
" " 4...O.C. "B" "
" " 5...O.C. "C" "
" " 6...O.C. "D" "
" " 7...O.C. Headquarters.
" " 8...71st Infantry Brigade.
" " 9...R.S.M.
" " 10...Transport Officer.
" " 11...Quartermaster.
" " 12...Medical Officer.
" " 13...Retained.
" " 14...Retained.
" " 15...War Diary.
" " 16...War Diary.

SECRET.

Copy No......15.

9th Battalion The Suffolk Regiment.
Operation No. 70.

Ref: Map LENS 11. 1/100.000.

1. To-morrow, 1st Proximo, the Battalion will move by march Route from its present area to COURCELLES-LE-COMTE via BAILLUVAL, BASSEUX, BELLACOURT, RANSART, ALINFER and AYETTE. Order of march :- DRUMS, H.Qtrs., "D", "C", "B" & "A" Coys. Companies will move at 100 yards interval. Transport will move with Battalion, divided into two portions; intervals of 100 yards to be maintained. The Battalion, including Transport, will be formed up on Main Road ready to move off at 8.30.a.m., head of Headquarters resting on Church.

2. 2/Lieut. R.E. Cook will be in charge of rear party.

3. An Advance Party consisting of 2/Lieut. C.H. Miller.M.C., C.Q.M.Sgts, and Sgt. Dent for H.Qtrs., will parade, with Bicycles, outside Orderly Room at 7.30.a.m. and will report to the Headquarters of 1st THE BUFFS at 10.a.m.

4. Officers' Valises, Mess Kit, Orderly Room Boxes, Band packs, H.Qtr. Stores, Rations and Dixies, will be ready to load outside Orderly Room at 7.45.a.m.

5. Blankets and Coy. Stores will be stacked outside Q.M.Stores by 7.a.m. Blankets will be rolled in Bundles of 10's and will be clearly labelled.

6. One Lorry will be at the disposal of the Battalion and will report at 7.a.m. This Lorry will make two journeys. One man per Coy. and H.Qtrs. unfit for marching will be detailed for loading and unloading Lorry. Qr.Mr. will make necessary arrangements.

7. 1. N.C.O. per Coy. & H.Qtrs. will remain behind to hand over Billets to the incoming Unit of the 16th Inf. Bde.
Major W.R. Elliston will hand over the Battalion's Billets in accordance with instructions issued.

8. All paillasses with straw, Billet Stores and Training Material will be handed over. Receipts in Triplicate to be forwarded to Orderly Room.

9. Attention of all concerned is directed to 6th Divisional Orders on March Discipline and cleanliness of Billets.

10. ACKNOWLEDGE.

Issued at 8.p.m.

G. Atherton Captain,

31.12.17. Adjutant, 9th Battalion The Suffolk Regiment.

P.T.O.

Copy No. 1. Commanding Officer.
" " 2. 2nd-in-Command.
" " 3. O.C. "A" Company.
" " 4. O.C. "B" Company.
" " 5. O.C. "C" Company.
" " 6. O.C. "D" Company.
" " 7. O.C. Headquarters.
" " 8. 71st Infantry Brigade.
" " 9. R.S.M.
" " 10. Transport Officer.
" " 11. Quartermaster.
" " 12. Medical Officer.
" " 13. Retained.
" " 14. Retained.
" " 15. War Diary.
" " 16. War Diary.

SECRET. Copy No....17.......

9th Battalion The Suffolk Regiment.
Operation Order No. 81.

Reference Map 57.C. 1/40.000.
MOEUVRES. 1/10.000

1. The Battalion will relieve 4th Seaforth Highlanders in the Right Sub-section to-morrow, 18th inst. Route :- LEBUCQUIERE, VELU, BEAUMETZ, DOIGNIES and DEMICOURT.

2. Disposition of Coys. will be as under :-

Right Front Company - "B" Coy.	post 1. to 6. - 1 Platoon.
	WALSH SUPPORT TRENCH in rear of posts 1 to 6. } - 1 Platoon.
	Coy. H.Q. in WALSH SUPPORT.
Left Front Company - "D" Coy.	Posts 7 to 9a - 1 Platoon.
	WALSH SUPPORT TRENCH in rear of posts 7 to 9a. } - 1 Platoon.
	Coy. H.Q. - K.7.b.30.15.
Support Company. - "A" Coy.	Coy. H.Q. - 4th Seaforth's Right Coy. H.Q. just South of Sunken Road at K.7.a.25.45.
Reserve Company. - "C" Coy.	in Dug-outs. Sunken Road South of DEMICOURT. J.18.d.4.8.
	Probable work from 19th inst:-
	1 Platoon Party No. 1. Dug-out Work. 1. Officer & 36 O.R. under 9th Royal Scots.
	1 Platoon Party No. 2. Dug-out Work. 1 Officer and 36 O.R. under 8th Royal Scots.

3. Coys. & Headquarters will parade on road in the following order ready to move off at 12.45.p.m. - "B", "D", Headquarters, "A" & "C" Coys. A distance of 200 yards will be maintained between Platoons when moving off.

4. Guides will meet Coys. and Headquarters at J.17.a.5.7.

5. All defence and work schemes, trench maps, aeroplane photographs and trench stores will be taken over in the line. Receipts will be forwarded to Adjutant (as soon as possible after relief). All Stores must be carefully checked by Officer per Coy. and H.Qtrs. proceeding to trenches in advance of Battalion.

6. Gum Boots, thigh, and petrol tins to be taken over in trenches and very carefully checked.

7. Completion of relief will be notified to Battalion Headquarters by wiring the following:- Your S.99. received at(hour).p.m.

8. Companies & Headquarters will send an advance party consisting of 1 officer per Coy. & Headquarters and 1 N.C.O. per Platoon into the line to-morrow morning. They will stay there for the remainder of the day and make themselves acquainted with their Coy. and Platoon fronts. This party will report at Brigade Headquarters BEAUMETZ (J.20.c.6.8) at 11.a.m. and will parade outside Headquarter Mess at 8.30.a.m.

P.T.O.

Continued.

9. Disposition Map will be forwarded to Battalion Headquarters by 7.a.m. 19th inst.

10. One Lewis Gun Limber will follow "B" Coy. and one "A" Coy.

11. ACKNOWLEDGE.

Issued at 10.pm .... [signature] Captain,

17.1.18. Adjutant, 9th Battalion The Suffolk Regiment.

Copy No. 1...Commanding Officer.
" " 2...2nd-in-Command.
" " 3...O.C. "A" Company.
" " 4...O.C. "B" Company.
" " 5...O.C. "C" Company.
" " 6...O.C. "D" Company.
" " 7...O.C. Headquarters.
" " 8...71st Infantry Brigade.
" " 9...R.S.M.
" " 10...Transport Officer.
" " 11...Quartermaster.
" " 12...Medical Officer.
" " 13...4th Seaforth Highlanders.
" " 14...Retained.
" " 15...Retained.
" " 16...War Diary.
" " 17...War Diary.

SECRET. Copy No..16.....

9th Battalion The Suffolk Regiment.
Operation Order No. 82.

---

1. To-morrow night of 22nd/23rd., the Battalion will be relieved in the trenches by 9th Battn. NORFOLK Regt., and after relief will occupy billets vacated by 9th Norfolk Regt. at LEBUCQUIERE forming Brigade reserve.

2. Two working parties each consisting of one Officer and 40 O.R. (total 2 Off. 80 O.R.) from both "A" and "C" Coys. will take over working parties from 9th Norfolks and will be accomodated at places detailed to Os.C. Coys. by Commanding Officer. Os.C. "A" and "C" Coys. will send officers to take over details to-morrow morning.

3. 2/Lieut. S.H. PHILLIPS with C.Q.M.Sgts. and Sgt. Dent for H.Q., will take over billets for Battalion (less parties of para 2.) from 9th Norfolks and will report at H.Q. 9th Norfolks at 10.a.m. to-morrow morning. 2/Lieut. S.H. PHILLIPS will arrange guides to be at entrance to LEBUCQUIERE from VELU at 9.p.m. to guide Coys. and H.Q. to their billets.

4. All trench stores, programme of work, defence scheme, aeroplane photos, petrol tins. gum boots, etc., will be handed over on relief, copy of stores to be handed over to be sent to Adjutant by 2.p.m. to-morrow 22nd inst.

5. H.Q.,"A", "B" and "D" Coys. (in LEBUCQUIERE) Officers Trench Kit, messing, etc., will be on dump at 6.p.m. Transport Officer will arrange the following :-

1 Limber for "B" and "D" Coys.
2 Limbers for H.Q. and "A" Coy.

6. Guides will be detailed according to Table "A" attached. All guides should know and have in writing the number of guide they are and Coy. and destination.

7. Transport Officer will arrange following :-
One Limber with rations for "A" Coy's working parties to be at A.D.S. DOIGNIES at 5.p.m. where guides from "A" Coy. will meet Limber and guide to dump. Thus Limber will return to Transport after dumping. One Limber with "C" Coy's rations and water for working parties to be at A.D.S. DOIGNIES at 4.p.m. where guides from "C" Coy. will meet Limber and guide it to dump. This Limber will then proceed to "C" Coy's DEMICOURT dump and pick up Coy. Lewis Guns, Officers Kit and Messing and take same to the dump where rations were dumped earlier in the evening, returning to LEBUCQUIERE with remainder of "C" Coy's Officers' Kits and Messing. One Limber for "B" and "D" Coys' Lewis Guns to be at point at 8.p.m. where Lewis Guns Limbers were unloaded on night of 18th/19th inst.

8. Transport Officer will arrange Transport of H.Q., "B" and "D" Coy.'s Officers' Valises, Mens Packs and blankets from FREMICOURT to LEBUCQUIERE, also Officers' Valises of "A" and "C" Coys. who are not on working parties and 20 blankets per Coy.

9. ACKNOWLEDGE.

Issued at.......... [signature] Captain,

21.1.18. Adjutant, 9th Battalion The Suffolk Regiment.

P.T.O.

Copy No. 1....Commanding Officer.
" " 2....O.C. "A" Company.
" " 3....O.C. "B" Company.
" " 4....O.C. "C" Company.
" " 5....O.C. "D" Company.
" " 6....71st Infantry Brigade.
" " 7....O.C. 9th Norfolks.
" " 8....Transport Officer.
" " 9....Quartermaster.
" " 10....Medical Officer.
" " 11....O.C. Headquarters.
" " 12....2/Lieut. S.H. PHILLIPS.
" " 13....R.S.M.
" " 14....Retained.
" " 15....2nd-in-Command.
" " 16....War Diary.
" " 17....War Diary.

TABLE "A" to accompany O.O. 82.

Battn. H.Q.

No. of Guides.	No. of Post.	No. of Men Main Post.	Nature of Post.	Coy. holding Front.
X 1.	Battalion H.Q.			
X 2.	Aid Post.			
X 3.	Bn. Details.			
		RIGHT FRONT COY.		
4.	1. Post.	1 N.C.O. and 6 man.	Bombers	)
5.	2. "	1 " " 7 "	Lewis Gun	)
6.	3. "	1 " " 6 "	Rifle.	)
7.	4. "	1 " " 6 "	Bombers.	) "B" Coy.
8.	5. "	1 " " 6 "	Rifle.	) consisting of
9.	6. "	1 " " 6 "	Lewis Gun.	) 2 Platoons.
X 10.	Company H.Q.			)
X 11.	Platoon in Support. WALSH SUPPORT.			)
12xxxxx7xxPost.		**LEFT FRONT COY.**		
12.	7. Post.	1 N.C.O. and 6 men.		)
13.	7a. "	1 " " 7 "		)
14.	8. "	1 " " 6 "		) "D" Coy.
15.	9. "	1 " " 8 "		) consisting of
16.	9a. "	1 " " 6 "		) 2 Platoons.
X 17.	Company H.Q.			)
X 18.	Platoon in Support in WALSH SUPPORT.			)
		SUPPORT COY.		
X 19.	One Platoon.	JAFFREY SOUTH.		) "A" Coy.
X 20.	One Platoon.	INNISKILLING Trench.		) consisting of
X 21.	Coy. H.Q.			) 2 Platoons.
		RESERVE COY.		
X 22.	One Platoon)	"C" Coy.		
X 23.	One Platoon.)	Consisting of		
X 24.	Coy. H.Q.)	Two Platoons.		

N.B. All Post guides will report to 2/Lt. G. COOPER at Medical Aid Post at 5.p.m.

X All Battn. H.Q., Coy. H.Q. and Platoon Guides will report to 2/Lt. F. BULLEN at Battn. H.Q. at 4.p.m.

SECRET. Copy No. 12

9th Battalion The Suffolk Regiment.
Operation Order No. 83.

---

1. Working Parties at present found by "A" & "C" Coys. will be relieved to-day by corresponding parties of 8th Battalion Bedfordshire Regiment.

2. Os.C. "A" & "C" Coys. will each send two guides to report to Adjutant LEBUCQUIERE at 4.45.p.m. to-day. These guides will guide relieving parties of 8th Bedfords to where parties of "A" & "C" Coys. are at present accommodated. Guides to places where Coys. are actually working will be furnished by "A" & "C" Coys. on arrival of relieving parties.

3. "A" & "C" Coys. will proceed to LEBUCQUIERE on being relieved.

4. Relief complete will be reported to Adjutant immediately the relieved Coys. arrive at LEBUCQUIERE.

5. Transport Officer will arrange for 2 Limbers to be at A.D.S. DOIGNIES at 5.p.m. to-day, for conveyance of Lewis Guns, Kit, etc., to LEBUCQUIERE. Transport Officer will also arrange for Officers'Valises Mens Packs, blankets, etc., of "A" & "C" Coys. to be brought to LEBUCQUIERE to-day.

6. ACKNOWLEDGE.

Issued at 12 noon
25.1.1918.

Captain,
Adjutant, 9th Battalion The Suffolk Regiment.

P.T.O.

Copy No. 1. Commanding Officer.
" " 2. O.C. "A" Coy.
" " 3. O.C. "B" Coy.
" " 4. O.C. "C" Coy.
" " 5. O.C. "D" Coy.
" " 6. R.S.M.
" " 7. Transport Officer.
" " 8. Quartermaster.
" " 9. Medical Officer.
" " 10. Retained.
" " 11. Retained.
" " 12. War Diary.
" " 13. War Diary.

Nominal Roll of Officers of the 9th Battalion The Suffolk Regiment who were present at the Officers FAREWELL DINNER on 29/ 1/ 1918.

Lieut.Colonel.	F. Latham. D.S.O.
Major.	T.B.Hall.
Captain	P.L. Scudamore
Captain.	H.C.Stanford.
Captain and Adjutant.	C. Allerton. D.S.O.
Captain.	R. England. M.C.
Captain.	L. Wilmot-Johnson.
Captain.	W.F.Fitch. M.C.
Captain.	C.V.Canning. M.C.
Captain and Qr.Mr.	R.Starling.
Lieut.	C.H.Woods.
Lieut.	J.C.Rowbotham.
Lieut.	H.L.Hayne.
Lieut.	H.E.Falkner.
Lieut.	A.G.Douglas.
2/Lieut.	A.H.Stoyle.
2/Lieut.	G. Hopkins.
2/Lieut.	F. Bullen.
2/Lieut.	J.A.Blanch.
2/Lieut.	J.W.Harding.
2/Lieut.	R.E.Cook.
2/Lieut.	E.L.Turner.
2/Lieut.	J.A.Bramley.
2/Lieut.	J.A.Simmons.
2/Lieut.	G.G.Cooper.
2/Lieut.	S.H.Phillips.
2/Lieut.	S.H.Habershon.
Lieut.	J.V.Lee. M.C. (2/1st R.E.K.Yeo)
Rev.	E.V.Blackburne. C.F.
Captain.	F.C.Lees. R.A.M.C.

F. Latham

Lieut.Colonel,

~~Lieut.Colonel~~,

1.2.1918. Commanding 9th Battalion The Suffolk Regiment.

CONFIDENTIAL.

Headquarters, "A".,
6th Division.

Herewith Original War Diary of the 9th Battalion The Suffolk Regt. from 1st to 16th February 1918.

Lieut-Colonel,

18.2.18. Commanding 71st Inf. Brigade.

Instructions regarding War Diaries and Intelligence Summaries are contained in F. S. Regs., Part II. and the Staff Manual respectively. Title pages will be prepared in manuscript.

WAR DIARY
or
INTELLIGENCE SUMMARY.
(Erase heading not required.)

Army Form C. 2118.

9 Suffolk Rgt
Vol 30

Place	Date	Hour	Summary of Events and Information	Remarks and references to Appendices
LEBUCQUIERE	1/2/18		Battalion preparing for disbandment	[initials]
	2/2/18		do do Orders received to send two drafts one consisting of 15 Officers and 300 O.R to be sent to the 11th Batt. Suffolk second of 12 Officers and 250 O.R's to be sent to the 12th Battalion	[initials]
"	3/2/18		Battn preparing drafts following Officers reported from divisional wing 2/Lts C.L.A. DUDDY. L. SUGDEN. H.L.S. SAVORY. H.A. PANTON. F. PRIOR. H.J.E. SLOANE. also 5 O.R.	[initials]
"	4/2/18		Batt. preparing drafts.	[initials]
"	5/2/18		Drafts for 11th and 12th Battns left Bn at one and 1.30 P.M. by lorries nominal roll of Officers attached who proceeded with drafts. The Divisional General said good bye to Battn at 9.30 am wishing Officers N.C.O.s and men the best wishes of the Division and thanking the Bn for the good work they had done since being with Division. Bugles were presented to the G.O.C. Division, Brigade, Brigade Major and Staff Captain, Captain P.I. SCUDAMORE, and the oldest member of the Battalion letters of thanks are attached. The silver bugle won by Bn at divisional sports was presented to the Commanding Officer (Lt. Col. F. LATHAM, D.S.O.) 2/Lts C.W. TALBOT and G.E. KELLY reported from divisional wing also 3 O.R.	[initials]

A6945 Wt. W11422/M1160 350,000 12/16 D. D. & L. Forms/C./2118/14.

309.

Captain A. Weyman, Brigade Major 71st Infantry Brigade, thanks the Officers, Warrant Officers, N.C.O.s and men of the 9th Battalion The Suffolk Regiment for their great kindness in presenting him with such a handsome memento of the Regiment on their disbandment. The Bugle will bring back pleasant memories of the cheery times he has had with the Regiment, and of the many friends he has known.

He takes this opportunity to say how proud he is of the honour done him by their very kind presentation, and how greatly he feels the disbandment of the 9th Battalion The Suffolk Regiment, after having served in the same Brigade with them since November 1915.

He wishes the Officers, Warrant Officers, N.C.O.s and men of the 9th Battalion The Suffolk Regiment the very best of Good Luck in the future.

5/2/18.

HQRS. 71st Inf Bde
6th Division
B.E.F.

Captain A. Wegman, Brigade Major 9th Infy Brigade, thanks the Officers, Warrant Officers, N.C.Os and men of the 9th Battalion The Suffolk Regiment for their great kindness in presenting him with such a handsome souvenir of the Regiment on their disbandment. The Brigade will long look pleasurably back on memories of the happy times he has had with the Regiment and of the many friends he has known. He takes this opportunity to say how proud he is of the honour done him by their very kind presentation, and how greatly he feels the disbandment of the 9th Battalion The Suffolk Regiment, after having served in the same Brigade with them since December 1915.

He wishes the Officers, Warrant Officers, N.C.O.s and men of the 9th Battalion The Suffolk Regiment the very best of good luck in the future.

5/2/18.

H.Q. 9th Infy Bde.
6th Division
B.E.F.

Captain F. F. Jones Staff Captain 71st Infantry Bde wishes to thank the Officers W.Os, N.C.Os, and Men 9th Bn The Suffolk Regt for their kind present of a Bugle on the disbandment of the Battalion.

this, I might add will remind me of many a most enjoyable time I have spent with them

5-9-1918

5/2/18

Dear Colonel Latham,

Thank you ever so much for sending me the Batt^n. Bugle as a memento of the "Old 9th". I shall prize it as one of my most cherished possessions in the years to come. It will serve to remind me – if there should be any need to do so – of the many good friends and happy associations I held in the Batt^n. now about to be disbanded.

Again thanking you for the kindly thought which prompted so an appropriate parting gift.

Yours very sincerely,

R. L. Scudamore.

Capt.

Army Form C. 2118.

Instructions regarding War Diaries and Intelligence Summaries are contained in F. S. Regs., Part II. and the Staff Manual respectively. Title pages will be prepared in manuscript.

WAR DIARY
or
INTELLIGENCE SUMMARY.
(Erase heading not required.)

Place	Date	Hour	Summary of Events and Information	Remarks and references to Appendices
LEBUCQUIERE	6/2/18		Surplus of Bn waiting orders	[illegible]
"	7/2/18		do	[illegible]
"	8/2/18.		do	[illegible]
"	9/2/18		do. Surplus of Bn ~~Leave~~ Transport moved by Route March to No 3 Camp COURCELLES.	[illegible]
"	10/2/18		Lt Col F Latham DSO proceeded on leave. Surplus of Bn left under command of Major T B HALL.	[illegible]
COURCELLES	10/2/18		Surplus of Bn under orders of IV Corps Reinforcement camp under Lt Col. L.H.K. FINCH DSO. 13th CHESHIRES.	[illegible]
"	11/2/18		do do do	[illegible]
"	12/2/18		do do do	[illegible]
"	13/2/18		do do do	[illegible]
"	14/2/18		do do do	[illegible]
"	15/2/18		do do do	[illegible]
"	16/2/18		Surplus of Bn transferred to No 5 Entrenching Battn under Lt Col L.H.K. FINCH DSO. Capt & QM R. Sterling and 12 O.R. sent to Base Details under orders to proceed to base. The 9th Bn the Suffolk Regiment ceased to exist after this date after being formed since beginning of the War and being through many actions	[illegible]

17/2/18.

T B Hall Major
Commanding 9th Bn the Suffolk Regt

A6945 Wt. W11422/M1160 350,000 12/16 D. D. & L. Forms/C./2118/14.

9th Battalion The Suffolk Regiment.

Nominal Roll of Officers of the above Battalion posted to 12th Battalion The Suffolk Regiment. 5.2.1918.

Captain.	R.	England. M.C.
Captain.	L.	Wilmot-Johnson.
Lieut.	A.G.	Douglas.
2/Lieut.	G.	Hopkins.
2/Lieut.	J.A.	Blanch.
2/Lieut.	J.W.	Harding.
2/Lieut.	E.L.	Turner.
2/Lieut.	C.C.	Dew.
2/Lieut.	S.H.	Habershon.
2/Lieut.	G.F.	Franklin.
2/Lieut.	S.E.	Clarke.
2/Lieut.	H.A.	Panton.

[signature] Capt for

Major,

16.2.1018. Commanding 9th Battalion The Suffolk Regiment.

9th Battalion The Suffolk Regiment.

Officers of
Nominal Roll of the above Battalion posted to 11th Battalion
The Suffolk Regiment 5.2.1918.

Captain. G.K. Moseley.
Captain. W.F. Fitch. M.C.
Captain. C.V. Canning. M.C.
Lieut. C.H. Woods.
Lieut. H.E. Falkner.
Lieut. A.H. Stoyle.
Lieut. F. Bullen.
Lieut. H. Almack.
2/Lieut. R.E. Cock.
2/Lieut. J.A. Simmons.
2/Lieut. G.W. Harvey.
2/Lieut. G.G. Cooper.
2/Lieut. W.B. Sapey.
2/Lieut. S.H. Phillips.
2/Lieut. G.L.A. Duddy.

Major,

16.2.1918. Commanding 9th Battalion The Suffolk Regiment.

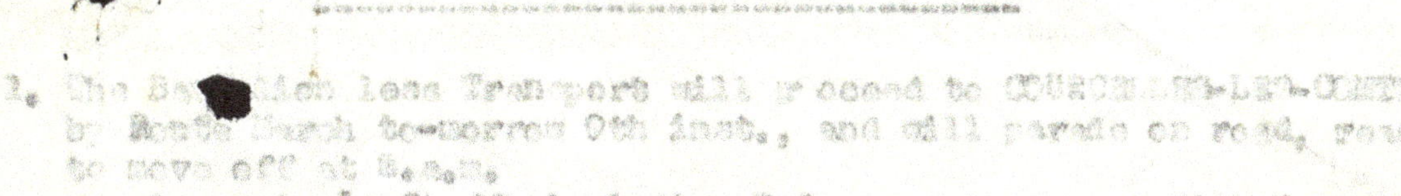

SECRET. 9th Battalion The Suffolk Regiment Copy No....11....

Operation Order No. 85

---

1. The Battalion less Transport will proceed to COURCELLES-LE-COMTE by Route March to-morrow 9th inst., and will parade on road, ready to move off at 8.a.m.
   Quartermaster's Staff, including B.1. men at present with Transport, will be picked up at FREMICOURT.

2. An advance party consisting of 2/Lieut. J.V. Tailby and C.Q.M.S. Acton, will proceed on bicycles from Battalion Headquarters at 6.a.m. and will report to Lieut.Col. FINCH, Commanding XXXXX Reinforcements IV Corps XXXX, at No. 3, Camp, COURCELLES, taking necessary information with ref. to accommodation required.

3. All blankets will be rolled in bundles of 10s, and ready to load at 7.15.a.m. Officers' Valises & Junior Officers' Messing will be ready to load at 7.15.a.m.

4. Transport Officer will arrange for 4 Limbers to be at Battalion Headquarters at 7.15.a.m. for conveyance of Officers' Kits, Men's Blankets, Orderly Room Boxes and Junior Officers' Messing.

5. Mess Cart will follow later during the day.

6. 3 Limbers and Mess Cart will return to Transport Lines on 10th inst. 1 Limber will remain with Battalion for drawing rations, etc.

7. Battalion will be billeted in No. 3. Camp, COURCELLES-LE-COMTE.

8. ACKNOWLEDGE.

Issued at......... [signature] Captain,

8.2.1918. Adjutant, 9th Battalion The Suffolk Regiment.

Copy No. 1..Commanding Officer.
" " 2..2nd-in-Command.
" " 3..Junior Officers' Mess.
" " 4..71st Infantry Brigade.
" " 5..Transport Officer.
" " 6..Quartermaster.
" " 7..C.Q.M. Sgts.
" " 8..A/R.S.M.
" " 9..Retained.
" " 10..Retained.
" " 11. War Diary.
" " 12..War Diary.

WO95/1625/2

6TH DIVISION

71ST MACHINE GUN COY.

6th Division

71st M.G. Coy.

January to December
1917

Aug 1916 – Jan 1918

71st Brigade.

6th Division.

71st BRIGADE MACHINE GUN COMPANY

AUGUST 1 9 1 6 :::

Instructions regarding War Diaries and Intelligence Summaries are contained in F. S. Regs., Part II. and the Staff Manual respectively. Title pages will be prepared in manuscript.

WAR DIARY
~~or~~
~~INTELLIGENCE SUMMARY.~~
(*Erase heading not required.*)

Army Form C. 2118.

Place	Date	Hour	Summary of Events and Information	Remarks and references to Appendices
Englebelmer	6 8/16.		One gun position bombarded by the enemy. 1. O. R. slightly wounded.	
In the trenches	8 8/16		Two gun emplacements heavily shelled. 3. O. R. slightly wounded. Mens kit destroyed. Lanes cut in enemy wire by artillery were kept open all night by our guns firing on them.	
In the trenches	9 8/16		One gun emplacement damaged by shell fire. 1. O. R. slightly wounded. Guns again played on lanes in enemy wire and kept them open.	
—do—	10 8/16.		3. O. R. slightly wounded. Guns again kept lanes in wire open. Fired on enemy transport on Cross roads at Beaumont Hamel, and made them retire.	
—do—	11 8/16.		Relieved by the 1st Guards M. G. Coy. and marched to Louvencourt arriving at midnight.	
Louvencourt	12 8/16		Overhauled Guns etc.	
In the trenches	14 8/16		Relieved 1st Guards M. G. Coy. at Englebelmer. Fired 4,300 rounds on enemy's front line and Communication trenches from 9-45 p.m. till 9-57 p.m.	
In the trenches	15 8/16		1. O. R. Killed. Fired 5,000 rounds on lanes in enemy wire.	
In the trenches	16 8/16		Fired on front line and communication trenches of enemy and also kept lanes in wire open. Fired 7,225 rounds.	
In the trenches	17 8/16.		Fired 6,275 rounds on enemy trenches and wire. 1. O. R. slightly wounded.	

2353 Wt. W2544/1454 700,000 5/15 D. D. & L. A.D.S.S./Forms/C. 2118.

Army Form C. 2118.

Instructions regarding War Diaries and Intelligence Summaries are contained in F. S. Regs., Part II. and the Staff Manual respectively. Title pages will be prepared in manuscript.

WAR DIARY
or
~~INTELLIGENCE SUMMARY.~~
(Erase heading not required.)

Place	Date	Hour	Summary of Events and Information	Remarks and references to Appendices
In the Trenches	18 8/16.		Fired 23,850 rounds on enemy front line and communication trenches and on enemy wire.	
In the trenches	19 8/16		Fired 11,225 rounds as above	
In the trenches	21 8/16		Fired 14,650 rounds in conjunction with the Artillery during a raid on the enemy front line trench. 1 O.R. wounded.	
In the trenches	22 8/16		Fired 3,750 rounds on lanes in Enemy wire.	
In the trenches	23 8/16		Fired 2,500 rounds as above. 1 O.R. wounded.	
In the Trenches	24 8/16		Fired 6,700 rounds on enemy wire, working parties dispersed, enemy transport held-up. Enemy M.G. open fire on No. 3. Gun position. We engaged it and it ceased fire. One new Gun emplacement constructed.	
— do —	25 8/16.		Fired 7,250 rounds on enemy wire and cross roads S. of BEAUMONT HAMEL Two alternative emplacements were completed on the right sector and the same number on the left. Map references: BEAUMONT HAMEL 1/10,000 Trench Map – Q10 d 0.5, Q10 d. 2 2½, Q16 b. 2¼.6½ Q.16 b 2.7. Sec: Lieut: A.B. FINDLAY, adjt, left on appointment 2nd in command 57th M.G. Coy.	[illegible]
— do —	26 8/16.		Fired 3250 rounds on enemy wire & cross roads S. of BEAUMONT HAMEL.	
	27 8/16.		Relieved by 144th Machine Gun Company. Marched from ENGLEBELMER 3 p.m. and arrived at LOUVENCOURT 5.30 p.m	[illegible]
LOUVENCOURT	28 8/16		Marched to BEAUVAL arriving at 1 pm.	

2353 Wt. W2544/1454 700,000 5/15 D. D. & L. A.D.S.S./Forms/C. 2118.

Army Form C. 2118.

Instructions regarding War Diaries and Intelligence Summaries are contained in F. S. Regs., Part II. and the Staff Manual respectively. Title pages will be prepared in manuscript.

WAR DIARY
or
INTELLIGENCE SUMMARY.
(Erase heading not required.)

Place	Date	Hour	Summary of Events and Information	Remarks and references to Appendices
BEAUVAL	29.8.16	8 am.	Marched to FLESSELLES via TALMAS.	
FLESSELLES	30.8.16		Coy. at disposal of O.C. for Training and Inspection.	
"	31.8.16.		LIEUT. G. HUDSON M.C. left on appointment as Second in Command 21st M.G. Coy.	

2353 Wt. W2544/1454 700,000 5/15 D. D. & L. A.D.S.S./Forms/C. 2118.

71st Brigade.

6th Division.

71st BRIGADE MACHINE GUN COMPANY

SEPTEMBER 1916.

Army Form C. 2118.

Instructions regarding War Diaries and Intelligence Summaries are contained in F. S. Regs., Part II. and the Staff Manual respectively. Title pages will be prepared in manuscript.

WAR DIARY
or
INTELLIGENCE SUMMARY.

(*Erase heading not required.*)

~~Head Quarters~~ Vol 2
71st ~~Bde~~ M Gun Coy

Place	Date	Hour	Summary of Events and Information	Remarks and references to Appendices
FLESSELLES	1.9.16.	10 am.	Attack practice 4 guns with 1 battalion. Demonstration of advancing to take successive lines of trenches. Points noted: In the advance teams did not get up and down with Infantry lines. Not sufficient use made of available cover or possible improvements with entrenching tools.	RD.
	2.9.16.	9 am.	2 Sections: attack practice open warfare.	

2353 Wt. W2544/1454 700,000 5/15 D. D. & L. A.D.S.S./Forms/C. 2118.

Army Form C. 2118.

Instructions regarding War Diaries and Intelligence Summaries are contained in F. S. Regs., Part II. and the Staff Manual respectively. Title Pages will be prepared in manuscript.

WAR DIARY
or
INTELLIGENCE SUMMARY

(Erase heading not required.)

Place	Date	Hour	Summary of Events and Information	Remarks and references to Appendices
FLESSELLES	1.9.16	10am	Attack practice 4 guns with 1 battalion. Demonstration of advancing to take successive times of trenches. Points noted; in the advance teams did not get up & down with infantry lines. Not sufficient use made of available cover or possible improvements with entrenching tools.	
	2.9.16	9am	2 Sections: Attack practice, open warfare.	
	5.9.16		Attack practice through woods to enemy entrenched position beyond. M.G Coy held in reserve till infantry cleared woods. M.G Coy orders were as follows. No 1. Section to send forward two guns to consolidate & to hold two in immediate reserve No 2 & 3 Sections. to employ overhead fire till suitable moment arrived to go forward to consolidate positions gained by infantry. No 4. Section to remain behind as brigade reserve	
ALLONVILLE	7.9.16		M.G Coy marched to billets at ALLONVILLE	
MERICOURT L'ABBÉ	8.9.16		M.G Coy marched to billets here.	
SANDPIT AREA	9th 11 9/16		M.G Coy marched to bivouacs	
BRIQUETERIE	12.9.16		M.G Coy H.Q. removed to LA BRIQUETERIE. No 2 section under the command of O.C. 2nd FORESTERS went to support trenches near ARROW HD COPSE No 3 section under the command of O.C. 9th SUFFOLKS went to firing line south of GUILLEMONT Sections 1 & 4 remained in reserve at H.Q.	

Instructions regarding War Diaries and Intelligence Summaries are contained in F. S. Regs., Part II. and the Staff Manual respectively. Title Pages will be prepared in manuscript.

WAR DIARY
or
INTELLIGENCE SUMMARY
(Erase heading not required.)

Army Form C. 2118.

Place	Date	Hour	Summary of Events and Information	Remarks and references to Appendices
GUILLEMONT	13.9.16	6am	71 I.B. attacked German lines to connect up with the division on the right & left. Half No 2 Section & No 3 Section went forward with attacking battalions. The objective of 1,000 yards depth was gained & consolidated.	
	14.9.16	11pm	No 1 & 4 Sections came with the 1st LEICESTERSHIRES & 9th NORFOLKS respectively, & passed through 2nd FORESTERS & 9th SUFFOLKS. Preparations were made for an attack on the following morning at 6.20 A M.	
	15.9.16	6.20am	The XIV Corps in conjunction with other corps & French troops to the South made an extensive attack on the German positions. The final objective of the 71st I B was a line to the east of LES BOEUFS & MORVAL. Considerable progress was made at first but the QUADRILATERAL caused heavy casualties & checked the advance on the right of the 71st I.B. consisting of 9th NORFOLKS & 9th SUFFOLKS. Later these regiments fell back. The disposition of the MG coy was as follows. No 1 Section sent two guns forward with the attacking waves. two guns followed close behind. Of the gun teams that went forward one team was completely knocked out & the gun & tripod blown up: the other team was reduced to a NCO & two men. No. 2 section brought up two guns when the 2nd FORESTERS came up to reinforce on the left. Casualties caused one gun to be dumped, the other team worked round to the division on the left.	

2449 Wt. W14957/M90 750,000 1/16 J.B.C. & A. Forms/C.2118/12.

Army Form C. 2118.

Instructions regarding War Diaries and Intelligence Summaries are contained in F. S. Regs., Part II. and the Staff Manual respectively. Title Pages will be prepared in manuscript.

WAR DIARY
or
INTELLIGENCE SUMMARY
(Erase heading not required.)

Place	Date	Hour	Summary of Events and Information	Remarks and references to Appendices
GUILLEMONT (Cont.)	15.9.16.		No. 3 Section remained in support till 9th SUFFOLKS reinforced. Two guns then went forward. Casualties reduced one team to NCO & two men & the other to three men & the main ammunition dump was blown up.	
			No 4 Section sent two guns forward with the attacking waves & two guns followed soon after. The officer in command & the N.C.O.s were knocked out & other casualties occurred	
			When the right of the 71st I.B retired, two guns from No1 Section were rushed to the right of the 1st LEICESTERSHIRES to enfilade the Valley running from COMBLES & to bring oblique fire to bear on enemy trench running towards sunken road in front of MORVAL.	
			Two guns from No 2 section used indirect fire on the QUADRILATERAL Two guns from No3 section were ordered to use traversing fire on the ridge in front in case of a counter attack	
			One gun from No 4 section was placed slightly to the rear on the right of the left flank with orders to remain there at all costs should the left flank retire.	
			Before the re arrangement was made much careful reconnaissance was necessary. Teams were badly disorganised. Some were without officers, some without N.C.O.s, others had a gun but no tripod, various ammunition carriers were killed or wounded, others had become detached. It speaks well for the moral of the company that in spite of intense machine	

Army Form C. 2118.

Instructions regarding War Diaries and Intelligence Summaries are contained in F. S. Regs., Part II. and the Staff Manual respectively. Title Pages will be prepared in manuscript.

WAR DIARY
or
INTELLIGENCE SUMMARY

(Erase heading not required.)

Place	Date	Hour	Summary of Events and Information	Remarks and references to Appendices
GUILLEMONT (cont)	15.9.16 & 16.9.16		gun fire & very heavy shelling, it was found possible to re-organise and re-equip so many gun teams with every essential in the way of ammunition, full complement of men, water & rations etc. that not only was any chance of a successful counter-attack nullified, but also that the relieving infantry of another brigade could go forward with full confidence that their advance & flanks were secure.	
GUINCHY				
CHIMPANZEE TRENCH	16.9.16	10pm	The M.G. Coy was relieved & bivouaced.	
TREUX.	18.9.16		Marched to billets at TREUX	
CITADEL AREA	22.9.16.		Marched to huts	
CARNOY	24.9.16.		Marched to bivouacs	

2449 Wt. W14957/M90 750,000 1/16 J.B.C. & A. Forms/C.2118/12.

Army Form C. 2118.

WAR DIARY
or
INTELLIGENCE SUMMARY
(Erase heading not required.)

Instructions regarding War Diaries and Intelligence Summaries are contained in F. S. Regs., Part II. and the Staff Manual respectively. Title Pages will be prepared in manuscript.

Place	Date	Hour	Summary of Events and Information	Remarks and references to Appendices
ARROW HEAD COPSE	25.9.16.		Occupied reserve trenches.	
TRENCHES	26-29/9/16.		Occupied trenches from LES BOEUFS to MORVAL.	
CRATERS	30.9.16.		Came from trenches & occupied dug-outs in CARNOY CRATERS AREA	
SANDPIT AREA	31.9.16.		Marched to bivouacs in SANDPIT AREA.	

2449 Wt. W14957/M90 750,000 1/16 J.B.C. & A. Forms/C.2118/12.

PAGE I.

Army Form C. 2118.

WAR DIARY
~~or~~
~~INTELLIGENCE SUMMARY~~
(Erase heading not required.)

71st Co., Machine Gun Corps

Vol III

Instructions regarding War Diaries and Intelligence Summaries are contained in F. S. Regs., Part II. and the Staff Manual respectively. Title Pages will be prepared in manuscript.

Place	Date	Hour	Summary of Events and Information	Remarks and references to Appendices
	30.9.16. 1.10.16.	12.15am.	The 71st Coy M.G.C was relieved in the line – LES BOEUFS – by the 169th Coy. M.G.C; the company then marched out to camp in the SANDPITS AREA near ALBERT.	
	2.10.16 3.10.16 4.10.16 5.10.16 6.10.16		Limber packing, drill etc under section officers.	
	7.10.16	8.35am.	Moved in camp F 17 b. (FRICOURT – MARIECOURT RD)	
	8.10.16	11.35am.	Moved in bivouacs S 28 c (NEAR BRIGETTERIE)	
	9.10.16.	8am	2nd in Command went to 16th 18th Brigades to see positions for guns	
	"	5.30pm	NO 2 section (A	
	"	6pm	No 1 & half NO 3 section to 9th Suffolks' H.Q with 2nd in Command 2nd Lts' Powell, Miller & Albrecht. Relieved 5 guns in centre divisional sector vacated by 16 & 18 M. G Coy	
	10.10.16.		Sent four guns in support line to support 2nd Sherwoods. 1 O.R wounded	
	11.10.16.		Four guns sent to front line, which did not seem to be adequately defended by machine guns. 1 O.R. wounded.	
	12.10.16.		Arranged that the three right guns should support 16th I.B. operations on our right. 2. O.R. wounded.	
	13.10.16.		Situation normal. During the night Lt Allen & two guns moved into positions in strong point in front of RAINBOW trench. We supported the 2nd SHERWOODS attack on the old gun pits in front of CLOUDY trench, which they captured.	Lt. ALLEN
	14.10.16		Enemy heavily shelled strong point blowing up one emplacement. 1 O.R. Killed & 2 wounded	
	15.10.16.	5.35am.	18th I.B. on our left attacked the trenches on our immediate front. We supported this attack. We carried out company relief during the night.	[initials]
	16.10.16		During the day our right guns did good work on retreating enemy parties vacating trenches on our right. At night we relieved three gun teams of 18 MG Coy, this left	

2449 Wt. W14957/M90 750,000 1/16 J.B.C. & A. Forms/C.2118/12.

PAGE II

Army Form C. 2118.

WAR DIARY or ~~INTELLIGENCE SUMMARY~~

(Erase heading not required.)

71st Co. Machine Gun Corps.

Instructions regarding War Diaries and Intelligence Summaries are contained in F. S. Regs., Part II. and the Staff Manual respectively. Title Pages will be prepared in manuscript.

Place	Date	Hour	Summary of Events and Information	Remarks and references to Appendices
	16.10.16		us with 11 guns in the line & 5 in reserve at forward H.Q. 2nd Lt NORRIS H slightly wounded & at duty	
			2 O.R. wounded.	
	17.10.16.		1 O.R. wounded }	
	18.10.16.		2 O.R. Killed 4 O.R. wounded } Enemy shell fire.	
	19.10.16.		Relieved by 24 M.G Coy Owing to congestion of trenches & very bad weather the relief was not completed until 5.30am 20.10.16.	
	20.10.16.	4.30am	Company moved to camp at SANDPITS near MEAULTE	
	21.10.16.		Company moved to CORBIE to Billets	
	22.10.16. } 23.10.16 }		Arranging refitting & replacement of equipment Etc. lost in action.	
	24.10.16	3pm	Entrained at CORBIE for ARAISNES	
	25.10.16.	3.30am	Arrived ARAISNES station & marched to CITERNE	
	26.10.16	10.50am	Inspected by GOC 6th Division	
	27.10.16	11.15am	" " " " 71st I.B.	
	28.10.16.	12noon	Marched to PONT REMY & entrained	
	29.10.16	3am	Detrained at FOUQUIERES station & marched to billets in FOUQUIERES	
	30.10.16		Carried out programme of work	
	31.10.16.	10am	Company inspected by G.O.C. 71st I.B.	

William Wilson Capt
OC. No 71 M.G. Coy.

2449 Wt. W14957/M90 750,000 1/16 J.B.C. & A. Forms/C.2118/12.

Page I

Instructions regarding War Diaries and Intelligence Summaries are contained in F. S. Regs., Part II. and the Staff Manual respectively. Title pages will be prepared in manuscript.

WAR DIARY
or
INTELLIGENCE SUMMARY.
(Erase heading not required.)

Army Form C. 2118.

11th Machine Gun Company

Vol 4

Place	Date	Hour	Summary of Events and Information	Remarks and references to Appendices
FOUQUEREUIL	1/11/16		Training under Section Officers.	
	2		" " "	
	3		" " " Week ending 3.11.16 Decrease 5 sick to Hospital	
	4		Morning. Route march. Afternoon. Work on limbers	
	5		Church Parade	
	6		Training under section officers, Work on limbers: Sgt Sprouts awarded Military Medal	
	7		Lecture on respirators. Packing limbers	
	8		Fitting ~~[illegible]~~ gas helmets. Drill under section officers	
	9		Trial of gas helmet in gas chamber: Small arm drill.	
	10		Inspection by Section officers: Regs. Part II Table C. Week ending 10.11.16 Reinforcements 6 O.R.	
			2 Officers transferred to Base. 5 O.R. sick to hospital.	
	11		Revolver Range practice. Belt filling	
	12		Church parade	
	13		Revolver drill. Respirator drill: completion of spare parts.	
	14		Inspection by O.C. Company	
	15		Fitting & completion of equipment: Limber packing.	

2353 Wt. W2544/1454 700,000 5/15 D. D. & L. A.D.S.S./Forms/C. 2118.

Page 2.

Instructions regarding War Diaries and Intelligence Summaries are contained in F. S. Regs., Part II. and the Staff Manual respectively. Title pages will be prepared in manuscript.

WAR DIARY
or
INTELLIGENCE SUMMARY.
(Erase heading not required.)

Army Form C. 2118.

1st Machine Gun Company

Place	Date	Hour	Summary of Events and Information	Remarks and references to Appendices
FOUQUEREUIL	16/11/16.		Instruction under section officers. Repair of limber spare part Boxes.	
	17.		Mechanism & gun stripping: Revolver & arm drill	
			Week ending 17.11.16. 1 increase from hospital: 3 reinforcements: 144.	
	18		Inspection by section officers. Box respirator drill: Gun drill.	
			Inspection of whole company by O.C. Coy.	
	19		Church parade.	
	20		Inspection by G.O.C. Brigade	
	21		Inspection by section officers. Combined drill. Box respirator drill	
	22.		Inspection by O.C Company. Route march.	
	23	224	Mechanism & limber cleaning & packing.	
LE PREOL	25		1 & 2 sections relieved No 95 M.G. Coy No 3 & 4 sections in billets.	
	31.		Four gun teams relieved.	

W. Allen Capt

2353 Wt. W2544/1454 700,000 5/15 D. D. & L. A.D.S.S./Forms/C. 2118.

PAGE 1.

Army Form C. 2118.

Instructions regarding War Diaries and Intelligence Summaries are contained in F. S. Regs., Part II. and the Staff Manual respectively. Title pages will be prepared in manuscript.

WAR DIARY
or
INTELLIGENCE SUMMARY.
(Erase heading not required.)

71st M. G. Coy

Vol 5

Place	Date	Hour	Summary of Events and Information	Remarks and references to Appendices
LE PREOL	1.12.16		Four Gun Teams Relieved	Reference
	2nd		700 Rounds fired on Cross Rds 22.B.8.6. 750 rds fired at 23.C.2.4; 1200 Rds fired at 22 C.8.0.	Trench Map
	3rd		850 " " " " 22.B.8.6; 1200 " " 23.C.2.4; 1400 " " " 22.C.8.0.	La Bassee
	4th		1250 " " from 22A.7.3 to 23.3.8.1; 500 " " 29A.9.5; 1250 " " 22.B.4.5.	36c N.W. 1.
			1 Gun & Tripod & 10 Belt Boxes blown up at Embankment Redoubt Emplacement knocked in & Rebuilt	1/10,000.
	5th		Three Gun Teams relieved; 2000 rds fired from 22A.7.3 to 23.3.8.1	
			850 rounds fired at 29.A.9.5; 850 " at 22 B.4.5	
	6th		750 " " " 23A.4.6; 1000 " " " 22B.4.5; 750 rds fired at 22B.8.5.	
			500 " " " 22A.9.5	
	7th		2500 " " " 23.A.4.6; 450 " " 22.B.4.5	
	8th		Four Gun teams relieved; 1000 rds fired ~~&~~ at track G.29.a.4.3½. 500 rds fired at Loan Farm G.29.a.2.1.; 25 rounds fired on La Bassee Rd G.24.B.2½.5.	
			~~500~~ 1. O.R. Wounded. 6.	
	9th		250 Rounds fired at La Bassee Rd 22.B.3.4. 750 rounds fired at Trench Rly 23 B.3.3.	
			1000 " " " Trench Track 23C.1.5. 750 " " 22 B.8.6	
	10th		750 " " " " from 23.C.9.9. to 23.D.2.8½ 500 rounds fired at from 23C.9.9. to 23 Central	
			500 " " La Bassee Rd from 23A.1.6 to 23A.7.7.	

WCS.

PAGE 2

WAR DIARY
or
INTELLIGENCE SUMMARY.
(Erase heading not required.)

71. M.G. Coy.

Army Form C. 2118.

Instructions regarding War Diaries and Intelligence Summaries are contained in F. S. Regs., Part II. and the Staff Manual respectively. Title pages will be prepared in manuscript.

Place	Date	Hour	Summary of Events and Information	Remarks and references to Appendices
LE PREOL	11th		500 Rds fired point La Bassee Rd A23.a.7.7.; 750 Rds fired on Trench Rly A23.b.2.3.; 500 Rds Village Line A23C.1.4½	
	12th		500 " " " 23 b.2.3.; 750 Rds fired 23.C.1.4.; 750 Rds fired at Track 28.B.3.L	
	13th		1000 " " at A28.a.3.5.; 750 rds on Trench Track from * 22D.9.7. to 23.C.4½	
			* Working Party was seen from Observation Post & dispersed by our fire.; 500 Rds fired at Roadway & Trench Rly from 23C.9.9. to 23D.2.9. Four Gun Teams relieved	
	14th		1000 Rds fired at A28.a.4.4. 500 Rds fired on Chateau Alley 22D.4.8½	
			750 Rds " Trench Track from 22D.9.7. to 23C.1.4½; 500 Rds fired on La Bassee Rd. 23A.6.0. to 23B.8.5.	
	15th		500 " " " " " " " " " " ; 500 " - - - - - - - - - - - -	
			1250 " " at A28.a.3.5. 500 rds fired on Chateau Alley 22D.4.8½	
	16th		1000 " " - - - - . 250 - - - A23b.3.9. to A23.b.9.6.; 750 rds fired on Trench Track	
			1570 " " on Roadway & Trench Rly	
	17th		1000 " " at A23a.1.5. to A23.a.9.8. 1000 fired at A23a.4.7.; 1250 rds fired on La Bassee Rd	
			~~2 O.R. Wounded~~ 23A 6.0 to 23 B.8.5. 1000 Rds fired on T. Track from 22D.9.7. to 23C.1.4½. 1000 Rds fired on Trench Rly. & Roadway 23C.9.9. to 23D.2.9. 1000 Rds fired at A22b and A23a.; 1750 fired on a line from 23A.7.7. to Canal. to a line from 22B.1.3. to 16A8.5 2 O.R. Wounded	
	18th		4 Gun Teams relieved. 700 Rds on La Bassee Rd. 23A 6.0 to 23B.8.5.; 500 Rd. Chateau Alley 22D.4.8½	
			500 Rds on T. Track 22.D.9.7. to 23C.1.4½ 1000 rds on A23 a.1.5. to A23A9.8.; 1000 Rds at A23a.4.7.	W.W.

Instructions regarding War Diaries and Intelligence Summaries are contained in F. S. Regs., Part II. and the Staff Manual respectively. Title pages will be prepared in manuscript.

PAGE 3

WAR DIARY
or
INTELLIGENCE SUMMARY.
(Erase heading not required.)

71. M. G. Coy.

Army Form C. 2118.

Place	Date	Hour	Summary of Events and Information	Remarks and references to Appendices
LE PREOL	19th		Fire opened on Enemy Working Parties	
	20th		Relieved by the 15th Coy M. G. C.	
NOEUX-LES	21			
-MINES	to		On rest in Billets. Re-equipped: Training programme included Box Respirator & Gas Helmet Drill	
	26		Gun cleaning, Limber Packing; Revolver Drill	
VERMELLES	26		Relieved the 162 Coy M. G. C. 14 Guns were put in the Line	
	27.28			
	29th		1000 rds fired on Enemy dump	
	30th		1 O.R. Killed. Gun buried but dug out at dusk. 1000 Rds fired on Enemy dump.	
	31st		1 O.R. Wounded. 750 Rds fired on Enemy dump	

Williamson Capt.
OC No 71 M. G. Coy.

2353 Wt. W2544/1454 700,000 5/15 D. D. & L. A.D.S.S./Forms/C. 2118.

PAGE I

Instructions regarding War Diaries and Intelligence Summaries are contained in F. S. Regs., Part II. and the Staff Manual respectively. Title pages will be prepared in manuscript.

WAR DIARY
or
INTELLIGENCE SUMMARY.
(Erase heading not required.)

71st Coy M.G.C

Army Form C. 2118.

Vol 6

Place	Date	Hour	Summary of Events and Information	Remarks and references to Appendices
VERMELLES	1.1.17		1000 rounds fired on CITE ST ELIE	
	2nd		500 rds fired on Enemy Commication Trench leading from St ELIE above the P in PUITS	
			1000 " " at C.T. leading from St ELIE in line with the S in PUITS; 1500 rds on Rly running away from PUITS 13	
	3rd		1750 rds fired on PUITS 13. and St ELIE; 3000 rds fired at St ELIE Communication Trench	
	4th		2000 rds " " St ELIE; 2000 rds on Rly leading from PUITS 13 an Enemy Gun retaliated but the cone fell 50x short	
	5th		1000 rds fired on St ELIE communication Trench; nothing further to report	
	6.		1000 rds " " PUITS 13 to St ELIE. 2500 rds fired on H.Y.A. 1260 rds fired on communications 92° E of R53a	
	7		2000 rds fired on St ELIE & communications leading thereto.	
	8.		1000 " " " St ELIE.	
	9.		7 Gun Teams relieved	
	10		500 rounds fired on St ELIE	WO
	11		2 Gun Teams relieved. 1500 rds fired on St ELIE.	

2353 Wt. W2544/1454 700,000 5/15 D. D. & L. A.D.S.S./Forms/C. 2118.

PAGE. 2.

Instructions regarding War Diaries and Intelligence Summaries are contained in F. S. Regs., Part II. and the Staff Manual respectively. Title pages will be prepared in manuscript.

WAR DIARY
or
INTELLIGENCE SUMMARY.

(*Erase heading not required.*)

71 M. G. Coy.

Army Form C. 2118.

Place	Date	Hour	Summary of Events and Information	Remarks and references to Appendices
VERMELLES	12.		1000 rounds fired on St ELIE	
"	13.		1,000 " " G5 b. 4½. 3.: 500 rounds fired on G6 b. 1 8.	
"	14.		1000 " " G6 a 3½ 6½ : 1000 " " new enemy	
"	"		trench in H 7c & H. 13 a: 750 rounds fired on St ELIE. 3 Gun teams relieved.	
"	15		1000 rounds fired on G 5b. 4½. 2.: 500 " " G6 A. 4. 2 to G6 b 1. 8½	
"	"		500 " " G6 a 3½ 5½.	
"	16.		500 " " G5b. 4½. 2.	
"	17.		500 " " St ELIE communications: 750 rds fired on G5a 4. 3.: 250 rds on G6. b ½. 8½.	
"	18		750 " " G5 b. 4½. 2½.: 250 rds fired at G6. b ½. 8½. 3 Gun teams relieved	
"	19.		1000 " " G5. b. 4½. 2½: 1000 " " G6. b. ½. 8½.	
"	20		1000 " " on CITE St ELIE. 3 Gun teams relieved	
"	21.		1000 " " " Do 500 rounds fired on G6 b. 9. 8½	
"	22		1000 " " CITE St ELIE 500 " " G 5a. 1. 6½.	
"	"		500 " " G6 b. 9. 8½.	
"	23		1000 " " CITE St ELIE. 1250 fired at G6 b 9. 8½: 1500 rds fired on G 5a 1. 6½.	
"	"		3 Gun teams relieved.	

W.C.

2353 Wt. W2544/1454 700,000 5/15 D. D. & L. A.D.S.S./Forms/C. 2118.

PAGE III

WAR DIARY
or
INTELLIGENCE SUMMARY.
(Erase heading not required.)

1/1 M. G. Coy.

Army Form C. 2118.

Instructions regarding War Diaries and Intelligence Summaries are contained in F. S. Regs., Part II. and the Staff Manual respectively. Title pages will be prepared in manuscript.

Place	Date	Hour	Summary of Events and Information	Remarks and references to Appendices
VERMELLES	24		1000 rounds fired on CITE ST. ELIE	
	25		2900 " " " "	
	-		450 - - - G5a.90.45. 1000 rounds fired on Enemy's C.Ts from G5a to G5b.	
	26		3 Gun teams relieved. 1000 rounds fired on CITE ST. ELIE.	
	26		1000 rounds fired on G5a 1.6½. 1250 rounds fired on G6b.9.8½	
	27		1500 - - - G5a 90.45. 2000 - - - G5d.10.20	
	-		1000 - - - CITE ST. ELIE 400 - - - Machine Gun at 7a.70.05	
	28		2000 - - G5a.60.63 to G5a 52.72: 500 rounds fired on G5b 4.6 to G5b.2.2.: 1600 rounds fired on Enemy CTs leading from ST. ELIE.	
	29		1500 rds on H7a.25.20, where work has been reported in progress: The range was lengthened to G7a.70.05 where a MG. is suspected. This brought retaliation which was however, short & wide: 1500 rds on G5a central 4000 rounds on roads G6a on the three occasions when transport could be distinctly heard. 1700 rounds on ST. ELIE	
	30.		1250 rds fired on road & communication to the right of Fosse 8.	
	-		1000 - - - G5b & G6a.: 1250 rds fired on H7a.2.5.	WW

2353 Wt. W2544/1454 700,000 5/15 D. D. & L. A.D.S.S./Forms/C. 2118.

PAGE IV

Instructions regarding War Diaries and Intelligence Summaries are contained in F. S. Regs., Part II. and the Staff Manual respectively. Title pages will be prepared in manuscript.

WAR DIARY
or
INTELLIGENCE SUMMARY.
(Erase heading not required.)

71 M. G. Coy

Army Form C. 2118.

Place	Date	Hour	Summary of Events and Information	Remarks and references to Appendices
VERMELLES.	30.1.17.		Enemy transport heard in ST. ELIE. This was fired on and	
	"		heard to gallop. 900 rounds fired on Engine Shed and	
	"		communications at ST. ELIE.	

Williamson Capt
O.C. No 71 M. G. Coy

2353 Wt. W2544/1454 700,000 5/15 D. D. & L. A.D.S.S./Forms/C. 2118.

Page I

Instructions regarding War Diaries and Intelligence Summaries are contained in F. S. Regs., Part II. and the Staff Manual respectively. Title pages will be prepared in manuscript.

WAR DIARY
or
INTELLIGENCE SUMMARY.
(*Erase heading not required.*)

71st M. G. Coy.

Army Form C. 2118.

Vol 7

Place	Date	Hour	Summary of Events and Information	Remarks and references to Appendices
VERMELLES	31/1/17		2250 rds fired on G.6 b.05.85 to A 30 d. 40.55. : 3000 rds on CITE ST. ELIE.	
–	1/2/17		1000 – – – G.6 b. 97 : 1750 rds on Transport heard at ST. ELIE.	
	–		1000 – – – H.1.C 7 6½ : 1200 – – H 7.a.2 9½ : 3000 on G.5 b. 4½. 2.	
	2/2/17		4000 – – – H.1.A 3½. : 1000 – – G 6 b 1. 8½. : 1250 " Transport heard at	
	–		CITE ST. ELIE : 1500 rds on G 6 a. 6 1 to G.6 b.1.9½. : 1900 rds on G.6 a 3.4 to G 6 a. 5 9½.	
	3/2/17		750 rds on Transport behind CITE ST ELIE. : 1500 rds fired on CITE. ST. ELIE.	
	–		3000 fired on H.1.C.8 5½. to H.1.C.03. : 2250 rds on G.6 a 6½ 1. to G.6 b.1 9½ : 2750 on G.6 b.9.7 to G 6 b 9.5	
	4/2/17		3000 – – H 1 b.2.3 to H.1 b. 4.4. 3500 fired on H 1 a.2½ to H 1 a. 4.1 : 3.250 on G 6 b.5.2 to G 6 b 4.3	
	5/2/17		500 rds " " Transport at CITE ST. ELIE. 4,250 " " CITE. ST. ELIE. 500 rds fired on G 6 b. ½. 8½.	
	–		3000 " " – G 6.b.5 2 : 3000 rds fired on H 1 a.2.1½ : 2,500 fired on H 1 b.2.3.	
	6/2/17		2000 – – G 6 b, 4.2 to H 2.5 b.2.5. 2000 rds fired on A 25 b.2.5 to A 30 a 2½ 10 : 1500 fired on	
	–		G.6 a. 6,10 to A.30.b.5 10 : 2500 fired on Cross Rds at CITE ST. ELIE : 2500 fired on Communication at CITE, ST. ELIE	
	7/2/17		2.500 rds fired on CITE ST ELIE Communication : 3250 fired on Cross Rds CITE. ST. ELIE	
	–		1,500 – – – G b 5. 4.2 to A.25 b. 25 : 1500 on A 25 b.2.5 to H 30 a 2½ 10 :	
	–		1,500 – – – G 6 a.6.10 to A 30 b.5.10 : 500 fired on G.6 d.9.6 to G.12.b.1.7.	
	8/2/17		25,000 rds " " C.T.'S Support Line & Roads in vicinity of the Raid.	WLS

T2134. Wt. W708–776. 500000. 4/15. Sir J. C. & S.

Page II

WAR DIARY
or
INTELLIGENCE SUMMARY.
(Erase heading not required.)

71st M. G. Coy.

Army Form C. 2118.

Instructions regarding War Diaries and Intelligence Summaries are contained in F. S. Regs., Part II. and the Staff Manual respectively. Title pages will be prepared in manuscript.

Place	Date	Hour	Summary of Events and Information	Remarks and references to Appendices
VERMELLES	9 2/17		10.000 rds fired on C.T.S & Roads	
	10 2/17		2.000 " " Communication near FOSSE. 8. ; 5000 fired on Communication near Quarries	
	11 2/17		4500 " " Do in G.6.6. 5000 fired on CT.S & Transport. A.A.A	
	12 2/17		25.000 & Barrages each side of the portion of enemy's line raided	
	13 2/17		5.000 fired on ST. ELIE & Roads. S of AUCHY.	
	14 2/17		6.000 " " enemy's CTS Pathways	
	15 2/17		5.000 " " CTS & Roadways.	
	16 2/17		Relieved by 62nd M G Coy & proceeded to BETHUNE	
	17 2/17 }		Programme of Physical Training, Gun Drill Re-equipping	
	27 2/17 }		In the afternoons, Recreational Training	
	28 2/17		Relieved 2nd Cav: Squadron M.G in the right sub-sector QUARRIES	8 guns
			" 111th M. G. Coy left HULLUCH	6 guns

[illegible] Capt.
O.C. No 71 M G Coy

Page I

Instructions regarding War Diaries and Intelligence Summaries are contained in F. S. Regs., Part II. and the Staff Manual respectively. Title pages will be prepared in manuscript.

WAR DIARY
or
INTELLIGENCE SUMMARY.
(Erase heading not required.)

11th M.G. Corps.

Vol 8

Army Form C. 2118.

Place	Date	Hour	Summary of Events and Information	Remarks and references to Appendices
VERMELLES	28 2/17		1500 rds fired on Fosse 8. : 1000 fired at 5 B. 4½.2. : 1/3/17 1000 rds fired at 5 A. 3½.3.	
"	2 3/17		750 " " at G. 5.A. 4.3; 750 fired at G. 6. B. ½. 8½ 500 rds fired at G. 5 B 4½. 2.	
			3000 " " " CITE ST. ELIE	
	3 3/17		2500 " " on Enemys Trenches & Rds G. 6 a G. 12. 6. ; 250 fired at enemys M. Gun 75 to 78	
	5 3/17		1000 " " Vertical Searching. 2000 rounds fired on CITE ST ELIE	
	6 3/17		450 " " " Enemy Trenches G 5 D. 125 rounds fired on Area round [illegible] 13 H 7.	
	7 3/17		1500 " " " " Machine Guns 2000 " " Enemy Trenches	
	8 3/17		2250 " " " Trenches 1000 " " " "	
	9 3/17		1000 " " " G 6 B ½ 8½. 1250 rds fired on A 29 D. 6·1½. 1000 rds on CITE ST ELIE	
			3500 " " " Enemy Trenches	
	10 3/17		1000 " " " H. 7. B. 4 to H. 14. a. 1250 rds fired on H. 8. B to H 15 a. 1000 rds on CITE ST ELIE	
	"		750 " " " H. 1 C. 4½ 5. 1000 rds fired at A. 29. D. 6. 1½. 500 rds on G. 6 B. 9. 7.	
			3000 rds fired on Enemy Trenches.	
	[illegible] 3/17		500 " " " fired at CITE ST. ELIE. 250 rounds fired at G. 6 B. ½. 8½	
			250 " " " " A. 29. D. 6·1½. 3000 " " " Enemy Trenches	
			1500 " " " area H. 8. B to H. 14 B & D. 1250 fired at H. 7 b. to H 14. a. 1500 on H 8 B to H 15 a	

W W Capt
OC Comdg 11th Coy M.G. Corps

T2134. Wt. W708–776. 500000. 4/15. Sir J. C. & S.

PAGE 2

Instructions regarding War Diaries and Intelligence Summaries are contained in F. S. Regs., Part II. and the Staff Manual respectively. Title pages will be prepared in manuscript.

WAR DIARY or INTELLIGENCE SUMMARY.

(Erase heading not required.)

71st M.G.C.

Army Form C. 2118.

Place	Date	Hour	Summary of Events and Information	Remarks and references to Appendices
Vermelles	12/7/17		1000 Rds fired on Area. H8b to H14 b.d. 1250 rds fired on area H7b to H14a.	
	〃		1000 〃 〃 〃 〃 H8b to H15a. 4000 〃 〃 〃 Enemy Com. Trench & Light Railway.	
	13/7/17		750 〃 〃 〃 〃 H8b to H14 b.d. 1000 〃 〃 〃 area H7b to H14a.	
	〃		1000 〃 〃 〃 〃 H8b to H15a. 1250 〃 〃 〃 〃 H1d to H7c	
	〃		1500 〃 〃 〃 Enemy Trenches	
	14/7/17		3000 〃 〃 〃 〃 〃 & 1000 〃 〃 〃 gaps in Enemy Wire	
	15/7/17		2000 〃 〃 〃 〃 〃 1000 〃 〃 〃 Enemy Front Wire	
			2000 〃 〃 〃 area G.6b to G.6d.	
	16/7/17		2000 〃 〃 〃 Enemy Trenches & 3500 〃 〃 〃 〃 Machine Gun	
	17/7/17		3250 〃 〃 〃 〃 M. Gun & 1000 fired on CITE ST ELIE. 1250 on Enemy Road	
	18/7/17		800 〃 〃 〃 〃 G.Ts. 1000 rounds fired on Enemy H8b to H14 b.d.	
	〃		1000 〃 〃 〃 〃 H7b to H14a, 3000 rounds fired on Enemy M.Gs. with Effect	
	19/7/17		3000 〃 〃 〃 Enemy M.G with good effect. 1250 fired on CITE ST ELIE	
	〃		1000 〃 〃 〃 〃 GTs. About 4 P.M, yesterday, a hostile aeroplane flying at about 1,000 ft was fired on. It dived abruptly & made for the German Lines	
			W.L.S. Capt	

T2134. Wt. W708–776. 500000. 4/15. Sir J. C. & S.

O.C. 71st Coy M. G. Corps

PAGE. 3

Instructions regarding War Diaries and Intelligence Summaries are contained in F. S. Regs., Part II. and the Staff Manual respectively. Title pages will be prepared in manuscript.

WAR DIARY or INTELLIGENCE SUMMARY. 41st M.G.C

(Erase heading not required.)

Army Form C. 2118.

Place	Date	Hour	Summary of Events and Information	Remarks and references to Appendices
Vermelles	20/3/17		2.000 rounds fired on. CITE St ELIE. 1000 rds fired on H1d.80.00 + H8d.55.95	
"	21/3/17		3,000 " " " Enemy Area. H1d to H8d. 5250 rds fired on Enemy M. Gun	
	22/3/17		3,450 " " " " Trenches. 3500 fired on area. H1d to H7b. 1000 fired on Hulluch	
	23/3/17		2.500 " " " " Area H1d to H1b. 4,000 rds fired on Enemy Trenches	
	24/3/17		3,000 " " " " Trenches	
	25/3/17		2.500 " " " " Communication Trenches & Cite St ELIE	
	26/3/17		2,500 " " " " Ditto Ditto.	
	27/3/17		Rounds fired Nil - - - - - -	
	28/3/17		3000, rds fired on Enemy Railway Track.	
	29/3/17		1000. " " " " Supply Dump. 2,000 rds on Enemy Com Trench	
	30/3/17		Nil report	
"	31/3/17		1,200 rds fired at CITE St ELIE	

William Wilson Capt.
O.C. Comdg 41 Coy M. G. Corps

T2134. Wt. W708-776. 500000. 4/15. Sir J. C. & S.

Page 2

Instructions regarding War Diaries and Intelligence Summaries are contained in F. S. Regs., Part II. and the Staff Manual respectively. Title pages will be prepared in manuscript.

WAR DIARY
or
INTELLIGENCE SUMMARY.

11th M. G. C.

(*Erase heading not required.*)

Army Form C. 2118.

Vol 9.

Place	Date	Hour	Summary of Events and Information	Remarks and references to Appendices
Vermelles	14/4/17		3,250 rds fired at Communication Trenches & Roads. 1500 rds fired at Rds behind St Elie	
"	18/4/17		1,250 " " " Enemy Roads. 1000 " " " Enemy Trenches	
"	19/4/17		500 " " " " "	
"	20/4/17		500 " " " Cite St Elie 2000 " " " " " & Rds	
"	21/4/17		1,500 " " " Do - Do 5000 " " " " " "	
"	22/4/17		4,500 " " " Enemy Support & Reserve Trenches & CTs	
"	23/4/17		1,000 " " " " " & " "	
"	24/4/17		2,500 " " " " Trenches & Roads behind St Elie	
"	25/4/17		4,000 " " " " Tracks & Roads	
"	26/4/17		3,250 " " " " Enemy Communication Trenches	
"	27/4/17		No rounds fired	
"	28/4/17		" " "	
"	29/4/17		" " "	
"	30/4/17		" " "	

T2134. Wt. W708-776. 500000. 4/15. Sir J. C. & S.

Page. 1

Instructions regarding War Diaries and Intelligence Summaries are contained in F. S. Regs., Part II. and the Staff Manual respectively. Title pages will be prepared in manuscript.

WAR DIARY
or
INTELLIGENCE SUMMARY.

(Erase heading not required.)

71st M G Corps

Army Form C. 2118.

Place	Date	Hour	Summary of Events and Information	Remarks and references to Appendices
Vermelles	April 1st/17		1.500 rds fired at Enemy Com. Trenches	
"	2.		No rounds fired	
"	3		No rounds fired	
"	4		1,000 " " at CITE ST. ELIE. 3500 rds fired at Enemy Com. Trenches	
"	5		4.250 " " Enemy Com. Trenches. 4250 rds " " Enemy Wire	
"	6		3,000 " " at C.Ts and roads in St Elie.	
"	7		1,000 " " Enemy Trenches & roads.	
"	8		No rounds fired	
"	9		4,000 rds fired at Enemy Trenches, 4000 rds fired at Enemy roads	
"	10		4,000 " " " " " and roads	
"	11		4.500 " " " " " , 2,000 rds fired at Enemy area G.12 b. 0.3.	
"	11		4.000 " " " targets on "barrage lines".	
"	12		4 250 " " " Enemy Trenches 14th 750 rds on En. Wire	
"	13		1,000 " " " " " 15th 750 rds fired at Enemy Wire	
"	14		2250 " " " " " 1500 rds fired at H13b. 13.10 to H13b. 90 35	

T2134. Wt. W708-776. 500000. 4/15. Sir J. C. & S.

PAGE 1

Instructions regarding War Diaries and Intelligence Summaries are contained in F. S. Regs., Part II. and the Staff Manual respectively. Title pages will be prepared in manuscript.

WAR DIARY
or
INTELLIGENCE SUMMARY.
(Erase heading not required.)

71 Coy M.G. Corps

Army Form C. 2118.

Vol 10

Place	Date	Hour	Summary of Events and Information	Remarks and references to Appendices
Maroc	1st May 1917		No rounds fired. Heavy enemy shelling of our lines. Armour piercing shell penetrated	
"	2nd "		one of our deep dug-outs, which was completely wrecked. Three of our men lost their lives	
"	3 "	"	Coy relieved by 138 M.G. Coy on the night of 2-3rd.	
Vermelles	4"	"	Coy relieved 16th M.G. Coy in the line on the night of 3-4th.	
"	5"	"	1500 rds fired on Enemy communication Trenches	
"	6	"	1500 " " " Do Do	
"	"		1500 " " " Trenches & Cross Roads. Usual shelling of our back areas	
"	7"		1000 " " " the QUARRIES N. of St ELIE. 1000 rds fired on Enemy Railway running through FOSSE 8. 1000 rds fired on Enemy Trenches.	
"	8th	"	2500 " " at Enemy Trenches & cross Roads	
"	9th	"	No rounds fired	
"	10th	"	5500 rds " at Enemy Support & Reserve Trenches as per O.O. 179	
"	11th	"	250 " " " " aeroplane which was flying very low over our lines	
"	12th	"	Night quiet. No rounds fired	
"	13	"	1000 rds fired at Enemy Support & Reserve Trenches	
"	14th	"	13,800 " " " Do. Do. Do.	

Instructions regarding War Diaries and Intelligence Summaries are contained in F. S. Regs., Part II. and the Staff Manual respectively. Title pages will be prepared in manuscript.

PAGE 11

WAR DIARY
or
INTELLIGENCE SUMMARY.
(Erase heading not required.)

71st Coy Machine Gun Corps

Army Form C. 2118.

Place	Date	Hour	Summary of Events and Information	Remarks and references to Appendices
	MAY			
Vermelles	15th		1500 rounds fired at Enemy Trenches & back areas.	
"	16th		2,000 " do do do do	
"	17th		4,000 " do do Cross Roads & C.Ts.	
"	18th		Coy relieved by 9th M G Squadron	
Fouquereuil	19th		Coy on rest at Fouquereuil	
Vermelles	29th		Coy relieves 9th M G Squadron & one Section M M Gun Battery	
"	30th		2,000 rds fired on Enemy Trenches.	
"	31st		1,500 " " " " Support & Reserve Trenches	

R M Scott Lieut for
O C Comdg No 71 Coy M G C.

T2134. Wt. W708–776. 500000. 4/15. Sir J. C. & S.

Page 1.

Instructions regarding War Diaries and Intelligence Summaries are contained in F. S. Regs., Part II. and the Staff Manual respectively. Title pages will be prepared in manuscript.

WAR DIARY
or
INTELLIGENCE SUMMARY.
(Erase heading not required.)

7/16 Coy M. G. Corps.

Army Form C. 2118.

Vol XI

Place	Date	Hour	Summary of Events and Information	Remarks and references to Appendices
Vermelles	1-6-17		9,000 rds fired on Enemy support & Reserve Trenches & CTS. Very quiet night	
"	2-6-17		Nothing of importance to report. Night extremely quiet.	
"	3-6-17		5000 rds fired on Enemy cross roads & light railways. Hostile artillery very active	
"	"		on VILLAGE LINES. with 4" & 5"·9 shells. No casualties. Situation normal.	
"	4-6-17		2000 rounds fired on Enemy Support & Reserve Trenches. R.50 position was shelled	
"	"		almost immediately it had opened fire with "minnies" & rifle Grenades. Casualties one.	
"	5-6-17		No rounds fired. At 11·30 P.M. an aeroplane crossed over our lines. The enemy sent up four green lights, as signals for the searchlights behind. Four were immediately brought into play from CITE ST ELIE & WINGLES, but nothing resulted from it. Our Support lines shelled heavily with "minnies"	
"	6-6-17		6000 rds fired as per O.O. The enemy sent up numerous Golden rain rockets. He immediately dropped a barrage on "no mans land", with aerial darts & Medium Trench Mortars also on front & support lines. Enemy Machine Guns were very active during the whole of the raid using the swinging traverse over our lines. The enemy seemed very alert & quite prepared for the raid	

T2134. Wt. W708–776. 500000. 4/15. Sir J. C. & S.

Page 2

Instructions regarding War Diaries and Intelligence Summaries are contained in F. S. Regs., Part II. and the Staff Manual respectively. Title pages will be prepared in manuscript.

WAR DIARY
or
INTELLIGENCE SUMMARY.
(*Erase heading not required.*)

Army Form C. 2118.

4/1 Coy M G Corps

Place	Date	Hour	Summary of Events and Information	Remarks and references to Appendices
Vermelles	6.6.17		3000 rds fired on working party at FOSSE 8 with good results	
"	"		3000 " " " A 30 central & CITE ST ELIE. The enemy opened out on front support & reserve lines at 5.30 AM with "minnies" & shrapnel & various other size shells. Heavy bombardment heard in the direction of Lens during the past 24 hours.	
"	7.6.17		5000 rds fired on Enemy working party at FOSSE 8 A 30 central & CITE ST ELIE. Heavy bombardment by Enemy Trench Mortars H & M. between 4.30 AM & 5.30 AM. on our front, support, & reserve trenches. Heavy bombardment continues in the region of LENS. Situation normal.	
"	8.6.17		2500 rds fired on Auchy - LA Bassee - Haines road running through A 9b & A 30 a & b (36 NW) large parties of enemy observed on this road. 2000 rounds fired on Enemy Back areas.	
"	9.6.17		4000 rounds fired on Enemy working party. Nothing unusual to report.	
"	10.6.17		Nothing unusual to report. Our artillery opened out very heavy about 11.30 PM. otherwise a very quiet night.	

T2134. Wt. W708-776. 500000. 4/15. Sir J. C. & S.

PAGE 3

Instructions regarding War Diaries and Intelligence Summaries are contained in F. S. Regs., Part II. and the Staff Manual respectively. Title pages will be prepared in manuscript.

WAR DIARY
or
INTELLIGENCE SUMMARY.
(Erase heading not required.)

2/1 Coy M G Corps

Army Form C. 2118.

Place	Date	Hour	Summary of Events and Information	Remarks and references to Appendices
Vermelles	11.6.17		5000 rounds fired on enemy support & reserve trenches during raid. At about 8.30 PM the enemy attempted to raid our trenches in the Cambrian sector but were caught by our Machine Gun fire & artillery. The enemys bombardment was very fierce & he sent up numerous red, green & yellow rockets. The enemy trenches were raided at 12:30 AM under the cover of an intense bombardment which lasted for about an hour & a half. Many loud explosions were heard & numerous rockets of all descriptions were sent up by the enemy.	
"	12.6.17		Night extremely quiet. 3 O.Rs admitted to hospital sick.	
"	13.6.17		7.000 rds fired on Enemy working party with good effect. Usual artillery duel. 1 O.R rejoined from Hospital.	
"	14.6.17		6,000 rounds fired on Enemy Support & Reserve Trenches CTs. Fires seen in the direction of LENS.	
"	15.6.17		No rounds fired. 1 Officer proceeded on Advanced course of Transport. 1 O.R from Hospital. 2 O.Rs admitted to Hospital.	
"	16.6.17		8,000 rounds fired on enemy back areas. Casualties nil. Night quiet	
"	17.6.17		No rounds fired. Heavy Enemy shelling on our support & front lines	

T2134. Wt. W708–776. 500000. 4/15. Sir J. C. & S.

PAGE 4

Instructions regarding War Diaries and Intelligence Summaries are contained in F. S. Regs., Part II. and the Staff Manual respectively. Title pages will be prepared in manuscript.

WAR DIARY
or
INTELLIGENCE SUMMARY.
(Erase heading not required.)

71st Coy M. G. Corps

Army Form C. 2118.

Place	Date	Hour	Summary of Events and Information	Remarks and references to Appendices
Vermelles	18/6/17		7000 rounds fired on enemy working party. Night extremely quiet	
"	19/6/17		Coy relieved by 147 Coy M.G.C. Coy moved to rest billets at Drouvin	
DROUVIN	20/6/17		Coy in strict training	
"	21/6/17		Parades for the day. Physical training, Setting & laying guns. Gun Drill, Gun & limber cleaning	
			4. O.Rs granted proficiency pay.	
"	22/6/17		Training as usual followed by route march & lectures by Section Officers	
"	23/6/17		Parades for the day. Physical training, Sight Setting, gun laying, judging distances.	
"	"		2 N.C.Os granted proficiency pay class I. 1.O.R. awarded 25 Days F.P. No 1.	
"	24/6/17		Parades for the day. Physical training. Gun Drill, Mechanism, Immediate Action	
			Sight Setting. 1.O.R granted proficiency pay class II.	
"	25/6/17		Training as before, followed by recreation.	
"	26/6/17		Training for the day. Physical training. Immediate action, Gun laying, sight-sighting Etc.	
Bully Grenay	27/6/17		Coy moves from Drouvin to Bully-Grenay. Arrival reported to 71st I.B.	
"	29/6/17		2 O.Rs admitted to Hospital	
Vermelles	30/6/17		Coy moves to Vermelles to relieve 147 Coy M.G. Corps	

No. 71 M.G. COMPANY
1-7-17
ORDERLY ROOM

J. Rushton Moore – Capt.
Comdg. No. 71 Coy. M.G. Corps.

PAGE 1

Instructions regarding War Diaries and Intelligence Summaries are contained in F. S. Regs., Part II. and the Staff Manual respectively. Title pages will be prepared in manuscript.

WAR DIARY
or
INTELLIGENCE SUMMARY.
(Erase heading not required.)

71st Coy. M. G. CORPS — Army Form C. 2118.

Vol 12

Place	Date	Hour	Summary of Events and Information	Remarks and references to Appendices
VERMELLES	JULY 1st 1917		No rounds fired. Heavy bombardment heard in the direction of LIENS. One O.R. admitted to Hospital. 3 O.R. rejoined from Hospital. 1 officer & 1 O.R. returned from MG course. 1 officer — f.	
DO	2nd	11 PM to 3 PM	6,000 rounds fired on Enemy centres of movement. Night extremely quiet	
		11-15 AM	500 rounds fired on Enemy aeroplane. 1 Officer proceeds on MG course. 1 O.R. returned from leave. 1 O.R. rejoined from Hospital. 1 O.R. granted proficiency pay	
DO	3rd	10-30 PM to 4 AM	3000 rds fired on area H.4a 9.6 & H1d 45.1 to H2a.05.4	
"		10 PM to 3 AM	3000 " fired on the vicinity of PUITS No 13. 2000 rds fired on Enemy Roads. H.1.c.4.0 to H1a.7.0	
"			500 " fired on Enemy aircraft. MOVEMENT. A great deal of movement was seen behind the enemy's line between 4-30 AM & 5-45 AM Parties of 4 & 5 were seen walking across fields behind ST ELIE. Situation NORMAL. REINFORCEMENT. 1 Officer joined from 178 Coy M.G. Corps. 2 O.Rs returned from leave.	
DO.	4th	8 PM to 4 PM	8000 rounds fired Trench Rly Road & CITE ST ELIE, Vicinity Puits 13 and Trenches in G.12.b. A balloon was seen drifting over our lines at Stand to	
DO	5th	10 PM to 4 AM	10000 rds fired on Tracks, Roads & Trench Rlys. Nothing unusual to report.	
DO	6th	10 PM to 4 AM	8,000 " " " vicinity of Puits 13 & Cite St Elie. 1 O.R. to Hospital	

Instructions regarding War Diaries and Intelligence Summaries are contained in F. S. Regs., Part II. and the Staff Manual respectively. Title pages will be prepared in manuscript.

WAR DIARY
or
INTELLIGENCE SUMMARY.
(Erase heading not required.)

Army Form C. 2118.

PAGE 2.

Place	Date	Hour	Summary of Events and Information	Remarks and references to Appendices
VERMELLES	4 7/17	10-0 PM to 4 AM	45,000 rounds fired on the following targets. Tracks & roads in the vicinity of PUITS 13 & CITE ST ELIE. Infantry Officers reported that our fire on CITE ST ELIE was very effective. The bullets could be seen striking the road & several parties were caught by our fire. 1 O.R. rejoined from Hospital.	
DO.	8 7/17	10.30 PM to 4 AM	50,000 rounds fired on the following targets. Vicinity of PUITS 13 & CITE ST ELIE. 1 Officer proceeded on a course. 1 O.R. admitted to Hospital.	
DO	9 7/17	10.0 PM to 4 AM	55,000 rounds fired on the following targets. Roads & cross roads & light Trench Railway. 1 Officer rejoined from Course. 1 O.R. rejoined from Base Depot.	
DO	10 7/17	10 PM to 4 AM	35,000 rounds fired on Enemy communication trenches, Dumps, Tracks etc. Situation NORMAL. 2 O.R rejoined from leave.	
DO	11 7/17	10 PM to 3-30 AM	50,000 rds fired on CITE ST ELIE, tracks, Dumps, & CTs. Enemy shelled our positions with 5.9. No casualties. Situation normal.	
DO	12 7/17	10 PM 3-AM	35,000 Rounds fired on Tracks, roads, light Railway. 3 O.R. granted leave.	
DO	13 7/17	9.0 PM 3.0 AM	30,000 " " " Tracks, roads Light Railway & Fosse 8. 1 O.R. admitted to Hospital.	
DO	14 7/17		30.000 rds. fired on Tracks, roads, light Railway, 500 rounds fired at Enemy aircraft.	

T2134. Wt. W708–776. 500000. 4/15. Sir J. C. & S.

Instructions regarding War Diaries and Intelligence Summaries are contained in F. S. Regs., Part II. and the Staff Manual respectively. Title pages will be prepared in manuscript.

PAGE 3

WAR DIARY
or
INTELLIGENCE SUMMARY.
(Erase heading not required.)

Army Form C. 2118.

Place	Date	Hour	Summary of Events and Information	Remarks and references to Appendices
VERMELLES	14.7.17	11.15AM	with good effect. The enemy airman returned the fire with his machine Gun, but was eventually driven off.	
DO	15.7.17	9.0.PM 3.0AM	Harrassing fire continued during the whole of the night. A marked decrease in Enemy trench mortars, "minnies" etc during the past three days. 30,00 rounds fired on the usual target. Situation normal. 1. Officer rejoined from course.	
DO.	16.7.17	9.30PM 3.30AM	Harrassing fire continued during the night, in which 30,000 rounds were expended on tracks, light railways, dumps, roads & CTS. 500 rounds fired on enemy M.G. which was giving constant trouble during the night. 2 O.Rs. from Hospital	
DO.	17.7.17	9.0PM 2.30AM	Harrassing fire continued throughout the night in which 30.000 rounds were expended on the usual target. Situation normal. 19.O.RS reported from Base Depot.	
DO	18.7.17	9.0PM 3.0AM	No rounds expended during the night. 1.O.R admitted to Hospital. 1.O.R rejoined from leave.	
DO	19.7.17		No " " " " " according to orders. A marked increase was noticed during day. Enemy trench mortars & "minnies" were very active. St Georges trench was heavily "minnied" eight & nine at a time. Situation normal. 1.O.R. rejoined from leave.	
DO	20.7.17		Nothing to report. The night was extremely quiet except for a little shelling of our front line. 1.O.R from leave.	

T2134. Wt. W708—776. 500000. 4/15. Sir J. C. & S.

Instructions regarding War Diaries and Intelligence Summaries are contained in F. S. Regs., Part II. and the Staff Manual respectively. Title pages will be prepared in manuscript.

WAR DIARY
or
INTELLIGENCE SUMMARY.
(Erase heading not required.)

PAGE. 4.

Army Form C. 2118.

Place	Date	Hour	Summary of Events and Information	Remarks and references to Appendices
VERMELLES.	21-7-17		Night was very quiet there being nothing to report.	
"	22-7-17	10.30PM	5000 rds fired on enemy centres of movement. Situation normal. 1.O.R accidently wounded.	
"				
"	23-7-17	11-0PM	2,000 rds fired on Enemy aircraft, which were very active during the day.	
"	24-7-17	9.15PM	88,000 rds fired in conjunction with raid. The coy was assisted by 16 guns from Divl. Coy & 4 Guns from 99 M.G. Coy who fired 150.000 rounds during the raid. The enemy were evendently taken by suprise, as the enemy, just before zero hour shelled our back areas, with the result that the raiding party were in the enemies trenches before the could drop his barrage. Everything ~~[illegible]~~ was a complete success. Casualties nil. One direct hit was obtained on one of our emplacements but no damage was done. Fire was opened out again at 2-30 AM according to instruction. A prisoner captured during the raid stated that a relief was taking place at 3.0 AM & our guns continued firing throughout the night. 1.O.R. from hospital. 2.O.Rs from leave.	
"	25-7-17		Coy being relieved by 139 M.G. Coy. Relief completed at 10.0 PM.	

T2134. Wt. W708—776. 500000. 4/15. Sir J. C. & S.

Army Form C. 2118.

WAR DIARY
or
INTELLIGENCE SUMMARY
(Erase heading not required.)

Instructions regarding War Diaries and Intelligence Summaries are contained in F. S. Regs., Part II. and the Staff Manual respectively. Title Pages will be prepared in manuscript.

PAGE 5

Place	Date	Hour	Summary of Events and Information	Remarks and references to Appendices
VERMELLES	26/4/17	9-0AM	Coy proceeded to training area by bus. Arrived at 12-30 PM.	
VILLERS BRULIN	27/4/17		Training was carried out during the day as follows. Physical training, General clean up, Kit inspection etc.	
"	28/4/17		Training as follows. Physical training, gun drill, Immediate action, gun & spare part cleaning.	
"	29/4/17		Parades carried out on the training grounds as follows, Physical training, Gun Drill, Mechanism. stoppages, immediate action, etc. 3. O.Rs transfer to 18th M G Coy.	
"	30/4/17		Parades as usual. 2. O.Rs proceeded on leave.	
"	31/4/17		Training as follows. Inspection by O.C. Coy, Gun drill, immediate action, & preparation for G.O.C. inspection. 1. Officer, 2. O.Rs. returned from leave. 6. O.Rs. transferred to 178 M.G. Coy.	

J. Rushton Moore Capt

Comdg. No. 71 Coy. M. G. Corps.

2449 Wt. W14957/M90 750,000 1/16 J.B.C. & A. Forms/C.2118/12.

Army Form C. 2118.

WAR DIARY
or
INTELLIGENCE SUMMARY 71st Coy Machine Gun Corps

(Erase heading not required.)

Instructions regarding War Diaries and Intelligence Summaries are contained in F. S. Regs., Part II. and the Staff Manual respectively. Title Pages will be prepared in manuscript. PAGE. I.

Vol 13

Place	Date	Hour	Summary of Events and Information	Remarks and references to Appendices
VILLERS BRULIN.	1-8-17	7-30 - 3-30.	Training carried out as follows. Physical training, Gun Drill, Mechanism, stoppages. Squad drill, & cleaning guns & packing limbers. Weather - Showery. Strength - 185 O.Rs. 11. Officers.	
"	2-8-17	7-30 - 3-30.	Training carried out as follows. Physical training. Visual training, Sight setting, & gun laying. Gun cleaning and overhauling belts. Afternoon lectures by Section Officers. Capt. J.K. Moore MC. proceeded on leave. Weather. Fair & showery. Strength - 185. Officers 10.	
"	3-8-17	7-30 - 3-30.	Training carried out as follows:- 7-7-30 AM. Filling guns, & belts & Packing limbers. 8-45 - 1-0 PM. Coy. march to the range for firing. Weather - Fine. Temperature 75 Deg. Strength. 185 O.Rs. 10. Officers.	
"	4-8-17	7-30 - 3-0 PM	Training carried out as usual. 7-7.30 AM. Physical training. 9-10-0 AM. Inspection by Comdg. Officer. Dress Full marching Order. 10-12 NOON Gun Drill. 12-1-0 PM. Gun cleaning Overhauling & repacking limbers. 2-3-0 PM. Overhauling & refilling belts. No. 8718, Pte Parker W. rejoined from leave. Weather No change. Temperature 78 Deg. Strength. 185 O.Ranks. 10 Officers.	
"	5-8-17	7-30 1-0 PM.	Coy attends Divine Service. Bathing parade. & Gun cleaning. Weather. Fine.	

2449 Wt. W14957/M90 750,000 1/16 J.B.C. & A. Forms/C.2118/12.

Army Form C. 2118.

WAR DIARY
or
INTELLIGENCE SUMMARY
(Erase heading not required.)

Instructions regarding War Diaries and Intelligence Summaries are contained in F. S. Regs., Part II. and the Staff Manual respectively. Title Pages will be prepared in manuscript.

PAGE 2

Place	Date	Hour	Summary of Events and Information	Remarks and references to Appendices
VILLERS BRULIN	6.8.17	7.30 to 3.30.	Training carried out as follows. Physical training, Mechanism, Squad Drill, gun cleaning, & Packing limbers. 2 O.Rs. rejoined from leave. Strength 11 Officers 185 O.Rs. Weather. Fair.	
"	7.8.17	"	Training carried out as follows. Packing limbers. Overhauling clothes, equipment etc. Inspection by O.C. Coy. Inspection by G.O.C. 71st I.B. Squad Drill. Strength 11 Officers 185 O.Rs. Weather. Warmer. Temperature 75°.	
"	8.8.17	"	Inspection & presentation of Medal Ribbons by Corps Commander. Afternoon - Recreational training. Weather. No change. Temperature 75°. Strength 11 Officers - 185 O. Ranks.	
"	9.8.17	"	Training carried out as follows. Physical training, Gun Drill with Mark IV auxiliary tripod, Gas helmet & Box respirators inspected by Brigade Gas N.C.O. Sight setting & laying. A route march lasting three quarters of an hour was carried out at night. Box respirators were worn during the march. Strength 11 Officers 185 O.Rs.	
"	10.8.17	"	Training as follows. Cleaning guns & tripods. Advanced Gun Drill. Inspection of Pack mules by G.O.C. 71st I.B. Strength 11 Officers 185 O.R. 6 O.Rs detailed to help civilians to gather in the harvest.	
"	11.8.17	"	Coy put through a revolver course. 2 O.Rs awarded 5 Days F.P. No 2.	

2449 Wt. W14957/M90 750,000 1/16 J.B.C. & A. Forms/C.2118/12.

Instructions regarding War Diaries and Intelligence Summaries are contained in F. S. Regs., Part II. and the Staff Manual respectively. Title Pages will be prepared in manuscript.

PAGE 3.

WAR DIARY
or
INTELLIGENCE SUMMARY

(Erase heading not required.)

Army Form C. 2118.

Place	Date	Hour	Summary of Events and Information	Remarks and references to Appendices
VILLERS BRULIN	12-8-17.	7.30 to 3.30.	Training carried out as follows. Physical training. Grenade throwing. combined Drill, Squad Drill, cleaning guns & packing limbers. Strength 11 Officers 185 O.Rs. 1. Officer rejoined from course. 1 Officer proceeded on course at 1st Army school. 2. O.Rs rejoined from leave. Signalling N.C.O transferred to 1st Batt. Loyal North Lancs. 1. N.C.O proceeded to England for commission.	
"	13-8-17	7.30 to 3.30.	Training carried out as follows. Physical training. Squad Drill. Mechanism & stoppages. Gun Drill, Afternoon Firing on revolver range. 2. O.Rs granted leave to U.K. 1. O.R rejoined from leave.	
"	14-8-17	7.30 3.30.	Training carried out as follows. Baths. Gun Drill, Revolver practice. Revolver shooting on range. On returning from leave Capt J.R. Moore assumed command of the coy.	
"	15-8-17	7.30 to 3.30	Training carried out as follows. Physical training. Gas Drill. Gun Drill, Immediate Action. Stoppages. Strength – 11 Officers 184 O.Rs.	
"	16-8-17	7.30 to 3.30.	Training carried out as follows. Preparing guns etc for pack mule training & route march. Route march with pack mules. 1. Officer granted leave. 1 O.R granted leave. Strength 11 Officers 184 O.Rs.	

2449 Wt. W14957/M90 750,000 1/16 J.B.C. & A. Forms/C.2118/12.

Army Form C. 2118.

Instructions regarding War Diaries and Intelligence Summaries are contained in F. S. Regs., Part II. and the Staff Manual respectively. Title Pages will be prepared in manuscript.

WAR DIARY
or
INTELLIGENCE SUMMARY
(Erase heading not required.)

PAGE. 4.

Place	Date	Hour	Summary of Events and Information	Remarks and references to Appendices
VILLERS BRULIN.	17.8.17	7.30 to 4. PM.	Training carried out as follows. Physical training, Gun. Drill, Immediate Action Squad Drill. Afternoon. 73. O.Rs inoculated. Strength – 11 Officers & 184 O.Rs.	
"	18.8.17	"	Training carried out as follows. Physical training. Light setting & laying. visual training, gas drill. Afternoon devoted to recreational training. Only 50% of the men attended parades owing to inoculation.	
"	19.8.17	"	Training carried out as follows. Physical training, gun drill, gas drill cleaning gun & packing limbers & Recreational training.	
"	20.8.17	"	Training as follows. All day firing on range & recreational training.	
"	21.8.17	"	9. Officers & 94. O.Rs inoculated. 48 hours excused duty.	
"	22.8.17		1. O.R. joined from Base Depot. Strength 11 Officers & 185 O.Rs.	
"	23.8.17		Training carried out as follows. Gas Drill, Squad Drill Immediate Action, gun cleaning & packing limbers. 1. O.R granted leave. 1. OR rejoined from leave.	
"	24.8.17	"	Training as follows. Physical training Immediate action, Gun Drill, Squad Drill, Overhauling guns, spare parts Etc. 1. O.R. rejoined from leave.	

2449 Wt. W14957/M90 750,000 1/16 J.B.C. & A. Forms/C.2118/12.

Instructions regarding War Diaries and Intelligence Summaries are contained in F. S. Regs., Part II. and the Staff Manual respectively. Title Pages will be prepared in manuscript.

PAGE 5.

WAR DIARY
or
INTELLIGENCE SUMMARY
(Erase heading not required.)

Army Form C. 2118.

Place	Date	Hour	Summary of Events and Information	Remarks and references to Appendices
VILLERS BRULIN	24.8.17		Training carried out as follows. Physical training. Packing limbers. Packed limbers inspected by O.C. Coy. Coy prepares for move.	
"	26.8.17	8-30 AM	Coy moves to NEOUX-LES-MINES by route march in full marching order. Arrived at Billet 2-10PM. 1. O.R. rejoined from Hospital.	
NEOUX-LES MINES	27.8.17	9-0 to 1.0PM	Cleaning guns & packing limbers. Strength 11 Officers 185 O.Rs. 1. O.R admitted to Hospital	
"	28.8.17	9-0 1.0PM	Training carried out as follows. Squad drill, gun drill & cleaning guns. 1. O.R. admitted to Hospital	
"	29.8.17	9-0 1.0PM	Squad drill, Inspection of Box respirators by Coy Gas N.C.O. Overhauling guns spare parts ammunition Etc.	
		2.0.PM	1 Section relieves 2 Sections of 178 M.G. Coy in the line. Relief complete 11-31PM Casualties NIL.	
"	30.8.17		Parades carried out as follows. Squad drill, Gun drill, cleaning guns, spare parts Etc. 1. O.R. joined from Base Depot. Strength increase 11 Officers 184 O.Rs.	
"	31.8.17		Parades as follows. Route March. & Lecture by Divisional Gas Officer. Strength 11 Officers & 184 O.Rs. 1. O.R. rejoined from leave	

R M Scott Lt 2nd i/c for O.C. 71st M. G. Coy

2449 Wt. W14957/M90 750,000 1/16 J.B.C. & A. Forms/C.2118/12.

Army Form C. 2118.

Vol 14

WAR DIARY
or
INTELLIGENCE SUMMARY

(Erase heading not required.)

Instructions regarding War Diaries and Intelligence Summaries are contained in F. S. Regs., Part II. and the Staff Manual respectively. Title Pages will be prepared in manuscript.

PAGE. I. 71st Coy MACHINE GUN CORPS.

Place	Date	Hour	Summary of Events and Information	Remarks and references to Appendices
NEOUX-LES MINES	1-9-17		Parades carried out as follows. Cleaning pack saddlery for G.O.C's inspection. 1 Section in the line reports enemy very restless during the night. Three barrages were promptly dropped on 'S O S' going up. Nothing followed. Casualties NIL.	
"	2-9-17		Divine Services for all ranks	
"	3-9-17		Operation Order for coming move received.	
"	4-9-17		Packing limbers Etc in preparation for the line. One Section on line relieved Casualties NIL.	
LES BREBIS	5-9-17	12 noon	Coy march to the trenches & relieve 18th M.G. Coy in the line. Relief complete 12 PM. Casualties NIL. No rounds fired during the night. REPORT. During the night the enemy opened up a heavy bombardment with gas shells & high explosives on VILLAGE LINE & also back areas. STRENGTH 11 Officers & 184 O.Rs.	
"	6-9-17		7,000 rounds fired on Enemy trenches. Intelligence Report. NIL. Enemy Operations Enemy artillery was active during the night on back areas especially LOOS. & MAROC was shelled with Gas & H.E shells. Casualties NIL.	
"	7-9-17		10,000 rounds fired on CTs Etc. Enemy Operations At 11.25 PM our S.O.S went up on 16th I.B. front. This was followed by various single red rockets, bursting into two. At 11.35 PM the artillery on both sides were very active.	

2449 Wt. W14957/M90 750,000 1/16 J.B.C. & A. Forms/C.2118/12.

Instructions regarding War Diaries and Intelligence Summaries are contained in F. S. Regs., Part II. and the Staff Manual respectively. Title pages will be prepared in manuscript.

WAR DIARY
or
INTELLIGENCE SUMMARY.
(Erase heading not required.)

Army Form C. 2118.

PAGE. 2.

Place	Date	Hour	Summary of Events and Information	Remarks and references to Appendices
LES BREBIS.	7-9-17		The Enemy Barrage appeared to be on the left Brigade front, also on our front line & communication trenches. At 11.45PM. The Enemy Barrage lifted on to the Reserve Trench - especially HURDLE TRENCH. 50. 5·9s fell round the guns & O.P. The majority of the of shells fell short. One gun was hit by shrapnel otherwise no damage was done. Casualties NIL. 1. O.R rejoined from Hospital. Situation. NORMAL.	
"	8-9.		No rounds fired during the night. ENEMY. OPERATIONS. Between 2.30PM & 3.15PM the enemy shelled our gun positions with 5·9s. No damage was done. Night quiet except for a little hostile shelling. Casualties NIL. Situation Normal.	
"	9-9.		10,000 rds fired on Enemy Trenches.	
			ENEMY OPERATIONS .... Enemy artillery put down a barrage of 77's and 4·2's during the raid by the Division on our left. Trench Mortars and aerial darts were active throughout the day.	
			Situation — Normal. CASUALTIES — Nil. STRENGTH. 11. OFF. 184. O.Rs.	
			MISCELLANEOUS. 1. OR. admitted to Hospital	
"	10-9.			

P. T. O.

T2134. Wt. W708-776. 500000. 4/15. Sir J. C. & S.

Instructions regarding War Diaries and Intelligence Summaries are contained in F. S. Regs., Part II. and the Staff Manual respectively. Title pages will be prepared in manuscript.

WAR DIARY
or
INTELLIGENCE SUMMARY.
(Erase heading not required.)

Army Form C. 2118.

PAGE. 3.

Place	Date	Hour	Summary of Events and Information	Remarks and references to Appendices
LES. BREBIS	1917 10-9		No. rounds fired. OUR. OPERATIONS. Our artillery was very active throughout the day. ENEMY DO. A hostile party attempted to raid our trenches, but were driven off by M.G. fire. Enemy artillery less active than usual. Situation Normal. Casualties NIL. Strength 11 Officers. 184 O.Rs.	
"	11-9.		No. rounds fired. OUR. OPERATIONS. Our Artillery active as usual. ENEMY DO. The enemy carried out a Gas Bombardment on our front line & Right Batt. Our S.O.S went up at 11-10 & 11-35 PM. Gun positions were shelled with "Whizz-bangs" at different periods during the day. Situation Normal. Casualties NIL. Strength 11 Officers & 184 O.Rs. 2 O.Rs proceeded on course.	
"	12-9.		6,000 rounds fired during the night. OUR. OPERATIONS. Harrassing fire carried out during the night. Enemy artillery shelled our positions during the day but obtain no hits. Situation NORMAL. Casualties NIL Strength. 11 Officers 184 O.Rs.	
"	13-9.		10,000 rds fired during the night on active areas. Situation Normal nothing to report.	

T2134. Wt. W708-776. 500000. 4/15. Sir J. C. & S.

Instructions regarding War Diaries and Intelligence Summaries are contained in F. S. Regs., Part II. and the Staff Manual respectively. Title pages will be prepared in manuscript.

WAR DIARY
or
INTELLIGENCE SUMMARY.
(Erase heading not required.)

Army Form C. 2118.

PAGE 4.

Place	Date	Hour	Summary of Events and Information	Remarks and references to Appendices
LOOS.	1917 14·9		7000 rounds expended during the night. Enemy Operations Enemy artillery searched our gun positions, but obtain no direct hits. Our Operations. Our Artillery & aeroplanes active throughout the day. Casualties. NIL. Situation Normal Strength 11 Officers 184 ORs. 2 ORs proceeded on leave.	
"	15·9		No rounds fired during night – Nothing of importance to report.	
"	16·9		Coy relieves 16th MG Coy in the line. Relief complete by 12 mid-night. Casualties NIL	
"	17·9		Nothing to report. Situation NORMAL Casualties NIL. Strength Decrease 11 Off. 181 ORs.	
"	18·9		Harressing fire carried out during the night on enemy centres of movement on which 12000 rounds were expended. Enemy Operations Our front & Support Lines were shelled at intervals during the day. Back area were also shelled. Situation normal. Casualties NIL. Strength No change.	
"	19·9		Harressing fire carried out as usual during the night. 1000 rds fired at Enemy aircraft which was flying very low. Enemy artillery less active than usual. Situation Normal Casualties NIL. Strength no change.	
"	20·9		No rounds fired. Night Extremely quiet, except for a few aerial darts & little shelling of our front line. Casualties NIL. Situation normal. Strength No change.	

T2134. Wt. W708–776. 500000. 4/15. Sir J. C. & S.

Instructions regarding War Diaries and Intelligence Summaries are contained in F. S. Regs., Part II. and the Staff Manual respectively. Title pages will be prepared in manuscript.

WAR DIARY
or
INTELLIGENCE SUMMARY.
(Erase heading not required.)

Army Form C. 2118.

PAGE. 5

Place	Date	Hour	Summary of Events and Information	Remarks and references to Appendices
LOOS	21-9-17		Harressing fire carried out during the night in which 15000 rounds were expended. Enemy Operations. Artillery active at various intervals during the day otherwise very quiet. Situation. Normal. Casualties NIL. Strength no change.	
"	22-9-17		Usual harressing fire carried out during the night in which 15000 rds were expended. One section relieved by 17th MG Coy. Relief completed by 9-30 PM. Casualties NIL. Enemy shelled the back areas, especially LOOS very heavily during the day, presumedly carrying out counter-battery work. Situation Normal.	
"	23-9-17		All Guns relieved by 139 & 137 MG Coy's. Relief complete by 12-30 AM 24th inst. Sections proceeded to LES-BREBIS for the day. Casualties NIL. Enemy Operations. About 5-20 PM. The enemy dropped an intense barrage on our support & front line; & at the same time shelled LOOS very heavily. This lasted for about an hour, but no infantry action followed. Enemy aeroplanes were very active	
CITE ST. PIERRE	24-9.		2 Sections relieved 13th Canadian Inf. G. Coy on night 24/25th. Relief complete by 12-30 AM morning of 25th. Casualties NIL. Enemy shelled back areas during the night, otherwise extremely quiet. No rounds fired. Situation Normal. Casualties NIL. Strength No change.	

Army Form C. 2118.

Instructions regarding War Diaries and Intelligence Summaries are contained in F. S. Regs., Part II. and the Staff Manual respectively. Title pages will be prepared in manuscript.

WAR DIARY
or
INTELLIGENCE SUMMARY.
(Erase heading not required.)

PAGE 6.

Place	Date	Hour	Summary of Events and Information	Remarks and references to Appendices
CITE St PIERRE	Sept. 25-9	1PM 5AM	Harressing fire carried out during the night in which 15,000 rds were fired on various active targets. Enemy retaliated by shelling our positions but obtained no direct hit. Situation NORMAL. Casualties NIL.	
"	26th	"	15,000 rds fired during night also 1,000 rds at Enemy aircraft. Leave HQ ~~received~~ shelled during the day. Enemy very active on back areas. Casualties NIL. Situation NIL. Strength 11 Officers 181 ORs. 1 Officer 1. OR granted leave.	
"	27th		10,000 rds fired on Enemy Machine Guns with good effect. 300 rds fired at enemy aircraft over CITE St PIERRE. This aeroplane was flying very low & succeeded in bringing down one of our 'planes'. Later in the evening he fetch one of our balloons down in flames. Situation NORMAL. Casualties NIL. Strength 11 Officers - 181. OR.	
"	28th		Harressing fire carried out during the night 12,000 rds expended on active targets. Enemy aeroplanes very active during the day. One brought down at about 6.30 PM falling towards his own line. Casualties NIL. Situation normal.	
"	29th		7000 rds fired during night. Enemy artillery very quiet during the night. Nothing of importance to report. Casualties NIL. Situation normal. Coy relieved by 76th M.G Coy. Relief complete by 9.30 PM. Coy returns to rest billets at Les Brebis	

T2134. Wt. W708-776. 500000. 4/15. Sir J. C. & S.

Instructions regarding War Diaries and Intelligence Summaries are contained in F. S. Regs., Part II. and the Staff Manual respectively. Title pages will be prepared in manuscript.

WAR DIARY
or
INTELLIGENCE SUMMARY.
(Erase heading not required.)

Army Form C. 2118.

PAGE 7

Place	Date	Hour	Summary of Events and Information	Remarks and references to Appendices
LES-BREBIS	30.9.17		9-0AM to 12noon coy prepares for move. 2PM Coy parades & march to DROUVIN for rest. Arrive at Billets 5PM. 2. ORs admitted to hospital. Strength 11 Off. 181 ORs.	

J. Rushton Moore Capt
OC 71st M Gun Coy

T2134. Wt. W708-776. 500000. 4/15. Sir J. C. & S.

Instructions regarding War Diaries and Intelligence Summaries are contained in F. S. Regs., Part II. and the Staff Manual respectively. Title pages will be prepared in manuscript.

WAR DIARY
or
INTELLIGENCE SUMMARY.
(*Erase heading not required.*)

Army Form C. 2118.

PAGE 1. 71st Coy Machine Gun Corps

Vol 15

Place	Date	Hour	Summary of Events and Information	Remarks and references to Appendices
DROUVIN	1-10-17		Parades carried out as follows. Inspection by OC Coy. Cleaning equipment & clothes. Orders received for one section to proceed up the line. 2 i/c proceeds to Adv Coy HQ of 18th M.G. Coy to make the necessary arrangements and reconnoitre the line. Section moves off at 5 PM and arrived at Adv. HQ by 10-0 PM. Casualties NIL. 2 ORs proceed on leave. 3 Sections remain in rest billets.	
"	2-10-17	9-0 to 1-PM	Parades carried out as follows. Cleaning & scrubbing clothes & equipment Etc. Limbers cleaned & polished. Spare parts & M.G. equipment checked & re-distributed. Coy paid out. Strength 11 Officers. 181 ORs.	
"	3-10-17	"	Parades carried out as follows 9-9.30 Cleaning equipment Etc. 10 AM OC's inspection. 10-30 to 11-30 Gun drill. 11-30 to 1 PM Cleaning limbers. Afternoon devoted to recreational training.	
"	4-10-17	"	Usual daily parades. Morning devoted to overhauling limbers. 1 OR from course of instruction. 5 ORs joined from Base Depot. Strength 11 Officers 185 ORs.	
"	5-10-17	"	Parades as follows. Inspection by OC Coy. Gun Drill & packing limbers.	
"	6-10-17	"	Usual daily parades. Strength 11 Officers 185 ORs.	
"	7-10-17	"	Parades as follows. Cleaning guns & limbers. Packing limbers.	

T2134. Wt. W708-776. 500000. 4/15. Sir J. C. & S.

Instructions regarding War Diaries and Intelligence Summaries are contained in F. S. Regs., Part II. and the Staff Manual respectively. Title pages will be prepared in manuscript.

WAR DIARY
or
INTELLIGENCE SUMMARY.
(Erase heading not required.)

Army Form C. 2118.

PAGE 2.

Place	Date	Hour	Summary of Events and Information	Remarks and references to Appendices
DROUVIN.	8-10-17		Parades carried out as follows. Preparing guns, limbers &c in preparation for move. Orders received for Lt Scott to proceed to MGTC. Capt Cozy joined coy & appointed 2nd/com vice Lt Scott to England.	
"	9-10-17		Coy parades 4 PM & march to Mazingarbe. Arrived in billets at 6-PM. 2 ORs Granted leave to UK. Strength 11 Officers 185 ORs.	
Mazingarbe	10-10-17		Coy march off at 4 PM to the trenches to relieve 18th M Gun Coy. Relief complete by 10 PM. Casualties 1. OR wounded. Strength decrease. 11 Officers 184 ORs. 2 ORs proceed on leave.	
LOOS	11-10-17	6 PM to 6 AM.	8.500 rounds fired on hostile communications. 1.750 rounds fired at hostile aircraft. Enemy aeroplanes returned the fire & succeeded in wounding No 4419 Sergt T Poole (Thigh). Enemy planes eventually driven off. Strength decrease 11 Officers 183 ORs. 2 ORs. granted leave.	
"	12-10-17		14,000 rounds fired during the night on enemy centres of movement. AUGUSTE CITY Rd was also harassed at intervals. "L" Battery Gun positions being dug. Situation, Normal Casualties NIL. Strength 11 Officers 183 ORs.	
"	13-10-17		Harrassing fire carried out during night in which 10,000 rds were expended on Enemy communications. Situation Normal. Casualties NIL.	

T2134. Wt. W708–776. 500000. 4/15. Sir J. C. & S.

Instructions regarding War Diaries and Intelligence Summaries are contained in F. S. Regs., Part II. and the Staff Manual respectively. Title pages will be prepared in manuscript.

WAR DIARY
or
INTELLIGENCE SUMMARY.
(Erase heading not required.)

Army Form C. 2118.

PAGE. 3.

Place	Date	Hour	Summary of Events and Information	Remarks and references to Appendices
LOOS.	14.10.17	6PM to 6AM.	10,000 rds fired on Enemy communications & Bite St Auguste Rd. 500 rds fired at hostile aircraft. Enemy shelled our forward positions, but obtained no direct hits. Casualties NIL. Situation normal. Strength 11 Officers & 1830 ORs.	
"	15.10.17	"	Harressing fire carried out on hostile communications, tracks roads &c on which 11,000 rds were expended. Situation normal. Casualties NIL.	
"	16-10.		12,000 rds fired on hostile CTS, tracks, roads &c. Situation Normal. Casualties NIL. 2 ORs proceed on leave.	
"	17.10.		Harressing fire carried out during the night in which 13,000 rds were expended. 300 rds fired at hostile aircraft. Situation normal. Casualties NIL.	
	18.10.		15,000 rds fired on enemy CTS. tracks roads &c 2000 rds fired at hostile aircraft which was flying very low. Situation Normal. casualties NIL.	
EMILE.	19.10.		Coy relieved by 18th M Gun Coy in the AUGUSTE sector. Relief complete by 9PM. Coy proceeds to the EMILE sector on relief by 18th M G Coy & relieves 16th Coy. Relief complete by 1AM the night 18/19th. Casualties NIL.	
	20.10.17		8,000 rounds fired during the night on enemy trenches etc. Enemy heavily minnied the front & support line from 1pm to 5.30PM. S.O.S was sent up about 4.30pm when the artillery opened out & dropped a heavy barrage on enemy lines.	
	21.10.17.		6,000 rounds fired on usual centres of movement. Casualties NIL. Situation normal.	

A5834 Wt. W4973/M687 750,000 8/16 D. D. & L. Ltd. Forms/C.2118/13.

Instructions regarding War Diaries and Intelligence Summaries are contained in F. S. Regs., Part II. and the Staff Manual respectively. Title pages will be prepared in manuscript.

WAR DIARY
or
INTELLIGENCE SUMMARY.
(Erase heading not required.)

Army Form C. 2118.

PAGE 4.

Place	Date	Hour	Summary of Events and Information	Remarks and references to Appendices
EMILE.	22/23 10.17		Coy relieved by 34th Coy, M.G.C. Relief started at 7pm & completed at 10pm. On relief complete Coy marched to billets in NOEUX-LES-MINES. Arrived in billets at 1am 23/23 inst.	
NOEUX-LES-MINES	23.10.17		Casualties during relief - 2 O.R.s wounded. Coy parade at 3.25PM and march to NOEUX-LES-MINES station where Coy entrained for LILLERS. Arrived LILLERS 5.30pm and marched to billets in LA TIMANDE. Arrived in billets 9pm. 1 O.R proceeds on leave.	
LA TIMANDE	24.10.17		Cleaning Clothes - Equipment Etc. 1 officer & 1 O.R. proceeds on leave	
	25.10.17		Physical training - C.O's inspection (Full Marching Order). Gun Drill - Cleaning Limbers - Football -	
	26.10.17		Walk & Run - Respirator, Iron Ration, Identity Disc Inspection - Judging Distance & Range Finding - Full Marching Order, Limber & Gun Inspection by O.C. - Football match 2 O.R joined from Base Depot.	
	[illegible]8.10.17		Church Parades - Cleaning Guns &3 O.R proceeded on leave.	
ORLENCOURT	29.10.17	9AM	Coy left LA TIMANDE and marched to billets at ORLENCOURT. Arrived [illegible].30pm	
LEINCOURT.	30.10.17	8AM	Coy left ORLENCOURT and marched to billets at LEINCOURT. Arrived 12.30pm	
	31.10.17		Walk & Run - Cleaning Equipment, Guns, Limbers Etc. - Gas Drill.	

J. Rushton Moore Capt
O.C. 71st Company M.G. Corps.

JRM

A5834 Wt. W4973/M687 750,000 8/16 D. D. & L. Ltd. Forms/C.2118/13.

1

Instructions regarding War Diaries and Intelligence Summaries are contained in F. S. Regs., Part II. and the Staff Manual respectively. Title pages will be prepared in manuscript.

PAGE. 1.

WAR DIARY
or
INTELLIGENCE SUMMARY.
(Erase heading not required.)

71 M.G. Coy

71st Machine Gun Company.

Vol 16

Army Form C. 2118.

6

Place	Date	Hour	Summary of Events and Information	Remarks and references to Appendices
LEINCOURT	1/4/17		Parades:- Physical training - Advanced Gun drill - Packing limbers - Inspection of limbers by C.O. - Cleaning & filling belts.	
"	2/4/17		Parades:- Physical training - Director practice - Range finding & judging distance - Cleaning guns - 1 O.R. admitted Hospital - 1 officer - 3 O.R. proceeded on leave.	
"	3/4/17		Parades:- Physical training - Director practice - Gun drill - Cleaning guns -	
"	4/4/17		Church Parades.	
"	5/4/17		Parades:- Physical Training - M.G. competition - Cleaning guns.	
"	6/4/17		Parades:- Physical training - Gun drill - Gas drill - Tank demonstration.	
"	7/4/17		Parades:- Route march & tank demonstration.	
"	8/4/17		Parades:- Physical training - Gun drill - Cleaning limbers - Kit inspection - 2 O.R's admitted Hospital.	
"	9/4/17		Parades. Physical training - Advanced Gun drill - Cleaning Guns - Cross country run. 5 O.R's proceed on leave.	
"	10/4/17		Parades. Preparing guns for range. - Firing on range - 1 O.R. from Hospital	
"	11/4/17		Church Parades	
"	12/4/17		Parades. Gun drill - Barrage drill - Cleaning Guns - Gas parade - 1 O.R. from leave.	

PAGE. II.

Instructions regarding War Diaries and Intelligence Summaries are contained in F. S. Regs., Part II. and the Staff Manual respectively. Title pages will be prepared in manuscript.

WAR DIARY
or
INTELLIGENCE SUMMARY.

(Erase heading not required.)

Army Form C. 2118.

Place	Date	Hour	Summary of Events and Information	Remarks and references to Appendices
LEINCOURT	13/11/17		Parade:- Physical Training - Barrage Drill - Inspection of S.B. Respirators - Orders for Coy transport to proceed to MANANCOURT & moves off at 5pm.	
"	14/11/17		Coy. prepares for move.	
"	15/11/17		Coy parades & march to FREVENT where they entrain for PERONNE. Coy detrains at PERONNE & march to Billets at MANANCOURT. Arrived 10.30 PM.	
DESSERT WOOD	16/11/17		Coy moves to DESSERT WOOD & remain there until the night of the 19/20th.	
TRENCHES	19/20th		Coy march to the trenches - 1 sub-section allotted to each Battalion	
"	20/11/17		2 Guns under Lt Ashlen went forward with 2nd Sherwood Foresters & consolidated in ~~TRENCH~~ the HINDENBURG LINE at L.9.a. 20.70. & then went forward with the infantry	
"	21 "		consolidating at L.20.d. on the 20th inst.	
"	22 "		2 Guns under 2nd Lieut Holwill went forward with the 9th Suffolks & consolidated in	
"	23 "		VALLEY TRENCH L.31.c. They moved up on 22nd to L.27.c.	
"	"		The enemy offered no opposition. These guns did not fire as	
"	"		2 Guns under Lieut J.W. Hendry went forward with 1st Leicesters & consolidated in UNSEEN TRENCH at L.26.c. & then moved up to L.27.a on the 22nd. These 2 guns did not fire as no target presented themselves.	
"	"		2 Guns under 2nd Lt. Curtis went forward with 11th Essex & consolidated at L.20.c. These guns fired on parties of the enemy as they were leaving their trenches doing considerable damage.	
"	"		No's. 2 & 4. Section under 2nd Lieut Bullman were formed into a Battery which fired on L.31.b. to cover the infantry advance.	

A5834 Wt. W4973/M687 750,000 8/16 D. D. & L. Ltd. Forms/C.2118/13.

Instructions regarding War Diaries and Intelligence Summaries are contained in F. S. Regs., Part II. and the Staff Manual respectively. Title pages will be prepared in manuscript.

WAR DIARY
or
INTELLIGENCE SUMMARY.

(*Erase heading not required.*)

Army Form C. 2118.

PAGE. III.

Place	Date	Hour	Summary of Events and Information	Remarks and references to Appendices
TRENCHES	20 21 22 23 / 11 / 17		They then moved forward to L.32.b 20.75 where they remained until the evening of 21st & then moved into RIBECOURT. until the afternoon of 23rd. On their way forward this Battery captured 2. Officers & 24. ORs. from a Battalion HQ, missed by the infantry. This Battery fired 8,000 rds.	
			Casualties 1. Officer & 13. ORs wounded. 2. ORs. Killed.	
"	24th.		All objectives held.	
"	28th		1. Officer & 17. ORanks joined from Base Depot.	
"	29th		Nothing of importance to report. 10. ORs proceed on leave. 1. OR to Hospital	
"	30th.	6.45 a.m	The enemy attacked the Divisions on our right & left. Our own front shelled all day.	
		12am.	Guns of No. 4. Section went up with 2nd Batt. Sherwood. Foresters. to form a defensive flank on our left.	
		4.30p	2 Guns of No 3. Section went up to the left to assist the guns of No. 4. Section. 29,000 rounds fired at enemy aircraft. We claim to have brought one enemy plane. down.	
			Casualties 1. Officer Killed.	

J Rushton Moore Capt.
Comdg: 71st Coy. M. Gun. Corps.

Instructions regarding War Diaries and Intelligence Summaries are contained in F. S. Regs., Part II. and the Staff Manual respectively. Title pages will be prepared in manuscript.

71st Coy. Machin[redacted] ...RY

SUMMARY.

(... not required.)

PAGE I.

Vol 17

Army Form C. 2118.

Place	Date	Hour	Summary of Events and Information	Remarks and references to Appendices
PREMY CHAPEL	1-12-17		5,000 rounds fired at hostile aircraft. New positions were consolidated by No 4 Section & shelters made for gun-teams. Hostile shelling less active during the night. Casualties NIL.	
"	2-12-17		No rounds fired during the night. 2 Guns were moved into position at L. 11 C. 80-70. Casualties. 1. O Rank wounded by half spent M.G. bullet.	
"	3-12-17		No rounds fired: 4. Guns under Lieut P.V. ALBRECHT were withdrawn & consolidated new positions at L.11.C.40.40. L.11.C 20.30... L.11.C 15.20. These guns were shelled at intervals but no direct hits were obtained. Casualties. NIL.	
"	4-12-17		On the night 4/5th all guns were withdrawn in conjunction with the infantry to the HINDENBURG SUPPORT system. Withdrawal commenced at 10 PM & was complete by 3-45 am the morning of the 5th. No trench stores, S.A.A. etc were left behind. Casualties NIL.	
RIBECOURT.	5-12-17		No rounds fired during night. Casualties 1. OR wounded.	
"	6-12-17		7,000 rounds fired at small parties of the enemy. Guns remained the same. Hostile shelling less active. Casualties NIL.	
"	7-12-17		5000 rounds fired at the enemy. A sniping gun firing from L.21.b. killed one & wounded several of the enemy. Adv Coy HQ shelled intermittently throughout the night with Gas shells. Casualties. NIL.	
VALLEY TRENCH	8-12-17		Adv. Coy HQ moves from RIBECOURT to VALLEY TRENCH. No rounds fired. Night extremely quiet. Casualties NIL	

A5834 Wt. W4973/M687 750,000 8/16 D. D. & L. Ltd. Forms/C.2118/13.

Army Form C. 2118.

Instructions regarding War Diaries and Intelligence Summaries are contained in F. S. Regs., Part II. and the Staff Manual respectively. Title pages will be prepared in manuscript.

[illegible]RY

[illegible] SUMMARY.

[illegible] not required.)

PAGE. I.

Place	Date	Hour	[illegible]mmary of Events and Information	Remarks and references to Appendices
VALLEY TRENCH	9.12.17	3.30 PM	5.500 fired at small parties of the enemy. 5000 rounds fired a hostile aircraft. At about 3.30 pm. a hostile aeroplane was brought down by one of our M.Guns, bursting into flames on reaching the ground. Casualties NIL.	
"	10.12.17		5000 rounds fired at hostile aircraft & small parties of the enemy. Warning orders sent round to all Section Officers of coming relief. Casualties NIL	
"	10th/11th		Coy relieved in the line by 58th M G Coy. Relief commenced 6.30PM & completed by 1-0AM 11th inst. Sections march from line on relief to hutments in ETRICOURT. Distance of 16 kilometres. - 5 ORs proceed on leave.	
ETRICOURT	14th		Coys moves by bus to BELLACOURT. Arrived in billets 5.15pm.	
BELLACOURT	16th		Training carried out as follows. Cleaning equipment - clothes etc. Gun cleaning.	
"	17th		" " " " " Physical training - Gun Drill - Range-finding - Judging Distances - Packing & oiling limbers.	
"	18th		" " " " " Physical training. Cleaning Guns - Belts etc. Inspection of Small box respirators & Gas Drill. Foot Inspection & lecture on same - Anti-Aircraft instructions.	
"	19th		" " " " " Physical training - Coy Drill under Capt Moore MC. Revolver practice - Barrage Drill - Cleaning Guns. Washing & oiling limbers	

Army Form C. 2118.

Instructions regarding War Diaries and Intelligence Summaries are contained in F. S. Regs., Part II. and the Staff Manual respectively. Title pages will be prepared in manuscript.

…RY
… SUMMARY.

(…not required.)

PAGE. III.

Place	Date	Hour	…mary of Events and Information	Remarks and references to Appendices
BELLACOURT		20th	Training carried out as follows. – Physical training – Gas Drill – Inspection by O C Coy. Revolver practice – Sight-setting & laying.	
"		21st	" " " " " 1- O.R. DIES in Hospital. 1 Officer admitted to Hospital. Gun Drill – Judging distances – Physical training – Revolver practice – Gas Drill – Lecture to Junior NCOs by Capt JR Moore MC.	
"		22nd	" " " " " Advanced Gun & Barrage Drill – Physical training. Gas Drill & Squad Drill. Revolver Snapping. Lecture to Junior NCOs by Capt JR Moore MC.	
"		23rd	" " " " " All day firing on range. 7. ORs granted proficiency pay.	
"		24th	" " " " " Physical training under Divisional instructor. Gun Drill. Squad Drill. Revolver snapping. Lecture by Capt JR Moore MC to Junior NCOs.	
"		25th	" " " " " Church parade. Christmas Dinner held in School at RIVIERE.	
"		26th	" " " " " Revolver Range – Physical training – Gun Drill. Lecture by Divisional Gas Officer.	

Instructions regarding War Diaries and Intelligence Summaries are contained in F. S. Regs., Part II. and the Staff Manual respectively. Title pages will be prepared in manuscript.

PAGE. 4.

[illegible]ARY

[illegible] SUMMARY.

[illegible]ot required.)

Army Form C. 2118.

Place	Date	Hour	[illegible]mary of Events and Information	Remarks and references to Appendices
BELLA COURT	27-12-17		Training carried out as follows - Route march - Full marching order. Lecture by Capt J.R. Moore MC. to Junior NCOs.	
"	28-12-17		" " " " " Physical training - Machenism - Stoppages - Close order Drill - marching & Passing orders in Box Respirator. Lecture. 1-OR to Hospital.	
"	29-12-17		" " " " " C.Os inspection - Firing on Range.	
"	30-12-17		" " " " " Church parade. Coy prepares for coming move. 5-ORs from Leave.	
"	31-12-17		" " " " " Physical training - Barrage Drill - Squad Drill - Firing on Revolver Range. Gas Drill & Cleaning Guns.	

[illegible] Moore Capt.
[illegible] M. Gun Coy

A5834 Wt. W4973/M687 750,000 8/16 D. D. & L. [illegible]orms/C.2118/13.

6th Division

71st M. G. Coy

January only

1918

71st Coy. Machine Gun Corps. Army Form C. 2118.

Instructions regarding War Diaries and Intelligence Summaries are contained in F. S. Regs., Part II. and the Staff Manual respectively. Title pages will be prepared in manuscript.

Page 1.

WAR DIARY
or
INTELLIGENCE SUMMARY.
(*Erase heading not required.*)

Vol 18

Place	Date	Hour	Summary of Events and Information	Remarks and references to Appendices
BELLACOURT	1/1/18		Coy parades 8-30 am & march to Billets in COURCELLES-LE-COMTE. Arrived in Billets 12-45 pm.	
COURCELLES	2nd		Training carried out as follows. Advanced Gun Drill - Physical training Mounting Guns in rough places. Gas Drill.	
"	3rd		Training carried out as follows. Barrage Drill - Sight setting & laying - Physical training - Adv. Gun Drill - Squad Drill.	
"	4th		Training carried out as follows. Physical training - Visual training Adv. Gun - Mechanism & Stoppages - Gas Drill	
"	5th		Training carried out as follows. - Route march. Dress. Full marching order. 4. ORs from Leave. 1. OR. admitted to Hospital.	
"	6th		Training carried out as follows. Divine Service for all ranks. 1. OR. from Hospital.	
"	7th		Training carried out as follows. Route march. Dress full marching order. 1. OR. proceeds for MG. course. 1. OR from MG course.	
"	8th		Training carried out as follows. Physical training - Barrage Drill Sight Setting & laying - Gas Drill. Lectures by Section Officers 1 OR admitted to Hospital. 1. Officer & 1. OR. from Base Depot.	
"	9th		Training carried out as follows. Adv. Gun drill - Sight setting & laying Close order drill. Gas Drill. 1. OR proceeds to MG Base Depot for transfer to England.	

Instructions regarding War Diaries and Intelligence Summaries are contained in F. S. Regs., Part II. and the Staff Manual respectively. Title pages will be prepared in manuscript.

WAR DIARY
or
INTELLIGENCE SUMMARY.
(*Erase heading not required.*)

Army Form C. 2118.

Page 2.

Place	Date	Hour	Summary of Events and Information	Remarks and references to Appendices
COURCELLES	10-1-18		Training carried out as follows. Physical training – Barrage Drill – mechanism & stoppages. Lecture by section officers. Kit inspection.	
"	11th		Training carried out as follows. Physical training – Gas Drill – Ad Gun Drill cleaning guns – belt boxes – ammunition etc. 2 – ORs admitted to Hospital.	
"	12th		Training carried out as follows. Route march. Dress full marching order. Kit Inspection. 3. ORs. admitted to Hospital. 2. ORs leave to U K.	
"	13th		Training carried out as follows. Cleaning & overhauling guns. tripods. Belt Boxes – spare parts – Belt filling & packing limbers.	
"	14th		Orders received for Coy to move to Billets in Fremicourt.	
"	15th		Coy paraded 8.45 a m & march to Fremicourt. Arrived 12.30 pm.	
FREMICOURT	16th		3. Sections parade at 12 NOON & march to the trenches & relieve 152 MG Coy Relief complete 5-30 pm. Casualties NIL.	
DOIGNIES	17th			
"	18th		No rounds fired. Gun positions searched with 5-9.s. Casualties NIL.	
"	19th		Nothing of importance to report.	
"	20th		No rounds fired. 50 yards of front line trench cleaned to depth of 1 ft. Casualties NIL.	
"	21st		No rounds fired. 2 Alternative Gun positions made. Casualties NIL.	

A5834 Wt. W4973/M687 750,000 8/16 D. D. & L. Ltd. Forms/C.2118/13.

Army Form C. 2118.

Instructions regarding War Diaries and Intelligence Summaries are contained in F. S. Regs., Part II. and the Staff Manual respectively. Title pages will be prepared in manuscript.

Page. III.

WAR DIARY
or
INTELLIGENCE SUMMARY.
(Erase heading not required.)

Place	Date	Hour	Summary of Events and Information	Remarks and references to Appendices
DOIGNIES	22-1-18		No rounds fired. Enemy seen working in front of Bourlon Wood & engaged by our artillery. Work continued on clearing trenches. Casualties NIL. 1. Officer & 1. OR admitted to Hospital. 1 Officer proceed on leave.	
"	23rd		No rounds fired. Nothing of importance to report. 1- OR Wounded (Gas).	
"	24th		Nothing of importance to report. 1- NCO proceeds to England for Commission. Operation order for relief received.	
"	25th		Coy. relieved by 16th MG Coy. Relief complete 10-0 p.m. Sections march from line to Billets at Lebucquiere. Casualties NIL.	
LEBUCQUIERE	26th		Parades spent in cleaning equipment - Guns etc. 1- OR joined from Hospital	
"	27th		Training carried as follows. Gun Drill - Physical training - Sight setting & laying. Cleaning and oiling limbers. 1- OR accidentally wounded.	
"	28th		Training as follows. Physical training - Barrage Drill - Gas Drill - Squad Drill. Recreational training. Court of Inquiry held re the wounding of Pte Skill. 2- ORs to Hospital	
"	29th		Training as follows. Physical training - Section Officers inspection. Barrage Drill. Squad Drill etc. 1- OR to Hospital.	
"	30th		Working party of 70 ORs & 3 Officers proceed to Reserve system for digging. 1. OR to Hospital	
"	31st		Working parties as above. 1- OR to Hospital	

H. J. Ashlin Lt
Comdg. 71st M G Coy.

A5834 Wt. W4973/M687 750,000 8/16 D. D. & L. Ltd. Forms/C.2118/13.

www.ingramcontent.com/pod-product-compliance
Lightning Source LLC
Chambersburg PA
CBHW080920230426
43668CB00014B/2161
* 9 7 8 1 4 7 4 5 0 6 2 8 1 *